# THE *GIDEON* CASE

UNIVERSITY PRESS OF FLORIDA

Florida A&M University, Tallahassee
Florida Atlantic University, Boca Raton
Florida Gulf Coast University, Ft. Myers
Florida International University, Miami
Florida State University, Tallahassee
New College of Florida, Sarasota
University of Central Florida, Orlando
University of Florida, Gainesville
University of North Florida, Jacksonville
University of South Florida, Tampa
University of West Florida, Pensacola

# The *Gideon* Case

## Inside the Supreme Court's
## Historic Right to Counsel Decision

BRUCE R. JACOB

UNIVERSITY PRESS OF FLORIDA

Gainesville/Tallahassee/Tampa/Boca Raton
Pensacola/Orlando/Miami/Jacksonville/Ft. Myers/Sarasota

*Cover:* Exterior of the United States Supreme Court Building. Credit: Shutterstock.

*Cover design by Mindy Basinger Hill.*

Copyright 2026 by Bruce R. Jacob

Published in the United States of America

31  30  29  28  25  26   6  5  4  3  2  1

DOI: https://doi.org/10.5744/9780813079547
Library of Congress Cataloging-in-Publication Data
Names: Jacob, Bruce R., author.
Title: The Gideon case : inside the Supreme Court's historic right to
counsel decision / Bruce R. Jacob.
Description: Gainesville : University Press of Florida, [2026] | Includes
index.
Identifiers: LCCN 2025027418 (print) | LCCN 2025027419 (ebook) | ISBN
9780813079547 (hardback) | ISBN 9780813075266 (ebook) | ISBN
9780813074221 (pdf)
Subjects: LCSH: Right to counsel—United States—History. | United States.
Supreme Court. | Gideon, Clarence Earl—Trials, litigation, etc. |
Wainwright, Louie L.—Trials, litigation, etc. | Jacob, Bruce R. |
Lawyers—United States—Biography.
Classification: LCC KF9646 .J33 2026 (print) | LCC KF9646 (ebook) | DDC
345.73/056—dc23/eng/20250618
LC record available at https://lccn.loc.gov/2025027418
LC ebook record available at https://lccn.loc.gov/2025027419

The University Press of Florida is the scholarly publishing agency for the State University System
of Florida, comprising Florida A&M University, Florida Atlantic University, Florida Gulf Coast
University, Florida International University, Florida State University, New College of Florida, University of Central Florida, University of Florida, University of North Florida, University of South
Florida, and University of West Florida.

University Press of Florida
2046 NE Waldo Road
Suite 2100
Gainesville, FL 32609
floridapress.org

GPSR EU Authorized Representative: Mare Nostrum Group B.V., Mauritskade 21D, 1091 GC
Amsterdam, The Netherlands, gpsr@mare-nostrum.co.uk

*Dedicated to my wife, Ann*

# CONTENTS

# PREFACE

## About the *Gideon* Case and the Author

*Gideon v. Wainwright*,[1] requiring state courts to provide counsel to represent indigent defendants in felony cases, is one of the great judicial decisions in American legal history. It has been called the most significant criminal law case ever decided by the United States Supreme Court. And it probably is one of the three most notable decisions of the Court during the twentieth century, the others being *Brown v. Board of Education*[2] (requiring the desegregation of public schools) and *Roe v. Wade*[3] (recognizing the right of a pregnant woman to choose to have an abortion). On June 24, 2022, the Supreme Court overruled *Roe v. Wade* in the *Dobbs v. Jackson Women's Health Organization* decision.[4]

Clarence Earl Gideon was the petitioner in the *Gideon* case. He had been convicted of breaking into a pool hall one night in the small community of Bay Harbor, next to Panama City in Florida's Panhandle, and stealing beer and wine and cash from the cigarette machine and jukebox. Before the Supreme Court, he was represented by appointed attorney Abe Fortas, a founding member of a prestigious Washington, D.C., law firm. Fortas later was to become a Justice of the Supreme Court.

Louie Wainwright, the Respondent, was the Director of the Division of Corrections of the State of Florida. While Gideon was confined at the Florida State Prison, he was in the custody of Florida's correctional system. Therefore, when suing to overturn his conviction, Gideon's legal actions were against Wainwright as the head of that system.

The Division of Corrections was represented in legal matters by the Florida Attorney General's Office in Tallahassee, Florida. I, an Assistant Attorney General in that office, was assigned to handle the *Gideon* case and represent the Division of Corrections director before the United States Supreme Court.

Map of places in Florida mentioned in the book. Map by Lee Ann Gun.

I began work on the case in March 1962 when I was 26 years old, and argued the case before the Court in January 1963, when I was 27. This book is the story of my experiences representing the Division of Corrections and the interests of the State of Florida before the Supreme Court in this landmark decision. It is the story of the case and those involved in it from the time it began, on June 3, 1961, to the present day. The year 2023 marked the sixty-year anniversary of this famous case.

# 1

## History at My Door

It was March 15, 1962. Nina (the first syllable rhymes with "eye") appeared at the door to my office and asked me to see Judge Bowen when I had time. Nina was Judge Reeves Bowen's secretary, and he was the head of our four-lawyer Criminal Appeals section of the Office of the Attorney General of Florida. We were on the ground floor of the old state Capitol, built in 1845. I told her I would see him immediately. I walked out of my office, turned right, and knocked on the half-open door of the office next to mine. Judge Bowen invited me in.

His office was always dark, with the window shades drawn shut. There was no light in his office except for what might be called a movable "spotlight" over his desk. He was about 60 years old and, in recent years, had begun to suffer from fading eyesight. But he did not allow this handicap to affect his work in any way. He could reach up to the light over his desk and move it with one of his hands to follow the words he was reading or writing on his desk. When he began working on a new criminal appeal, Nina would read the entire appellate record, including trial transcripts, to him. This might consist of thousands of pages. He would listen intently and remember every piece of information in the record, down to the last detail. He argued his cases before the courts without any notes. He was an exceptional lawyer.

As I sat down across the desk from him, he told me that our office had been asked by the United States Supreme Court to file a typewritten response to a petition for certiorari by an inmate named Clarence Earl Gideon. "I'd like you to take care of this," he said, and he handed the letter to me from across the desk. Enclosed with the letter was a copy of the certiorari petition.

"This might be the case the Court will use to overrule *Betts v. Brady*,"[1] he said, "because he has not alleged any special circumstances, just that he was indigent and should have had a court-appointed lawyer." The *Betts* case had required appointed counsel if there was a special circumstance involved, such as the fact that the defendant was extremely young or inexperienced. The four of us in the Criminal Appeals section were well aware that the Supreme Court had been moving in the direction of overturning the *Betts* decision and extending a right to state-paid counsel to any defendant in a state criminal felony case who could not afford a lawyer.

When *Betts* was decided in 1942, there were three dissenting Justices, Hugo Black, William Douglas, and Frank Murphy. And a few years later, in *Adamson v. California* and *Bute v. Illinois*,[2] there were four Justices opposed to the holding in *Betts*—the three original dissenters, plus Justice Wiley Rutledge. I thanked Judge Bowen for the assignment and returned to my office.

It was a day that would change my life. The assignment would be the central focus of my life for the next 12 months, even as I got married and was hired by one of Florida's fastest growing law firms. More than 60 years later, there are still memories of that day and that case. *Gideon v. Wainwright*,[3] requiring state courts to provide counsel to represent indigent defendants in all felony cases, is one of the great judicial decisions in American legal history. It would be the subject of a book and movie (of the same name, *Gideon's Trumpet*) that starred one of the most famous actors of the twentieth century, Henry Fonda.[4] Another famous actor in the film was José Ferrer. My role would be played by an actor named Nicholas Pryor, who had parts in some TV shows and in a variety of movies, including Tom Cruise's dad in *Risky Business.*

How did I happen to be one of the lawyers, in 1962, handling criminal appeals and post-conviction cases in the Office of the Attorney General of Florida? I was born in Chicago on March 26, 1935. My family lived in Hinsdale, a western suburb of Chicago until I was 16. When I was near the end of my third year of high school, we moved to Sarasota, on the Gulf Coast of Florida, and it was there that I graduated from high school. Then, after one year at Principia College, a small liberal arts college for Christian Scientists on the bluffs overlooking the Mississippi River near Alton, Illinois, I transferred to Florida State University, where I received the B.A. degree in January 1957.

That same January, I began studying law at the Stetson University College of Law. The main campus of Stetson University was in DeLand, north of Orlando, but the law school had moved to what formerly was a hotel in Gulfport, a small community next to St. Petersburg, on Florida's west coast, in 1954. The law school had been compelled to move because after World War II, veterans were entitled to the G.I. Bill of Rights, which provided them financial assistance for college, so many more students than usual were attending universities and colleges. The undergraduate program needed more

Professor and former Oregon Supreme Court justice James Tenney Brand (*center*) and the Stetson Moot Court Team, the author (*left*) and Wallace Storey (*right*), 1958. Courtesy of Stetson University College of Law.

room and had taken over the space on the DeLand campus formerly occupied by the law school.

I graduated from law school in June 1959. During my years there, my most significant experience was being a member of the two-person team that represented our school in the regionals of a national appellate moot court competition. The hypothetical problem for the competition assumed that we were before the United States Supreme Court and were arguing about constitutional questions arising from the fact situation given to us. We were to write a brief following the Supreme Court's rules and orally argue the case before a panel of volunteer lawyers in Atlanta, acting as competition judges. The preparation of the brief and the oral arguments took place through the summer and fall of 1958.

My team partner had a job 70 miles away during the summer, so the task of writing the brief fell largely to me. Under competition rules, I was allowed to receive limited help from a faculty member. The faculty member assigned to assist with the brief was Professor James Tenney Brand, a retired justice and chief justice of the Oregon Supreme Court. I spent a lot of time with him,

Dean and former Florida Supreme Court justice Harold L. (Tom) Sebring. Courtesy of the State Archives of Florida.

learning how to write a complex appellate brief. He was scrupulously careful not to give me more help than was allowed by the rules of the competition, but what I learned from him was invaluable. I was being tutored on brief writing by one of the best teachers of the art of writing appellate briefs in the United States.

During the three weeks before the oral arguments in the competition, during the fall of 1958, Justice Brand and our dean, Harold L. (Tom) Sebring, sat as a panel in our courtroom, asking questions of the two of us to prepare us for the oral arguments. Sebring had been a justice and chief justice of the Florida Supreme Court. The two of them had been among the 25 or so judges for the Nuremberg War Crimes Trials in 1946 and 1947, and they had met there. Sebring was one of the three judges of the "Medical Case," trying Nazi doctors who had performed inhuman medical experiments on inmates of concentration camps. Brand had been the chief judge of the three-judge panel in the "Justice Case," in which leading Nazi judges and prosecutors were tried for war crimes. The play and movie *Judgment at Nuremberg* are about his case. In the movie, actor Spencer Tracy plays the part of Justice Brand.

Brand and Sebring were highly intelligent men and good lawyers. As former Nuremberg judges and former state supreme court justices, they had had extraordinary careers in the law. And if one word could be used to describe the most important attribute of each of these men, it is "integrity." Getting to know them and working with them as we did was one of the best learning experiences I have ever had. Unfortunately, we lost the competition, but we received an unbelievable educational experience from Justices Brand and Sebring. Also, the competition got me interested in appellate work as a possible career.

After graduating from Stetson in June 1959 and passing the bar exam, I was sworn in as a member of The Florida Bar in a ceremony at the Florida Supreme Court in Tallahassee in late November 1959. After the ceremony, a friend who had graduated from the University of Miami School of Law and planned to practice in Miami mentioned that he had heard that the Florida Attorney General's Office was hiring new lawyers. I thanked him and immediately walked from the Supreme Court building, across a huge parking lot,[5] to the historic Capitol building. I went to the main office of the attorney general and asked if it was true that they were hiring new lawyers. I had been an undergraduate student at Florida State University, in Tallahassee, had enjoyed my time there, and liked the idea of living there. Also, I was interested in public law and therefore was very interested in working in that office. Without delay, his secretary ushered me into the office of the attorney general, Richard W. Ervin, for an interview. I told him that I was a member of the Florida National Guard and would be leaving one week later for Fort Jackson, South Carolina, for six months of active duty in the Army. But, I told him I would like to work in his office when the six months ended. He asked me to send him a letter about one month before I was scheduled to be discharged from active duty, and if there was a job opening at that time, the job would be mine. He said this without first even seeing my résumé. I may have sent a résumé later.

It seems strange now that I was interviewed on the spot by the attorney general himself, but this did not seem unusual in 1959 in Florida. The Attorney General's Office consisted of only about 22 lawyers in Tallahassee, two in Miami, and a part-time attorney in Lakeland. We also probably had an additional 40 secretaries and other staff, for about 65 total employees.

Today, the Florida Attorney General's Office has 14 offices and almost 1,300 lawyers and other employees. The state of Florida then had a population of about 5 million compared with approximately 23 million in 2025. Florida then was basically an agricultural state with money coming mainly from citrus, cattle, and tourism. The Florida of 1959 was much different than

Richard W. Ervin Jr, Attorney General of Florida. This was a photo of him given to the author (in 1961 or 1962), saying "To Assistant Attorney General Bruce R. Jacob, with my sincere appreciation for the fine public service he is rendering the State of Florida."

the state today. In those days, it did not seem odd to walk into the Florida Attorney General's Office and to be interviewed by the attorney general himself immediately.

Richard Ervin became a friend and one of the persons in the legal profession I most admire. He was a knowledgeable lawyer and a kind, thoughtful, and quite unassuming man. Any state would be fortunate to have an attorney general like him. He later served as a justice and chief justice of the Florida Supreme Court.

In the Army, I first went through basic training and then clerk-typist school. After that, I was assigned as a clerk-typist to "Courts and Boards," where I typed charges in summary and special court-martial proceedings and also acted as a court reporter during special court-martial trials. I would sit in the middle of the courtroom, just a few feet away from witnesses as they testified, and take detailed notes regarding their testimony. Then I would type a summary of what each witness said. Attorneys reviewed my summaries in the Judge Advocate General Corps office at Fort Jackson to decide whether to uphold each conviction.

In April 1960, I wrote Attorney General Ervin, letting him know that I would be discharged from active duty during the last week of May and would be able to begin working in his office. I received a reply telling me I could start on June 1, 1960, and that my salary would be $4,800 per year. Because of inflation, that was like $51,179 in 2025. It was a good starting salary for the times. Some of my classmates made only $3,600 per year, and those who began in Miami had to work for several months for free. They would be put on the payroll only after showing they could do satisfactory work.

My beginning title was Special Assistant Attorney General. After I had been working there for six months, the title changed to Assistant Attorney General. Every six months, I received a raise in my annual pay of $600. By the time I left the office in September 1962, I was earning $7,200 annually, which would be $75,736 in 2025 dollars.

I began in the "civil" or general section of the office. The first sit-ins by demonstrators seeking to end racial discrimination at lunch counters throughout the South took place in February and March 1960. Later the "Freedom Riders," African American and white protesters against racial segregation, traveled by bus throughout Alabama and Mississippi, sitting down at "white only" lunch counters. In late 1960 or early 1961, our office received requests from editors of two law school law reviews to write articles about the legal aspects of these anti-segregation demonstrations. The demonstrators were being immediately arrested, charged, and convicted of crimes, such as breach of the peace, disorderly conduct, and unlawful assembly. Attorney General Ervin asked me to work on those two articles. Since criminal law was involved, he also asked Judge Reeves Bowen to oversee my work.

Bowen was a scholar. He had attended the University of Florida College of Law in the 1920s when the LL.B. (Bachelor of Laws) was the standard law degree. But if a student had attained a high enough grade point average, he (there were no women students in those days) was invited to stay for a fourth year of law study and obtain the J.D., Juris Doctor degree. Today, the J.D. is the standard law degree after three years. Bowen had elected to stay the extra year and obtain the J.D. Before joining the Attorney General's Office, he had served as the county judge in his hometown of Chipley in the Panhandle of Florida.

We began working together on the law review articles. I did the research and would write a draft. He would review the draft of a section that I had prepared and come to my office, located in another part of the ground floor of the Capitol, to discuss that section with me. When we were finished, we gave our articles to Ervin for his review, and the articles were published.[6]

During the summer of 1961, shortly after Judge Bowen and I had finished working together on the law review articles, one of the four lawyers in the Criminal Appeals section decided to leave the Attorney General's Office to go into private practice. Judge Bowen approached me and said that he and the two remaining lawyers in the section, George Georgieff and Jim Mahorner, had taken a vote to decide which lawyer in the office they wanted to invite to join them, and the vote was to invite me. I readily accepted their invitation. Being able to work in that section was a privilege. I would be briefing and orally arguing criminal appeals before the appellate courts of Florida, including the Florida Supreme Court. I would be preparing returns (responses) to habeas corpus petitions and representing the state in hearings in habeas cases in Florida circuit courts and United States district courts. Also, I would act as a hearing officer in extradition cases and make recommendations to the governor on whether to extradite or not persons wanted for crimes in other states. I would hear testimony and legal arguments before making my recommendation to the governor. I would research and write legal opinions for police and sheriff's departments throughout the state. I would be a legal adviser to the Division of Corrections. Also, there was the possibility of arguing a case before the United States Supreme Court.

The Supreme Court makes major decisions in only about 75 cases per year. There are two lawyers orally arguing each of these (one on each side), which means that only about 150 lawyers per year orally argue cases before

Judge Reeves Bowen as a young lawyer. From the *Bench and Bar of Florida,* vol. 1, 1935.

the Court. There could be a few more lawyers who have filed amicus curiae (friend of the court) briefs who are allowed to argue orally before the Court. In the early 1960s, there were about 300,000 lawyers in the United States, so with only about 150 out of 300,000 arguing each year, it is clear that extremely few American lawyers ever got to make an oral argument before that Court. For me, it would be a great privilege to be one of the few lawyers to argue a case before the Justices of the Supreme Court.

The first thing Judge Bowen asked me to do when I became a member of the Criminal Appeals section was to carefully read the Florida Constitution and every statute of our state on the subject of criminal law. I was asked by him to study the Florida Rules of Appellate Procedure carefully. After that, he taught me how to respond and file returns in habeas cases. Next, he handed me the record in my first appeal. It might have been a kidnapping case, an armed robbery, or a burglary. Or perhaps manslaughter or second-degree murder, or even first-degree murder. He told me to read the record carefully, including transcripts of testimony, and then come back to discuss the case with him. When I returned to his office, he would ask many questions about what I had learned. In my first weeks on the job, he almost always said, "You don't understand the case well enough, Bruce. Go back and study the record again." After I studied the case more intensely, I would return to his office, and this time he would ask more questions and tell me that I now understood the facts of the case. Then we would discuss the legal issues involved, and only after a lengthy discussion with him and much legal research by me would I begin to write the brief.

Listening to him and talking with him about law was like taking an individualized postgraduate course on legal history, legal philosophy, and the practice of law from one of the country's great professors. His knowledge was vast, and he loved the law and the legal process. He was patient, caring, and painstaking. It was mainly from him that I learned how to think about law and how to be a lawyer.

In early April 1962, I mailed our response to Gideon's petition to the Office of the Clerk of the Supreme Court. It was typewritten and consisted of thirteen legal-sized pages fastened together with blue paper backing, as required by Supreme Court rules. The argument was that an indigent defendant was entitled to appointed counsel, under *Betts v. Brady* and the cases following *Betts*, if there was a special circumstance involved that would make it difficult for that defendant to get a fair trial without having an attorney. But there had been no special circumstance alleged in the habeas petition before the Florida Supreme Court or in Gideon's petition for certiorari to the Supreme Court of the United States.

I have often been asked why I, who was 26 years old, the youngest and newest lawyer in our office, was chosen by Judge Bowen to handle the *Gideon* case. I think the answer is simple—I was the only one of the four of us who had not yet argued a case before the United States Supreme Court, and in fairness, I deserved the next opportunity to take a case before that Court. Judge Bowen had argued there several times. George Georgieff had had a case or two there, and Jim Mahorner had just argued *Carnley v. Cochran*[7] a year earlier.

Bowen and I had worked together on the law review articles. He had read much of my writing—drafts of law review articles, appellate motions and briefs, and habeas corpus returns. He knew that I liked legal history and constitutional law. He knew I was a hard worker.

Also, he had heard me orally argue at least one appeal. The First District Court of Appeal is located in Tallahassee, but it sometimes sat in courthouses of small towns. On one occasion, Judge Bowen and I each had an appeal to be argued in Crestview, west of Tallahassee in Florida's Panhandle, on the same morning. We drove there together the day before, spent the night, argued our cases the next morning, and returned to Tallahassee that afternoon. My argument that day was in a criminal contempt case involving an approach by the defendant to a grand jury member, in an attempt to persuade the grand jurors to act favorably for him in a matter being considered by them.

Thus, Judge Bowen knew a lot about my research and writing ability and had at least one opportunity to hear me orally argue an appeal. I believe he assigned the *Gideon* case to me because I was next in line to argue before the Supreme Court and because he was familiar enough with my work to be confident that I had the ability and enough experience to do a good job in the *Gideon* case.

But I am getting ahead of myself. Let's turn to where the case against Clarence Earl Gideon began, at a pool hall in a small community in the northwestern part of the state of Florida.

# 2

## The Crime and the Arrest

In the early morning of June 3, 1961, 22-year-old Henry Cook rode with friends on the 60-mile drive from Apalachicola west to Panama City along the Gulf Coast of Florida's Panhandle.

He and his friends had attended an all-night dance in Apalachicola and were now traveling home.[1] When they arrived at the small community of Bay Harbor, just east of Panama City, his friends dropped Cook off across the street from the Bay Harbor Pool Room. It was about 5:30 a.m.[2] He did not want to go to his home, which was nearby because he was afraid that his parents would "get on" him about coming home after a night of drinking.[3] The poolroom opened at 7:00 a.m., and Cook decided to "hang around" until it opened.[4] The poolroom was located on the west side of Everitt Avenue. He would later testify that as he was waiting for it to open, standing on the sidewalk, he looked through the front window and saw Clarence Gideon inside the poolroom. Gideon was about eight feet away, standing by a cigarette machine.[5] The front of the cigarette machine had been removed. Gideon, Cook later testified, was stealing coins from the machine in the darkened pool hall. Cook had known Clarence Gideon for about six months, and he said he was certain it was Clarence Gideon who was just inside the window.[6] The lights in the poolroom were not on, but there was enough early morning light to make it possible for Henry Cook to know that the man he was seeing was Gideon.[7] Cook later testified that he observed Gideon through the window for about a minute or more.[8]

Gideon then walked toward the back door of the poolroom. Cook walked a few feet to the north and, looking through the gap between the poolroom and the building to the north, the Bay Harbor Bar,[9] he said he could see Gideon in the alley that ran behind the poolroom and the other buildings along the west side of Everitt Avenue.[10] Gideon had emerged from the back door and had begun walking northward along the alley. Cook walked north along the sidewalk in front of the buildings, observing Gideon in the alley through

Side view of the Bay Harbor Pool Room. Reprinted with permission from CBS News.

Interior view of the Bay Harbor Pool Room. Reprinted with permission from CBS News.

gaps between the buildings. He said Gideon walked to the telephone booth at the north corner of the half block where the buildings stood.[11] His pants "bulged out," presumably from stolen coins, and he was carrying a bottle of wine. He acted "kinder drunk,"[12] according to Cook. Gideon set down the wine bottle as he entered the telephone booth. He made a phone call and stayed seated inside the booth until a taxi picked him up and drove away.[13] He left the half-empty wine bottle.

After the taxi had left, Cook walked to the east side of Everitt Avenue, opposite the phone booth, where a woman named Irene Rhodes had been sitting on her porch at Prescott's Apartments. She had just walked across the street to pick up the half-empty wine bottle left by Gideon, had drunk the wine, and had walked back across the street to her apartment.[14] Cook spoke with her.[15] She agreed with Cook that it was Clarence Gideon—a person she also knew—who emerged from the alley's north end and got into the phone booth.[16] Gideon lived in the Bay Harbor Hotel, a rooming house on the east side of Everitt. The rooming house was across from the poolroom, where he spent a lot of time.[17]

Cook walked back to the poolroom. He looked through the window again and saw the cigarette machine with its front removed. He saw money bags on the pool table.[18] Empty beer cans were on the counter.[19] Within 10 minutes after he had returned to the poolroom, police arrived, and Cook spoke with them. It is possible that no one had notified the police, and they just came on a regular patrol.[20] The police found a large garbage can against a side window near the rear of the building, and the intruder had broken and climbed through that window.[21] Once inside, he had broken into the jukebox and cigarette machine and taken an undetermined amount of money, all in coins. Beer had been drunk by him, and he had taken some wine.[22]

The taxicab driver, Preston Bray, drove Gideon to a bar in nearby Panama City.[23] Gideon paid Bray with coins.[24] Gideon drank at the bar until he was arrested by police later that morning. When he was arrested, he had had and paid for some drinks and still had $25.28, all in coins.[25] Using an inflation calculator, we estimate that $25.28 in 1961 would be worth $266.96 in 2025 dollars.

The information (the criminal charge) filed against him on June 19, 1961, stated that Gideon "did unlawfully and feloniously break and enter a building of another, to wit, the Bay Harbor Poolroom, property of Ira Strickland Jr., lessee, with intent to commit a misdemeanor within said building, to wit, petit larceny."[26] The dividing line between grand larceny and petit larceny at the time was $50. The prosecutor could not charge him with intent to commit grand larceny because Strickland had no way of knowing exactly how much in coins had been taken from the jukebox and cigarette machine.[27] It could have been less than $50, and therefore Gideon was charged with having the intent to commit petit larceny. Even though his intent was to commit a misdemeanor, the crime was a felony because it also involved the more serious act of breaking into a building.

On June 29, Gideon appeared for arraignment, a hearing to enter a plea, before the Circuit Court of Bay County, in Panama City. He had been in jail and did not have an attorney. He requested permission to obtain and consult counsel before being arraigned. The arraignment was postponed until July 31.[28] On July 31, he was arraigned by Judge Robert L McCrary Jr. He did not yet have counsel, but he pled not guilty to the charge against him. The trial was set for August 4.[29]

**Gideon's Path Walking Up the Alley and Cook's Path Walking Up the Sidewalk**

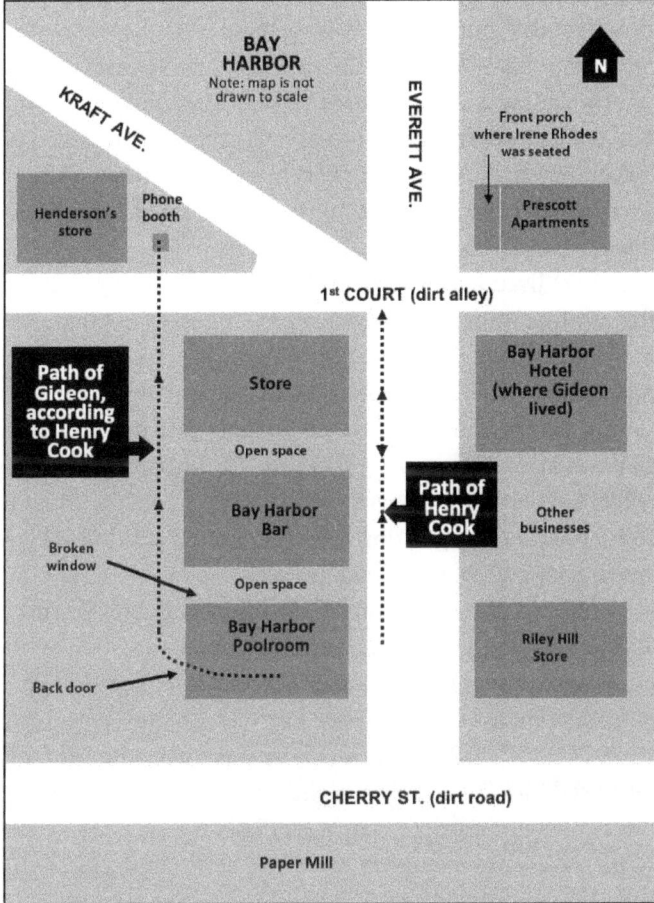

Clarence Gideon's path walking up the alley behind the poolroom, and Henry Cook's path walking up the street in front of the pool-room, in the early morning of June 3, 1961. Drawn by Lee Ann Gun.

The area where these events took place was a half-block section of Everitt Avenue, a north–south street, with commercial buildings and rooming houses on the sides of the street. On the west side, from north to south, were Henderson's Grocery, the phone booth, the Bay Harbor Bar, and the Bay Harbor Pool Room. On the east side, from north to south, among other buildings, were Prescott's Apartments (where Irene Rhodes lived), the Bay Harbor Hotel (the rooming house where Clarence Gideon stayed), and the Riley Hill Grocery.

Everitt Avenue ended at the south end of this half block, and at the end of the street, immediately to the south, was the manufacturing plant of the International Paper Company, where wood pulp was processed into paper. It was the most impressive feature of the area, dominating everything for miles around. Its smokestacks soared at least 100 feet into the sky, emitting smoke and fumes, and the papermaking process caused an acrid odor that pervaded the entire countryside for 10 or 15 miles in every direction. Those living in nearby Panama City were exposed to the caustic smell, which burned the eyes, the nose, and the throat.

I (the author) lived and worked in Panama City during the summer of 1957, after my first semester of law school. This was four years before the break-in of the poolroom. I worked on a Dr. Pepper truck, delivering cases of Dr. Pepper and other beverages to every grocery store, bar, restaurant, filling station, or other business around Panama City that sold soft drinks. Although it was many years ago, I still can specifically remember being inside the Riley Hill Grocery, which was almost directly across the street from the Bay Harbor Pool Room, delivering soft drinks, and I am almost certain that we delivered drinks at the poolroom as well.

It was a rundown area consisting of old, dingy buildings set just north of the paper mill, which towered overhead. It was the place where the paper mill workers lived, bought groceries, drank beer, and played pool.

The defendant in this case, Clarence Earl Gideon, was born in Hannibal, Missouri, in 1910. His father died when he was three, and his mother and stepfather raised him.[30] He had an eighth-grade education.[31] At 14, he ran away from home but returned home a year later.[32]

At 15, he broke into a country store and stole some clothing. He was apprehended and convicted as a juvenile. He was paroled a year later.[33] He got married, and then at 18, he received a 10-year sentence to the Missouri state penitentiary for burglary, larceny, and robbery. Apparently, his marriage ended around this time. He was released on parole when he was 22 years old.[34]

From Fred Turner, the lawyer appointed to represent Gideon at his second trial, after Gideon's victory before the Supreme Court, I learned that in 1934 Gideon and his accomplices decided to rob a bank. They needed machine guns for the crime and broke into a United States armory to obtain them. They put the machine guns in the back seat of their "touring car," which had open sides. The car got stuck, and a deputy sheriff stopped to help them. The officer saw the machine guns and arrested Gideon and his accomplices.[35] They were convicted in federal court in Missouri, and he was given two three-year sentences for unlawful possession of government property. He was granted conditional release (parole) from these sentences in 1937.[36]

In 1939, he was charged under the Missouri second-offender habitual criminal statute for burglary and larceny. He was sentenced to 10 years for the burglary and five for the larceny, with the sentences to run concurrently. He escaped from prison in 1943 but was apprehended in 1944. The burglary and larceny sentences were commuted, but he was given 10 years for the escape.[37] He left prison in 1950 and married a second time, but the couple separated in 1951.[38] He was arrested in 1951 in Texas for burglary in the nighttime, receiving a sentence of two years,[39] and was released after serving 13 months.[40]

In 1953, he was diagnosed with tuberculosis and received 18 months of treatment for that illness in a hospital in New Orleans. He left the hospital in 1954.[41]

He married a third time in 1955, and he and his wife moved to Orange, Texas,[42] where they bought a pool hall and beer parlor and called it Smitty's Bar. At the time of the Bay Harbor, Florida, break-in in 1961, Gideon was using "Smitty" as a nickname.[43] After spending six months in Orange, he left his wife, and they divorced.[44]

Later in 1955, he married his fourth wife, Ruth Ada Carpenter Babineaux, who was his spouse at the time of the Bay Harbor break-in. She had three children, and they soon had two of their own.[45] They moved to Panama City, Florida, in 1957 and, in 1959, had a sixth child.[46]

In December 1959, Gideon entered a hospital in Tallahassee, where for eight months he again was treated for tuberculosis.[47] In 1960, he became a cook on a barge for a construction company in Baton Rouge, Louisiana. However, he was laid off in January 1961 when the health department learned he had had tuberculosis.[48] He returned to Panama City and attempted to earn a living by "running" gambling games.[49] However, during the first months of 1961, he often was without work.[50] He was unable to support his wife and children,[51] and his wife was suing him for divorce and child support.[52]

By the summer of 1961, he had spent one year in a juvenile correctional institution and about eighteen years in adult prisons. And when not in prison, he often was on parole.

At the time of the break-in, Gideon was five feet, eleven inches tall, and weighed 140 pounds. He had gray hair. He was an alcoholic.[53]

What was Clarence Gideon like? Well, for one thing, he wasn't the glum loner as he was portrayed in the 1980 movie *Gideon's Trumpet*. Henry Fonda was the actor who played the part of Clarence Gideon in that film.

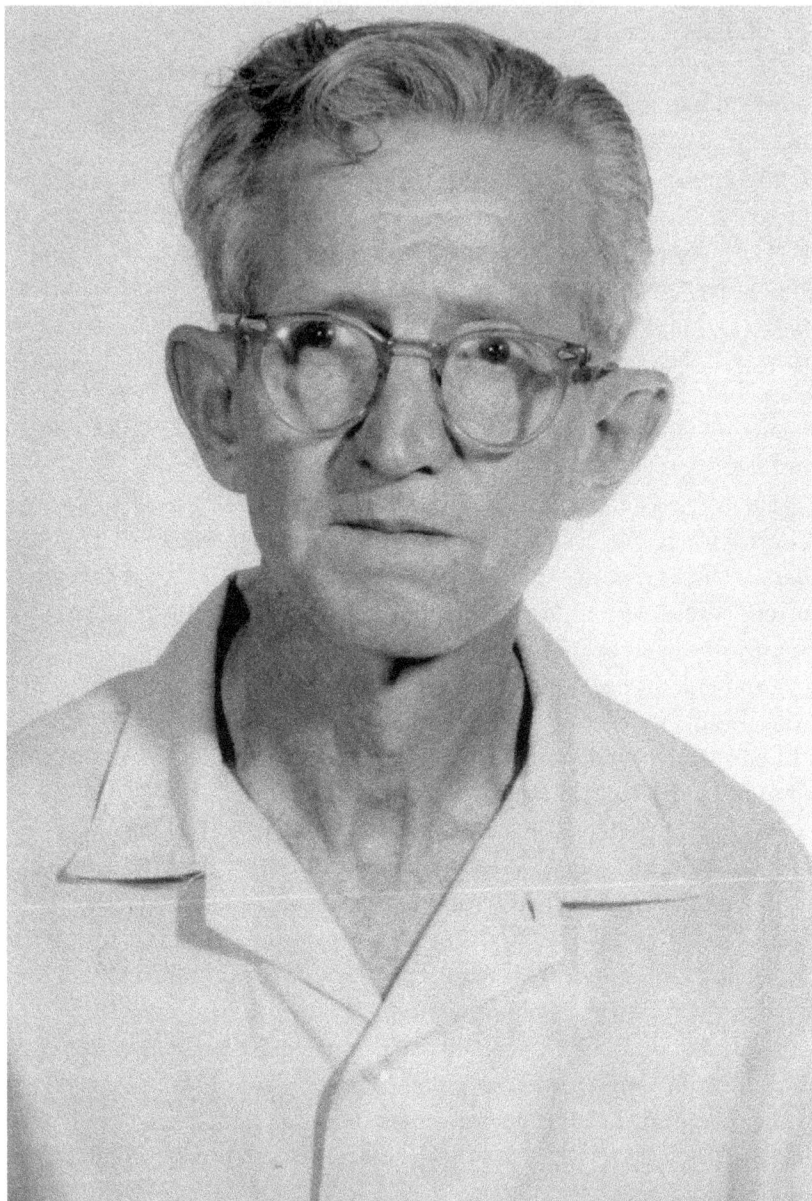

Clarence Earl Gideon. Photo by Woody Wisner, 1963, courtesy of the State Archives of Florida.

Those who knew Gideon say he was friendly. He enjoyed being with people. He liked to talk.

On May 11, 2022, I took part in an exchange of email messages with Gary Yates of Tallahassee regarding, among other things, the *Gideon* case. Gary lives in Tallahassee but was raised in Panama City. Here is some information he has generously provided to me about Clarence Gideon:

> My Mom and Dad had a shoe store and grocery store in Springfield/Millville area, so they knew just about everybody there back in the late 50s and 60s. My Uncle (now deceased) worked at International Paper, which is right next to the Bay Harbor Pool Room. He occasionally interacted with Gideon in that area. According to his children, his impression was that Gideon had a decent personality and a dry sense of humor. As you have written, not so much of the character that Henry Fonda played. My Mom remembered selling him some groceries on credit and that he actually paid her (unlike lots of other residents).

# 3

## The Right to Counsel Colloquy

August 4, 1961, was the day set for Clarence Gideon's trial. He had been in jail since his arrest on June 3. He had been trying to obtain an attorney to represent him at the trial but was unsuccessful. The reason probably was a lack of money to pay a lawyer's fee.

The trial judge was Circuit Judge Robert L. McCrary Jr. The prosecutor was Assistant State Attorney William E. Harris. Following the formal opening of the court, this colloquy took place:

> The Court: The next case on the docket is the case of the State of Florida, Plaintiff v. Clarence Earl Gideon, Defendant. What says the State? Are you ready to go to trial?
>
> Mr. Harris: The State is ready, your Honor.
>
> The Court: What says the Defendant? Are you ready to go to trial in this case?
>
> The Defendant: I am not ready, your Honor.
>
> The Court: Did you plead not guilty to this charge by reason of insanity?
>
> The Defendant: No, sir.
>
> The Court: Why aren't you ready?
>
> The Defendant: I have no Counsel.
>
> The Court: Why do you not have Counsel? Did you not know that your case was set for trial today?
>
> The Defendant: Yes, sir, I knew that it was set for trial today.
>
> The Court: Why, then, did you not secure Counsel and be prepared to go to trial?

The Defendant answered the Court's question but spoke in such low tones that it was not audible.

The Court: Come closer up, Mr. Gideon. I can't understand you. I don't know what you said, and the reporter didn't understand you either. At this point, the Defendant arose from his chair at the Counsel Table and walked up and stood directly in front of the Bench, facing his Honor, Judge McCrary.

The Court: Now, tell us what you said again so that we can understand you, please.

The Defendant: Your Honor, I said: I request this Court to appoint Counsel to represent me in this trial.

The Court: Mr. Gideon, I am sorry, but I cannot appoint Counsel to represent you in this case. Under the laws of the State of Florida, the only time the Court can appoint Counsel to represent a Defendant is when that person is charged with a capital offense [an offense for which a defendant could be put to death if convicted]. I am sorry, but I will have to deny your request to appoint Counsel to defend you in this case.

The Defendant: The United States Supreme Court says I am entitled to be represented by Counsel.

The Court: (Addressing the reporter) Let the record show that the Defendant has asked the Court to appoint Counsel to represent him in this trial, and the Court denied the request and informed the Defendant that the only time the Court could appoint Counsel to represent a Defendant was in cases where the Defendant was charged with a capital offense. The Defendant stated to the Court that the United States Supreme Court said he was entitled to it.

(Addressing the Defendant) Are you now ready to go to trial?

The Defendant: Yes, sir.[1]

Two main participants in Gideon's 1961 trial were Gideon himself and the trial judge, Robert McCrary. We have already learned about Gideon's background. Who was Judge McCrary?

In conversations and telephone interviews with three persons in Panama City who knew him well, I learned the following information about Judge McCrary. He graduated from the University of Florida and the University of Florida Law School. He was 45 years old and married with three children. He was of average height and was heavyset. According to a person who knew him when he was on the bench, "he was all business" and he "followed the law."[2] He was "calm and thoughtful, a very good judge."[3] He kept order and did not tolerate disturbances in his courtroom. He did not easily get angry.[4] Fred Turner, Gideon's appointed attorney at the second trial after Gideon had won his case in the Supreme Court, was less complimentary than others. When I asked him what Judge McCrary was like, he told me that McCrary had been an Army officer, a Lieutenant Colonel in the field artillery in World War II, and "he sometimes looked straight ahead, with blinders."[5] When not on the bench, McCrary was a "people person."[6] He was kind, jovial, good-natured, and a good friend.[7] You could count on his word.[8]

When he said that under the law he could only appoint counsel in a capital case, not in a noncapital felony case such as Gideon's, Judge McCrary was wrong. When Clarence Gideon told McCrary that the Supreme Court had said he was entitled to the appointment of counsel, he also was wrong. They both were wrong because their statements on August 4, 1961, were inconsistent with the decision of the Supreme Court in the case of *Betts v. Brady*,[9] which was the law of the land as of 1961 regarding the right to counsel in noncapital felony cases in state courts.

Under the 1942 *Betts* decision an indigent defendant in a state felony prosecution was entitled to the appointment of counsel if there was a special circumstance involved in the case, which would make it difficult for the defendant to receive a fair trial without the benefit of counsel. In addition to the special circumstances mentioned in chapter 1, special circumstances included such things as illiteracy of the defendant, the fact that the charges against the defendant were complex, or the defendant's difficulty understanding the English language.

There were no special circumstances in Gideon's case. He was over 50 years old. He had previous experience as a defendant in criminal cases and, therefore, was familiar with court procedures. Accordingly, under the principles of *Betts v. Brady*, he was not entitled to the appointment of counsel.

Even so, in his colloquy with Judge McCrary, Gideon seemed certain he was entitled to counsel. What led him to erroneously believe that under Supreme Court precedent Judge McCrary should have appointed an attorney for him? One reason might have been that he previously, in 1934, had been tried and convicted in a federal court, where counsel was being provided to indigent defendants. Also, he previously had been tried and convicted in Missouri state courts, and Missouri had a statute requiring appointment of counsel in felony cases.[10] He could have mistakenly thought that the United States Supreme Court had mandated the Missouri statute and practice.

Judge McCrary was mistaken when he said that under Florida law, the only time he was allowed to appoint counsel was in a capital case. He was

Circuit judge Robert L. McCrary Jr. Reprinted with permission from CBS News.

indeed required by Florida statute to appoint in a capital case, but his power to appoint was much broader. *Betts v. Brady* required appointment if one or more special circumstances were implicated, and *Betts* was as much a part of the law of Florida as the statute of the state requiring an appointment of counsel for the indigent defendant in a capital case.[11] After all, United States Supreme Court decisions construing portions of the United States Constitution are the law of the land.

McCrary was required by *Betts v. Brady* to be aware of the existence of special circumstances and to appoint counsel if a special circumstance was present in a case. Did McCrary conduct an inquiry to make such a determination in Gideon's case? Virgil Q. Mayo, one of the lawyers who practiced in that judicial circuit in 1961, said to me in a telephone interview that McCrary and the other two judges in the circuit would appoint counsel if an indigent defendant was incompetent to handle his own defense.[12] However, Mayo and Fred Turner, who also practiced before those judges, told me that it was not Judge McCrary's custom, or the custom of the other judges in the circuit to conduct inquiries specifically to determine the existence of special circumstances that would require appointment under *Betts v. Brady*.[13]

Bay County, Florida, where the Gideon trial took place, is in Florida's Panhandle, a remote, sparsely populated area. It is possible that McCrary had little contact with judges from other parts of the state and was unaware of the *Betts* decision. Turner commented that if Judge McCrary knew of the *Betts* decision, it might have been only a vague idea somewhere in the back of his mind.[14] Both Mayo and Turner were unsure whether McCrary knew about the *Betts* case.[15]

Another reason why McCrary was wrong when he told Gideon that he could appoint only in a capital case is that, as a trial judge, he had inherent powers to appoint counsel in any case before him. Members of the bar are required to accept such appointments, without compensation, as part of the privilege of practicing law.[16]

However, McCrary would have encountered practical problems if he had appointed counsel very often because there were so few lawyers in Bay County. According to Martindale-Hubbell, in 1960 there were 36 lawyers in that county: 34 in Panama City, and one in each of the two other towns.[17] One of the 36 was not admitted to practice in Florida, and another was William Harris, the assistant state attorney who prosecuted cases in that county. That would have left 34 lawyers, some of whom were not trial lawyers, to handle the cases of the indigent defendants in the county. Of the 34, only two—Turner and Mayo—were experienced criminal defense lawyers.

In 1961, an attorney appointed by a court to represent a defendant in a capital case in Florida was paid a fee of only $90, and the counties did not have any funds to pay lawyers who might be appointed in noncapital cases.[18]

The population of Bay County was 67,131 in 1961. The number of felonies in that county that year could be estimated at 1,650.[19] Not all defendants would have been indigent, but with this volume of crime and so few lawyers available for appointment, and no funds to pay for lawyers in noncapital cases, the circuit judges in that county would have had difficulty appointing counsel for very many of the indigent defendants appearing before their court. It is clear that there were inherent problems in implementing *Betts v. Brady* in areas such as Bay County, Florida, in 1961.

# 4

# Gideon's Trial, Conviction, and Sentence

Counsel was not appointed for Gideon, and he had to try his own case. The trial began when six men were called as prospective jurors. In Florida, 12 jurors are needed in capital cases, but only six in noncapital trials, and Gideon's case was noncapital. The prosecutor, William Harris, asked questions of the six and stated that he accepted each as a juror.

Judge McCrary then began talking to the six men. He asked whether any of them knew the defendant, Clarence Earl Gideon. They all answered no. He then asked this question: "Will you give him the same fair trial and consideration, since he is not represented by counsel, that you would if he were represented by counsel?" They all answered yes.[1]

The judge asked several other questions that would have been asked by the defense attorney if Gideon had been represented by counsel. Another question, for example, was whether any of them would have any bias or prejudice against Gideon. Would they pay close attention to all of the testimony, and "if, after you have heard all of the testimony, there is a doubt in your mind that this defendant is not guilty of the crime he is charged with . . . will you give him the benefit of the doubt and acquit him?"[2]

McCrary's next and last question during his brief interrogation of the prospective jurors on behalf of the defendant was, "You will be fair to him as well as to the State in rendering your verdict in this case?"[3]

In those days, when an attorney did not represent a defendant, it was the belief among some lawyers and judges that the trial judge could protect the defendant by doing many of the things a defense attorney would have done for them, thereby making sure that the trial would be fair. This was one of the justifications given for not appointing counsel for indigent defendants in the absence of special circumstances. Some attorneys then, and virtually all today, realize how fallacious it was to believe that the trial judge could adequately protect a defendant's interests in such a situation. A judge should be an impartial decision-maker, while a lawyer is an advocate. It was foolish to think that one person could simultaneously play both roles.

After asking these questions of the prospective jurors, McCrary said this to Clarence Gideon:

> **The Court:** Now, Mr. Gideon, look these six Gentlemen over and if you don't want them to sit as a Jury to try your case, just point out one, or more, all six if you want to, and the Court will excuse them, and we will call another, or some others, to try your case. You don't have to have a reason, just look them over, and if you don't like their looks, that's all it takes to get them excused; just point out any one, two, three, four, five, or all six of them if you want to, and the Court will excuse them.

Gideon did not object to any of the prospective jurors. He responded to Judge McCrary by saying, "They suit me all right, your Honor."[4]

The members of the jury were sworn, and the next phase of the trial consisted of opening statements. Prosecutor Harris gave his. Then, at this point, the defendant walked around the counsel table and stood facing the jury, and told them what he expected the evidence on his behalf to show.[5]

The opening and closing statements or arguments were not recorded by the court reporter, so we do not know what Gideon said. It was the practice at the time for court reporters not to record opening or closing arguments unless specifically requested to do so.[6]

We can speculate about what Gideon said in his opening statement by reviewing his testimony at his second trial, after the Supreme Court reversed his conviction and remanded the case back to Bay County for a new trial.

In his first trial, he chose not to take the stand and give testimony, but in the second trial, he waived his constitutional right not to testify and did take the witness stand to give his version of the events that took place on June 3, 1961.

At the second trial, Gideon's testimony was that he often got up early and called a taxi to take him from Bay Harbor to Panama City, but it was his habit to walk across Everitt Avenue and call from the phone booth. By making the call there, he would not awake others at his boarding house, which was called the "Bay Harbor Hotel."[7]

William Harris began presenting evidence for the State of Florida. In telephone interviews with lawyers who knew him I learned what he was like. He was a tall, muscular man.[8] He was a capable trial lawyer,[9] and had a "presence" in the courtroom.[10] He was described as being "quick," and lawyers said he could be "funny" in court proceedings.[11] He was "old school, rough, tough, a fine lawyer."[12] He was "plain spoken."[13] He was described as "gruff on the outside," but "with a heart of gold" and a "great sense of fairness."[14] "Everyone liked him."[15]

He called two witnesses for the State. One was Ira Strickland Jr., the owner of the Bay Harbor Pool Room, and the other was Henry Cook. Strickland testified on direct examination by Harris that he had closed the business at 12 o'clock midnight the evening of June 2, 1961. He had locked the door, and the windows had been closed and fastened.[16] The next morning, police were waiting for him when he arrived at the poolroom. The cigarette machine and jukebox had been broken into. There had been money taken from each machine, but there was no way of knowing exactly how much had been stolen. The intruder had entered through a side window near the rear of the building. That window did not have any bars on it.[17]

Gideon cross-examined Ira Strickland. The following are some of the exchanges that took place between the two of them.

**By the Defendant:**

Q. Where does the "Juke" Box sit in the building?

A. In the extreme front of the building.

Q. Where does the Cigarette Machine sit in the building?

A. It also sits in front of the building.[18]

\* \* \* \* \*

Q. How was the window broken?

A. When I arrived that morning, the window was broken out. There was a garbage can that had been removed from the back and carried around to the side, and I assumed the purpose of it was to enter the building through the window.[19]

Gideon apparently wanted to know whether the intruder had entered through an open door and therefore would not be guilty of "breaking." This is why he asked the next questions.

Q. Mr. Strickland, did you ever go off and leave your building unlocked?

A. Yes, sir.

Q. You have?

A. Yes, sir, I have, for a short while.

Q. Did you ever go off and leave it unlocked overnight?

A. No, sir.

Q. Did you ever leave your building open?

**The Court:** I don't think that has any bearing on this case. The testimony here is that the building was securely locked on the night of the entrance into it through a broken window. That particular time is all we are interested in here; what has been done prior to this time would have no bearing on this case.

**By the Defendant:**

Q. You locked the building that night?

A. Yes, sir.

Q. You are positive of that?

A. I am positive, yes, sir.[20]

Gideon next turned to questions about the merchandise that had been taken during the break-in. Answers by the witness were not very satisfactory to Gideon.

Q. Do you know positively what merchandise was removed from the building?

A. No, sir, I don't. I do know there was some Wine and Beer taken out, but I can't tell you exactly how much; it was removed from the shelves in the Bar.

Q. I wish you would tell this Court and Jury just what this person took out of the building.

A. I can't tell them exactly what was taken out. I don't know.

Q. What do you mean by "I don't know?" You have said that certain things were taken out or removed from the building. Now, will you tell the Court and Jury just exactly what was taken out, how much of each item was taken, that you have stated was taken, including the money you say was in the "Juke" Box and Cigarette Machine?

**The Court:** This witness has testified that he did not know how much Wine or Beer was taken. He has also stated that he had no way of knowing how much money was in the "Juke" Box and Cigarette Machine because they were both automatic machines, and he had no way of knowing. Do you want to ask him any more questions?

**The Defendant:** No, sir, that's all.[21]

That ended the testimony by that witness. The second and last witness called by Harris was Henry Cook. In response to questions by Harris, Cook said that he arrived back from Apalachicola at about 5:30 a.m. on June 3, 1961, and that he saw the man he knew as Clarence Gideon, the defendant in this trial, now sitting in the courtroom, through the window of the darkened poolroom standing by the cigarette machine. He stated that he watched him for about a minute "or a little more."[22]

Cook testified that Gideon left the poolroom by the back door, walked up the alley to the corner, and called a cab. Gideon was carrying some wine. His pockets bulged out.[23]

After Gideon left in the cab, Cook said he walked back to the poolroom, where, through the window, he could see the money box on the pool table. The cigarette machine was "all torn up." The face of the machine was lying on the table with the money box.[24]

He also saw the window near the rear of the building and the garbage can placed by the window. The window was broken out.[25]

Gideon then began his cross-examination.

### By the Defendant:

Q. Have you ever been convicted of a felony?

A. No, sir, never have.[26]

* * * * *

Q. Was it dark or daylight?

A. It was dark enough that I had to put my head up to the window to see you—but I seen you.

Q. And where did you go after that?

A. I walked up to the corner.

Q. You walked up to the corner, eh?

A. Yes, sir.

Q. When was the next time you seen me?

A. When I saw you walk up and get in the Cab.

Q. Didn't you just get through saying you saw me come out the back door of the Pool Room?

A. You said the "next time"—I first saw you through the window, in the Pool Room, standing up by the Cigarette Machine—the next time I saw you was when you came out the back door and walked up to the corner and called a Cab—and the next time I saw you was when you walked up and got in the Cab.

Q. How could you see me come out of the back door?

A. I seen you come out just as I walked by.

**Q.** You say that I come out of the building and walked up to the corner; how did you see me?

**A.** You were there about the same time I was—it was you—I'm definitely sure of that.

Gideon next asked questions about the wine and about the window that supposedly was the point of entry by the intruder.

**Q.** You said I was carrying something—what was I carrying?

**A.** A pint of Wine.

**Q.** A 'what'?

**A.** A pint of Wine.

**Q.** A pint of Wine?

**A.** Yes, sir, a pint of Wine.

**Q.** Do You know positively that I was carrying a pint of Wine?

**A.** Yes, I know you was.

**Q.** How do you know that?

**A.** Because I seen it in your hand.

**Q.** And you saw me with a pint of Wine?

**A.** Yes.

**Q.** How far away from me were you?

**A.** I was twenty yards, or less, something like that.[27]

\* \* \* \* \*

**Q.** Did you see that the window was broken out?

**A.** Yes, I saw it.

**Q.** How was it broken?

**A.** Well, it was broken all to pieces, it was laying outside on the ground.

**Q.** No glass left in it at all?

**A.** There might have been a small piece left in the corner, but that's all if there was any.

**Q.** All the glass was on the outside of the building?

**A.** All that I saw was on the outside.[28]

That ended the cross-examination of Henry Cook. Next, Gideon examined his witnesses, who had been subpoenaed beforehand. Apparently, while he was in jail awaiting trial, he had been allowed to have the subpoenas issued and served on eight witnesses.

The first of his witnesses was Henry Berryhill Jr., a police officer who had been patrolling the area around the poolroom at 5:00 or 5:15 the morning

of the break-in. He found a door open in the building and met Henry Cook
at the front of the building. Cook told him that he saw Clarence Gideon
leaving the building. Berryhill said that entrance into the building had been
gained through a window near the back of the building. The window had
been broken from the outside.[29]

Duell Pitts followed Berryhill. He also was a police officer, and he confirmed that the window had been broken from the outside because most of
the glass was on the inside.[30]

The fifth witness called to testify by Clarence Gideon was Arthur Widin-
camp, the owner of the building where the pool hall was located and the
father-in-law of Ira Strickland Jr. His main addition to the evidence was to
testify that the window in the back of the pool hall that had been broken,
with the glass gone, was large enough for a person to crawl through.[31]

Gideon's third witness was Preston Gray, the cab driver who picked him
up at the telephone booth and drove him to the bar in Panama City, a couple
of miles from Bay Harbor.

They had this exchange:

**Q.** Was it anything out of the ordinary for me to call you?
**A.** No, sir, you called me all the time.
**Q.** That morning, did I have any Wine, Beer, Whiskey, or other
intoxicating drinks on me or with me?
**A.** No, sir, not that I could see.[32]

\* \* \* \* \*

**Q.** Would you say I was intoxicated that morning?
**A.** No, sir, I wouldn't.[33]

William Harris then cross-examined Gray:

**Q.** Do You know whether or not [Gideon] was unemployed at that
time, and had he been unemployed for some time?
**A.** I knew he was working at the Pool Room—now, whether he was
getting paid or not, I don't know.[34]

\* \* \* \* \*

**Q.** How much was the cab fare?
**A.** A dollar ($1.00).
**Q.** Did he give you a tip?
**A.** Yes, sir.
**Q.** How much tip did he give you?

**A.** Fifty cents.

**Q.** What kind of money did he pay you with?

**A.** Quarters.[35]

Irene Rhodes was the fourth witness called to the witness stand by the defendant. She was the woman sitting on her porch across the street from the telephone booth on the morning of the crime. Under direct examination by the defendant, she agreed that the night before the break-in, she and the defendant had been drinking together.[36] She also said that on the morning of the crime, she was on her front porch.[37] Gideon then asked:

**Q.** When did you first know the place had been broken into?
And her answer was:

**A.** When the young man . . . what's his name, Cook . . . Henry Cook, when he walked up to the porch and told me.[38]

Here are more of Gideon's questions and her answers:

**Q.** Did he [Cook] leave down there before I left the Telephone Booth?

**A.** Yes, He left and called the "Cops."[39]

* * * * *

**Q.** When you first saw me, where was I?

**A.** When you came out of the Alley and walked over to call a taxi.[40]

* * * * *

**Q.** Is it common for me to come out through the Alley?

**A.** That's right. I didn't think a thing about it—and when you called a Cab, I didn't think anything about that, either. I just thought you were going downtown.

**Q.** This, Mr. Cook, when he come from toward the Pool Room to your place, where you were on the porch, that was about a half-block, wasn't it?

**A.** About a half-block, yes.

**Q.** Could he have seen me come out the back door of that place from where he was?

**A.** No, I don't think so.[41]

William Harris cross-examined her, asking:

**Q.** Did you go over to the phone booth where this man made the phone call from?

**A.** Yes.

**Q.** Why did you go over there?

**A.** Well, I just went over there, that's all.

**Q.** He had put that Wine down there, and you went over there and got it didn't you?

**A.** Yes.

**Q.** You saw him when he put it there, didn't you?

**A.** It was there, I saw it there, and I picked it up.[42]

On redirect examination, Gideon asked:

**Q.** Was it [the wine] inside or outside the booth?

**A.** Outside.[43]

\* \* \* \* \*

**Q.** What kind of wine was it?

**A.** I don't know. I didn't pay no attention to it. I gave it to my Landlord.

**Q.** Gave it to your Landlord.

**A.** Yes, because he was sick.[44]

A witness named G. F. Hall had been subpoenaed by Gideon. He apparently was an employee of the Bay Harbor Pool Room. Gideon asked him several questions, but none of his answers contributed anything new to the body of information already testified to in the case. Gideon's seventh witness was Robert Richardson, a bartender at the Bay Harbor Bar, located in the building to the immediate north of the poolroom. He testified that on the morning the crime was committed, he had seen an "Oil Can or a Drum, it was a big can . . . setting up beside the window."[45]

Gideon's last witness was Velva Estelle Morris, the owner of the Bay Harbor Hotel, where Gideon lived, on the east side of Everitt Avenue, across the street from the Bay Harbor Pool Room. Here are some exchanges between Gideon and Mrs. Morris:

**Q.** On the morning this crime was committed, when the Bay Harbor Pool Room was broken into, did I go anywhere the night before?

**A.** Well, I think you went up at bedtime and went to bed. There wasn't too many in the hotel that night. I'm almost positive you went upstairs and went to bed.

**Q.** Isn't it true, Mrs. Morris, that I don't ordinarily use the Telephone in the hotel when people are sleeping?

**A.** Yes, that's true. Most of the men are considerate of the sleepers in using the Telephone in the house.

**Q.** Is it not true that I went to the corner and used the Public Telephone when the guests are asleep in the hotel?

**A.** Yes, that is true. Most of the men did that because it disturbs the sleepers. . . .[46]

\* \* \* \* \*

**Q.** Mrs. Morris, during the time I lived at the hotel, did you ever know of me being out drunk?

**A.** No.

**Q.** Did you ever see me drunk?

**A.** No.

**Q.** Did you ever hear of me getting drunk?

**A.** No.[47]

Mr. Harris then cross-examined this witness. He wanted to know how true her testimony was that Gideon had been in bed the night of the break-in. Here are his questions and her answers:

**Q.** Mrs. Morris, you don't know whether this man went to bed at all that night, do you?

**A.** Why, yes, he went to bed; that is, he went upstairs. I saw him when he went up. I was sitting in the Lobby.

**Q.** What time was that?

**A.** About ten o'clock.

**Q.** Was that the last time you saw him?

**A.** Yes, that was the last time I saw him when he went upstairs.

**Q.** He went upstairs?

**A.** Yes, he went upstairs.

**Q.** But you don't know whether he went to bed or not, do you?

**A.** Why no, I don't know that. I know he went upstairs; I saw him go up, and I never heard him come down.[48]

At this point, the testimony of witnesses ended. Judge McCrary said this to Gideon:

Do you wish to take the stand and tell the Jury your version of this case, Mr. Gideon? As I told you before, you are not required to take the witness stand, and it will not be held against you if you do not take it, but it is your privilege, and you may do so at this time if you desire to.[49]

Gideon's response was, "I don't care to take the witness stand, your Honor."[50]

The next part of the trial consisted of the closing arguments for each side. Gideon talked to the jurors for approximately 11 minutes. Then Harris spoke for about nine minutes.[51]

The judge orally gave his instructions to the jury, letting the jurors know that the defendant comes into court with the presumption of innocence and that he should only be found guilty if the evidence proved him guilty beyond a reasonable doubt.[52] The judge explained the elements of the crime—that to convict, the jurors had to find that Gideon did break and enter the building in which the Bay Harbor Pool Room was located, with the intent to commit petit larceny.

The jury found the defendant guilty on the day of trial, August 4, 1961. However, sentencing was postponed to allow the probation office to conduct a presentence investigation report to provide information to assist the judge in deciding what sentence to impose.

On August 25, 1961, Judge McCrary imposed the maximum sentence on Gideon for his crime, committing him to the State Prison at Raiford, near Starke, Florida, for a period of five years. Gideon probably received the maximum because of his past criminal record, which included state criminal offenses in Missouri and Texas and the federal crime in Missouri.

# 5

## Petition for Review to the Florida Supreme Court

The commitment papers were signed by Judge McCrary on August 30, 1961.[1] Gideon was transported under armed guard to the State Prison at Raiford, in the northeast corner of the state, and he arrived there a few days after August 30. He had made the comment during his interview for the presentence investigation that he had been "framed" and this indicated that he would probably seek review of his conviction soon after beginning to serve his sentence.

There were two types of review available to him. One was review by direct appeal from the conviction and sentence. The other was through a petition for writ of habeas corpus.

In 1961, a direct appeal was ordinarily used by a convicted defendant with sufficient funds to hire a lawyer for the appeal. However, indigent defendants could take their appeals by themselves. There was not yet a constitutional right to counsel for an indigent in a criminal appeal. It would not be until March 18, 1963, when the Supreme Court would decide that a state must provide a lawyer, at public expense, for an indigent convicted defendant who wished to appeal. That case was *Douglas v. California*,[2] and it was announced by the Court on the same day that the decision in *Gideon v. Wainwright*[3] was announced.

In 1956, the Court had decided the *Griffin v. Illinois* case,[4] dealing with appeals by indigent convicted defendants. The Court held that under the Equal Protection and Due Processes Clauses of the Fourteenth Amendment, a state must provide a trial transcript, at state expense, or some other means of perfecting an appeal, for an indigent convicted defendant seeking appellate review of their conviction. But the principle requiring equality for poor persons inherent in that decision had not been extended to providing counsel for indigent criminal appellants, at least not by 1961.

The procedures for a direct appeal are complicated from a layperson's standpoint. In 1961, a convicted defendant initiated the appeal by filing a one-page notice of appeal with the clerk's office of the trial court. The notice had to be filed within 30 days after the conviction or sentence, whichever was later. This was, and is, a "jurisdictional" time period, meaning that if the notice is not filed within that period, the appellate court will not gain the authority—the "jurisdiction"—to consider the case.

Along with the notice of appeal, an indigent defendant taking their own appeal had to file an "affidavit of indigency," stating that they were a pauper and did not have enough money to pay the costs of the appeal, together with a "motion for leave to proceed in forma pauperis." When this was done, the judge would declare the appellant indigent and that appellant would not have to pay the costs of the appeal, including the costs of the typing of transcripts of testimony.

The appellant next filed "designations to the clerk," specifying which portions of the record would be required for the appeal. The court reporter typed the transcripts, and the clerk put together the "record" (the charging document—called an "information" if filed by the prosecution, or the "indictment" if issued by the grand jury—motions, orders, and transcripts of testimony) for transmittal to the district court of appeal for that geographical area of the state. This was an intermediate appellate court. If it was a capital case, the appeal instead was taken directly to the Florida Supreme Court. The appellant also filed, with the case papers, the "assignments of error"— the grounds being asserted for overturning the conviction. The clerk of the trial court transmitted the papers in the case to the clerk's office of the appellate court.

The briefs for the convicted defendant (appellant) and the state (appellee) were prepared and filed in the appellate court. If indigent, the appellant would use the prison library to prepare their brief. If represented by a lawyer, the case was argued orally by both sides before the three-person intermediate appellate court panel. If the defendant was indigent, in prison, handling their own appeal, the decision in noncapital cases was made by the intermediate appellate court on the basis of the briefs. In that situation, there was no oral argument. If it was a capital case, it went directly from the trial court to the seven-justice Supreme Court of Florida. If it was a capital case, the defendant-appellant would have been represented by an attorney. Florida statutes required appointment of counsel in death cases, both at the trial level and for the appeal.

If the district court of appeal ruled against the appellant, there was the possibility of seeking review of that decision by the Florida Supreme Court. If the issues in the case involved only state law, the case stayed within the state judicial system. However, if there was an issue of federal law involved, such as an issue of federal constitutional law, there was the possibility of further review in federal courts, including the Supreme Court of the United States. So, if the defendant-appellant lost his case in the state judicial system, further review by federal courts was possible, but only if there was an issue of federal law involved.

The alternative—the one Gideon chose—was to file a petition for a writ of habeas corpus. The writ of habeas corpus is an ancient English common law order of court that frees persons unlawfully restrained of their liberty. It is called the "Great Writ," with good reason because it protects the freedom of individuals from arbitrary governmental power. At our country's founding, we assimilated the remedy of habeas corpus from the English common law, making it part of our own jurisprudence.

Our Founding Fathers included the right to habeas corpus in the United States Constitution. The provision regarding this right or "privilege" reads as follows:

> The Privilege of the Writ of Habeas Corpus shall not be suspended, unless when in Cases of Rebellion or Invasion the public Safety may require it.[5]

This provision is contained in the body of the Constitution, not in the Bill of Rights, which was added later. Because of this, an argument can be made that the Founding Fathers considered the "privilege" of habeas corpus to be the most important right of all, even greater than the rights outlined in the Bill of Rights, such as freedom of speech, freedom of press and religion[6]; the right to bear arms[7]; the right to be secure against unreasonable searches and seizures[8]; protection against being tried twice for the same offense[9]; the right to be tried by a jury[10]; and the right to be protected against cruel and unusual punishments.[11] These were added after the guarantee of the privilege of habeas corpus already had been included in the body of the Constitution.

So, in the federal system, individuals who are confined or otherwise restrained of their liberty unlawfully may assert their right to be free through the use of the remedy of habeas corpus. Also, the states have adopted state constitutional provisions and statutes guaranteeing individuals the right to relief through habeas in the state courts. In Florida, habeas corpus is a fundamental state constitutional right. Every circuit judge, district court of appeal judge, or Florida Supreme Court justice has the power to issue a writ of habeas corpus. Also, a district court of appeal as a body and the Florida Supreme Court as a body have the power to issue writs of habeas corpus.[12]

The term "habeas corpus" comes from medieval Latin, meaning "have the body." After receiving a petition for the writ, the court issues the writ addressed to the jailor, warden, or other person who allegedly is unlawfully depriving the petitioner of his liberty. That individual must have the body of the petitioner before the court on a given day and time to determine whether the restraint of the petitioner's freedom is lawful. A habeas case takes precedence over other cases on the court's docket because of the importance of protecting individual freedom.

One does not need to have legal training to institute a habeas proceeding. The petition can be no more than a letter sent to the court by the person deprived of his liberty. The petition is filed in the district or circuit where the "respondent," the jailor, lives or works.

The respondent files a "return," a response that answers the allegations of the petition, arguing that the confinement is not unlawful. The return may have exhibits attached to it, such as copies of the case's conviction, sentencing, and commitment papers. An evidentiary hearing, including testimony by witnesses, will be held, if needed, before the judge to clarify the facts involved in the case.

A habeas petition can be filed on behalf of a defendant before trial. For example, suppose charges have been filed against a defendant based on a statute that is so ambiguous or vague that it is difficult to know exactly what the defendant is charged with. In this situation, the court could order the defendant's release from jail or bail restrictions, ending the prosecution.

Petitions for habeas relief may also be filed on behalf of convicted inmates who claim their convictions are unlawful. For example, the convicted defendant may have lost a direct appeal and subsequently filed a "post-conviction" habeas petition. Or, a convicted defendant could bypass the direct appeal and instead file a habeas petition challenging the conviction as the initial method of seeking a review of the conviction. This was true in 1961. Today the convicted inmate in Florida challenging their conviction first uses Rule 3.850 of the Florida Rules of Criminal Procedure to challenge the conviction.

A direct appeal involves the original trial-level case moving upward, vertically, through the court system. A habeas petition, on the other hand, is a new, independent case collaterally challenging the results of the original trial.

Many issues can be raised either through a direct appeal or habeas corpus. Constitutional issues, such as whether there has been a denial of the right to trial by jury, can be raised either way. An issue that can be raised only by direct appeal is the question of whether the evidence was sufficient to uphold the conviction. For example, a killing does not amount to first-degree murder unless it is premeditated, which requires the clear intent to kill before the act of killing takes place. That intent can exist in the defendant's mind for a very short period, perhaps for only a few seconds, but there must be some time involved. If the intent is formed suddenly, instantaneously, and at virtually the same instant that the killing takes place, there is not enough time for premeditation, and therefore the offense would be second-degree murder. In a direct appeal, the appellate court would have the transcripts of the testimony of any witness present at the time of the killing. The appellate judges would be able to study and evaluate the testimony of that witness in determining whether there was enough time for premeditation to be formed in the defendant's mind and whether the defendant should have been convicted of second-degree murder rather than murder in the first degree.

The members of the appellate court in an appeal are limited in their review to the "record" in the case—the information or indictment, motions, court orders, and transcripts of testimony. There is no such limit in habeas cases. The habeas court can go outside the record in making its decision, using information not introduced at the trial. For instance, suppose that after the trial, the convicted defendant learns that the prosecuting witness (the victim) paid a bribe to one of the jurors during the trial for a promise by that juror that he would persuade the other jurors to convict. The issue of whether that actually took place can be raised in a habeas proceeding, even though there is nothing in the case record to support that claim because the act of bribery would have taken place outside the trial court proceedings.

If a state prisoner-petitioner files their petition for habeas relief in a Florida circuit court and loses, they may appeal that denial to the district court of appeal. If they lose there, it might be possible to obtain review in the state supreme court. Also, as noted earlier, a convicted defendant could initially file the habeas petition in a district court of appeal or the Florida Supreme Court, challenging the conviction.[13]

If the case involves an issue of federal law, when all state judicial remedies have been exhausted, and the petitioner has not been successful in the state courts, that petitioner can seek federal habeas corpus relief in federal courts.

Clarence Gideon did not take a direct appeal from his conviction. He could have filed a petition for habeas in the circuit court where the prison was located. The nearest circuit court was in the town of Starke. But a more expeditious way of obtaining review of his case was to file a habeas petition in the Florida Supreme Court in Tallahassee. The respondent in that proceeding was H. G. Cochran Jr., the director of the Division of Corrections at the time, with offices in Tallahassee. Gideon mailed his handwritten petition to the Florida Supreme Court, and it arrived there and was filed on October 11, 1961, not much more than one month after he had arrived at the State Prison at Raiford, Florida. Here are the two pertinent paragraphs of his petition:

4. I was without funds and without an attorney. I asked this court to appoint me an attorney but they denied me that right. I told this court of the 14th District of Florida, County of Bay, that United States Supreme Court had ruled that the State of Florida should see that everyone who is tried for a Felony charge should have legal counsel. But the court ignored this plea.

5. I, Clarence Earl Gideon, claim that I was denied the rights of the 4th, 5th, and 14th amendments of the Bill of Rights.[14]

The petition was only a page or so in length. Gideon did not allege that there was a special circumstance present in his case.

If the petition had alleged a possibly meritorious ground for relief, the Florida Supreme Court would have asked the Office of the Florida Attorney General to prepare and file a return, a response, in the case. However, since the petition did not allege any special circumstances, the petition had no merit under then-existing law, and on October 30, 1961, the Florida Supreme Court denied the petition with a one-sentence rejection, which read as follows:

The abovenamed petitioner has filed a petition for writ of habeas corpus in the above cause, and upon consideration thereof, it is ordered that said petition be and the same is hereby denied.[15]

# 6

## The Petition for Writ of Certiorari to the United States Supreme Court

After he had lost his habeas corpus case in the Florida Supreme Court, Gideon had further review options open to him. He had raised an issue of federal law—whether the Fourteenth Amendment required appointment of counsel for an indigent state defendant in a noncapital felony case regardless of the existence of a special circumstance. Because an issue of federal law was involved and the state courts had denied relief, he could seek review in federal courts—either by a petition for federal habeas corpus in the United States District Court for the Northern District of Florida or through a petition for writ of certiorari directly to the Supreme Court of the United States. If he began and lost in the district court, he could appeal to the United States Court of Appeals for the Fifth Circuit,[1] and if he lost there, he could petition the United States Supreme Court for a writ of certiorari. Of these two choices—beginning in the federal district court or seeking certiorari directly in the Supreme Court—Gideon decided to petition the Supreme Court for a writ of certiorari without going through the lower federal courts.

Certiorari is the method the Supreme Court uses to selectively bring cases the Justices believe to be most significant before them for decision. Petitioners seeking review by certiorari have no right to have their cases accepted and decided by the Supreme Court whether their cases have merit or not. Acceptance of a case by the Court is a discretionary matter. It requires the votes of four of the nine Justices for a writ of certiorari to be granted and the case accepted for review. So certiorari is the method the Court uses to selectively decide which cases coming to it from the highest courts of states and from lower federal courts it wants to hear.

The number of certiorari petitions granted is small in comparison with the number filed. Only a small percentage of paupers' petitions filed are granted, certainly less than 5 percent, with the Court fully hearing their cases.[2] So, statistically, Gideon's chance of success was small.

Gideon had 90 days following the October 30, 1961, decision by the Florida Supreme Court in which to file his petition for a writ of certiorari in the United States Supreme Court. The petition was received and filed at the Court on January 8, 1962, well within that jurisdictional time limit.

Who actually wrote the petition? It was written by Gideon and signed by him, but the words were dictated to him by a fellow inmate who had been a lawyer and municipal judge who became one of the most notorious murderers in the history of Florida. That inmate's name was Joseph A. Peel Jr.

I learned about Peel's role from W. Fred Turner, who had become Gideon's lawyer for the second trial, after the Supreme Court's decision. Fred Turner told me that the fellow inmate and former lawyer, Joe Peel, had stood behind Gideon, hovering over Gideon's shoulders, and had dictated the petition for certiorari to Gideon. So the petition is in Gideon's handwriting, but the words were Peel's, not Gideon's.

Peel was serving two life terms for being an accessory before the fact to the murders of Circuit Judge Curtis E. Chillingworth and his wife, Marjorie. The Chillingworths disappeared from their oceanfront home on Manalapan, an island community just south of Palm Beach, late on the evening of June 14, 1955. There were blood stains on a walkway outside the home. The judge's wallet had been left at the house. Clearly, he and his wife were victims of foul play. But for the next four years, police could not gain any information about what happened to the Chillingworths.

Then a man named Floyd "Lucky" Holzapfel bragged to a friend that he knew what had happened to Judge and Mrs. Chillingworth. Two undercover policemen pretended to become friends with Holzapfel. The three spent two days together, drinking in a motel room. In the room next door, other police were recording Holzapfel while he was heavily drinking and relating the details surrounding the killings of the Chillingworths to the two "friends."

He said that Joe Peel had paid him and George "Bobby" Lincoln $2,500 to kill Judge Chillingworth. That amount would be worth $29,877 in 2025 purchasing power. Holzapfel and Lincoln drove a motorboat to the beach in front of the home of the Chillingworths. It was 10:00 p.m. Holzapfel knocked on the door. The judge answered the door in his pajamas. Holzapfel told him that he was stranded and needed help. Bobby Lincoln, who had been hiding in the bushes, rushed to the door, knocked out the light on the house, and helped Holzapfel overpower Chillingworth. They bound and gagged him. Mrs. Chillingworth came to the door, and she, too, was bound and gagged. Peel had not asked Holzapfel and Lincoln to kill her, but they decided they had to kill her since she could identify the two of them.

Holzapfel and Lincoln dragged the couple to the water's edge and forced them into their boat. They drove the boat about four miles out into the Atlantic Ocean. They attached weights to Mrs. Chillingworth and threw her overboard. They put weights on the judge, but before they could throw him out of the boat, he jumped overboard and attempted to swim away. They drove the boat to where he was trying to swim and hit him over the head with a shotgun barrel so hard that the gun broke apart. He vanished beneath the water. Neither body was ever recovered, and the couple was declared legally dead in 1957.

Joe Peel was born in 1924. He graduated in 1949 from the Stetson University College of Law, when it was located on the DeLand campus of Stetson University, and then moved to barracks of a former military air base just north of DeLand.[3] He became a lawyer in 1949 and began practicing law in West Palm Beach. In 1952, he was appointed municipal judge, a part-time position that allowed him to continue in the private practice while also being a judge.

In 1953, in his private practice, Peel represented both the husband and wife in a divorce when there was a clear conflict of interest involved. As a result, Circuit Judge Chillingworth, also in West Palm Beach, reprimanded Peel in a disciplinary proceeding and warned Peel that if he got into similar trouble again, he (Chillingworth) would see to it that Peel would be disbarred.

As a municipal judge, Peel had the power to issue search warrants. When Peel issued a search warrant for police or sheriff's deputies to raid a gambling den or seize a moonshine still, Peel would tip off the gamblers or moonshiners, making it possible for them to avoid being disrupted in their criminal activities. These criminals paid "protection" money to Peel, as much as $3,000 per week ($35,560 in 2025 dollars).

Peel represented a woman in a divorce and advised her that the divorce was final when, in fact, he had not obtained a divorce for her. She relied on what he told her and remarried and had a child with her new husband. Then she learned that she was not divorced from her former husband, that her new "marriage" was bigamous, and her child was illegitimate.

In June 1955, Peel was scheduled to appear before Judge Chillingworth to answer the charge of professional misconduct in this divorce matter. Chillingworth had warned him in 1953 that he (Chillingworth) would seek disbarment if Peel ever again got into this kind of trouble, so Peel realized that he probably was about to lose his law license.

Peel talked with Holzapfel and Bobby Lincoln, who were confederates in his protection scheme on behalf of gamblers and moonshiners, and asked them to kill Judge Chillingworth. Eventually, Peel was disciplined in the bigamy case, but with Chillingworth gone, the punishment was a 90-day suspension of his ability to practice law rather than disbarment.

After the disclosures by Holzapfel, Bobby Lincoln agreed to cooperate with authorities and was given immunity from prosecution. He never served time for the crimes. Holzapfel was charged with the murders, was tried, found guilty, and sentenced to death. Subsequently, the death sentence was commuted to life in prison. He died in prison in 1996.

Peel resigned from his judgeship and surrendered his license to practice law on October 1, 1960. He was arrested on October 4, 1960, and charged as an accessory before the fact to the murders of the Chillingworths. He was found guilty in the murder of Judge Chillingworth on March 31, 1961, but the jury recommended mercy, sparing his life. He then pled guilty as an accessory before the fact for the killing of Mrs. Chillingworth and received a penalty of life imprisonment for that crime. Thus he began to serve two life sentences. In 1982, he was dying of cancer and was released on parole for humanitarian reasons. He died nine days later. He was 58 years old when he died.[4]

In October 1985, while I was the dean of the Stetson College of Law, I was interviewing alumni, staff, and faculty to create an institutional history of our school. One of the people I spoke with was Ray Jordan, who had been the Stetson University College of Law librarian during the 1940s and early 1950s when the school had been located in DeLand. (In 1954, the school moved to Gulfport, Florida, next to St. Petersburg, and has been there since then.) I asked her if she had known Peel, a law student in those days. She said yes and then elaborated:

> Joe Peel? He was the nicest chap. Very good looking and a big man on campus. The girls were just crazy about him, and I honestly had a hard time getting it through my head that he could have gotten involved in something like that. I thought back on it and I just wonder if he just must have been one of the early drug users or something because it was completely out of character.

In the petition for certiorari, Peel and Gideon did not mention *Betts v. Brady* and did not allege any special circumstances. The portion of the petition regarding the denial of his need for an attorney reads as follows:

[A]t the Time of petitioner's trial he ask the lower court for the aid of counsel. The court refused this aid. Petitioner told the court that this court had made decision to the effect that all citizens tried for a felony crime should have the aid of counsel. The lower court ignored this plea.

Your petitioner was compelled to make his own defense, he was incapable adequately of making his own defense. Petitioner did not plead nolo contender [nolo contendere] but that is what his trial amounted to.[5]

A nolo contendere plea has the same effect as a plea of guilty. The defendant does not admit guilt but says he does not wish to contest the charges against him. By pleading nolo instead of guilty, the defendant avoids having the plea used against him in a related civil case. For example, if the defendant is charged with embezzlement and pleads guilty, that plea can be used as evidence in a civil case against him by the victim, seeking money damages, but a nolo plea cannot be used against him.

Joe Peel had been a lawyer, which might explain why no special circumstance was alleged. Even if Gideon had not been aware of the *Betts v. Brady* decision during his trial, he certainly found out about it after he entered the Florida State Prison. Inmates were filing petitions alleging they had been indigent at the time of their trials but had not been given appointed counsel, even though special circumstances had been present in their cases. It was widely known that the way to try to set aside a conviction of an indigent convicted defendant was to allege that a special circumstance had been present in the case. However, a lawyer such as Peel would have realized that the Supreme Court was on the verge of overruling *Betts* and that the way to enable the Court to do this would be to file a petition for certiorari alleging no special circumstances. This would raise the issue of whether lawyers should be appointed in all cases, not only those involving special circumstances. He also would have known that if Gideon failed at the Supreme Court this time, he could start again, filing a petition for habeas corpus in Florida courts alleging special circumstances, such as his limited education, his bouts with tuberculosis, or his alcoholism. In those days, there was no time limit for filing a habeas petition, and not much restraint against filing multiple habeas petitions.

So the petition for certiorari in the case of *Clarence Earl Gideon v. H.G. Cochran, Jr.* was filed at the Supreme Court in January 1962. It would take

In The Supreme Court of the
United States of America

Clarence Earl Gideon | Petition For Writ
Petitioner | of Certiorari
vs | Directed To
H.G. Cochran, Jr, Director, | the Supreme
Division of corrections | Court State
State of Florida | of Florida
Respondent |

to, the Honorable Chief Justice of
Earl Warren and associate Justices
of the United States Supreme
court.
    Come now Clarence Earl Gideon
appearing in proper person, Who
affirms he is a citizen of the
united States of America, and
appearing as his own counsel,
Who petitions this court For a
Writ of Certiorari directed to
the Supreme court state of
Florida. To review the order of
and Judgement of, the court
below denying the petition
of Writ of Habeus Corpus
    Petitioner submit that the

First page of Gideon's petition for writ of certiorari, January 1962.

the votes of at least four Justices for the petition to be granted, and the case heard by the full court.

The papers in paupers' cases were sent by the Clerk of the Supreme Court to the office of Chief Justice Earl Warren. Warren had three law clerks who, among other things, were responsible for scrutinizing in forma pauperis petitions. One of those clerks would prepare a memorandum regarding the facts and issues in a case and circulate that memo to the nine Justices. However, the law clerk could suggest to the Chief Justice that state authorities be first asked to file an informal, typewritten response before circulating the certiorari petition to the Justices. That is what was done in Gideon's case. A letter was mailed by Assistant Clerk Michael Rodak Jr., to Richard W. Ervin Jr., Attorney General of Florida, dated March 8, 1962, requesting a typewritten response to Gideon's petition. The attorney general was asked to file the response within 30 days.

# 7

## The Florida Attorney General's Office

That was where I entered the case, as I explain in chapter 1.

I did research and prepared the response. In early April 1962 I mailed our response to Gideon's petition for certiorari to the Office of the Clerk of the Supreme Court. The argument was that an indigent defendant was entitled to appointed counsel, under *Betts v. Brady,* and other Supreme Court cases based on *Betts,* if there was a special circumstance involved that would make it difficult for that defendant to get a fair trial without having an attorney. But there had been no special circumstance alleged in the habeas petition before the Florida Supreme Court or in Gideon's certiorari petition in the Supreme Court of the United States.

Through April, May, and early June of 1962, we waited for a letter from the Supreme Court letting us know whether the petition for writ of certiorari from Clarence Gideon had been granted or rejected. There was no way of knowing how long the Court would take to make that decision. It could be weeks or many months. During that period, I continued handling my usual workload in the Criminal Appeals section of the Attorney General's Office. While in that section, I usually worked on about 25 matters at any given time. This would include six or seven direct appeals in various stages of completion. (I was the lawyer in a total of 19 appeals, including the *Gideon* case, during my 15 months in the Criminal Appeals section.) In a couple of those appeals, I would be studying the record in each and reading the transcripts of testimony carefully. In one of those cases, I might be working on the statement of the facts to be incorporated later in our brief. In some of the appeals I would be researching the law in our library, across the hall from our Criminal Appeals section offices. I would be writing drafts of my briefs, which were typed by our secretaries. And I would be preparing for oral arguments and arguing cases before the appellate courts.

In some of the appellate cases, I would be preparing, filing, or orally arguing motions, such as a motion to strike a certain portion of the brief filed by the appellant. For example, the appellant's lawyer might have made an incorrect material statement, and in that situation, I would move to strike so that the misinformation would not be used by the members of the court in their deliberations.

Each of us in our section was asked to research and write formal and informal legal opinions for public officials. As an example, a sheriff might ask our office for a formal opinion regarding the meaning of a phrase in a criminal statute. Our opinion would be issued publicly and used by law enforcement officers, judges, and lawyers as the correct legal interpretation of that phrase unless and until the Florida Supreme Court or a district court of appeal, in an opinion, adopted a different meaning. In other words, our formal opinions on legal questions were the equivalent of the "law" of the state (such as the state constitution, statutes, judicial case law, court rules) except as changed by an opinion of a court.

We also wrote informal opinions when requested to do so by public officials. For example, a sheriff might want to know whether he was adequately compensating his employees under state statutes. We would write an opinion explaining the statutes involved and advise him whether he was accurately following them or not. This would be mainly for that one public official's benefit, and our response would not rise to the level of a formal opinion.

I also worked on a number of habeas corpus cases. An inmate at a prison near Marianna might file a petition for habeas in the circuit court there, alleging that one of his constitutional rights was violated at his trial or sentencing. I would obtain and study the trial transcripts if available and phone the prosecuting attorney to find out what happened in the case. When I understood the facts, I would prepare and file a return. Then I would go to Marianna for the hearing before a circuit judge. The inmate would have been brought into the court and would testify. I might have witnesses who would testify, and we would discuss the legal issues involved. Then the judge would decide whether the conviction should be set aside and the inmate released from custody.

Inmates would send letters to us or the Division of Corrections with allegations, such as claims of mistreatment. The Division would forward these letters to us, and we would investigate to determine whether their allegations were true. I recall one letter forwarded to me by the Division of Corrections in which the inmate claimed that he should be entitled to release from confinement about 120 days earlier than the release date that the Division had set. I researched the statutes involved and found that the inmate was correct—that he should be released earlier. I phoned the office of the Division of Corrections and advised that he should be released 120 days earlier, and sent them a letter to that effect, with a copy to the inmate.

We frequently received phone calls from sheriffs, police chiefs, and other public officers asking for our advice. A police chief might want to talk with one of us for advice on whether his department had enough evidence to go before a court seeking a search warrant in a particular case. A phone rang during one lunch hour when I was alone in our offices. It was a circuit judge calling, and he was in the middle of a first-degree murder trial. Just before the lunch break, the defense attorney had told the judge that his client wanted to change his plea in the case from not guilty to nolo contendere. The court was in recess for lunch, and the judge needed to know whether he could accept such a plea. I told him I would find the answer and would call back immediately. I went across the hall to our library, did some quick research, and found the answer. I phoned back and told him the answer was no. He thanked me profusely.

The Attorney General's Office was a marvelous place to work; I liked all my colleagues. Every morning at 10:00, the lawyers who were not in court or otherwise away from the office would gather in our large conference room for coffee. We would discuss the cases we were working on, state or national news, Florida governmental problems, and other such subjects. Often Attorney General Ervin was able to attend these sessions.

In the morning arguments before the Florida Supreme Court, the chief justice would announce that the court would be taking a break and he was inviting all the lawyers in the courtroom to come into the area behind the bench for coffee, donuts, and other pastries. For 20 minutes or so, we would sip coffee and talk with the justices. Sometimes one or two of them would even remove their robes, which apparently were not very comfortable. I got to know several of the justices fairly well during these sessions. We could not talk about the cases we were arguing that morning in these informal sessions, but there was no other limit to what we could discuss. I really enjoyed these coffee break meetings with the justices.

I argued several capital cases, plus other cases, such as *Davis v. State*,[1] in the Florida Supreme Court. In *Davis*, a group belonging to a gun club asked a sheriff's deputy to follow them to the local dump, where Davis, one of the members, used a handgun to shoot at some rats. The sheriff's deputy arrested Davis, charging him with violating a statute that made it a crime to possess a handgun without having a license. This was a test case to determine whether the statute was constitutional. One of the issues was whether the statute violated the Second Amendment to the United States Constitution. We argued about the meaning of that Amendment, and I learned much about that provision.

Here is what the Second Amendment says:

> A well regulated Militia being necessary to the security of a free State, the right of the people to keep and bear Arms, shall not be infringed.

A leading case regarding the Second Amendment at the time was the 1939 case of *United States v. Miller*.[2] The members of each state militia (now the National Guard) needed "arms" for military use. A main reason for the Second Amendment was to protect against the potential threat posed by standing armies. A standing army could be dangerous. In ancient Rome, the commanding general of the army could march his army into Rome, depose the rulers, and proclaim himself emperor. Our Founding Fathers wanted the states to have strong militias. They believed that the states, the people, and our system of laws and government would be best protected by militias, consisting of citizen soldiers. And for these militias to be "well regulated," strong and effective, their members, as a group, needed to be able to have arms. The Second Amendment, originally, did not provide a constitutionally based right to non-militia individuals.

We won the *Davis* case, but in recent years, the Supreme Court, in two cases, interpreted the Second Amendment to give private individuals the right to own handguns in their homes to protect themselves and their families. Those cases are *District of Columbia v. Heller*[3] and *McDonald v. City of Chicago*.[4] So *United States v. Miller* has been replaced by *Heller* and *McDonald*. Also, more recently, in 2022, the Supreme Court decided a third very significant case regarding gun rights. In it, the Court held that people have a right to carry guns in public for self-defense. The case name is *New York State Rifle and Pistol Association v. Bruen*.[5]

One of the capital cases I handled was *Rankin v. State*,[6] a first-degree murder case. The crime took place in the Raiford Penitentiary. About 10 inmates had been put into 10-by-8-foot wire cage, for disciplinary reasons. Several of them made an inmate kneel while they put a rag around his neck and pulled it tighter and tighter until they strangled him to death. After the killing each of the men in that cage was required to give his statement on what had taken place. Rankin was one of the perpetrators, and he had given a statement.

At the trial, however, he denied that he had given the statement. But the prosecutor read each line of the statement and asked Rankin if he remembered telling that line to the investigator. Each time Rankin denied making that particular part of his statement, but the prosecutor read each line of Rankin's entire statement into the record before the jury in this fashion. This was being done under the reasoning that Rankin was being "impeached." But the Florida Supreme Court ruled that this went well beyond impeaching the defendant. The prosecutor, under these circumstances, should not have been allowed to get the entire statement before the jury in this manner. Also, testimony was allowed that told the jury that the victim had been married and had left a widow. The court found this to be prejudicial. The conviction was set aside.

# 8

## The Summer of 1962

### Working on the *Gideon* Case

On about June 8, 1962, we received, in the mail, a copy of the order of the Supreme Court granting certiorari in our case. Here is what it said:

> The 890 Misc. GIDEON v COCHRAN. The motion for leave to proceed in forma pauperis and the petition for writ of certiorari to the Supreme Court of Florida are granted. The case is transferred to the appellate docket. In addition to other questions presented by this case, counsel are requested to discuss the following in their briefs and oral arguments: "Should this Court's holding in Betts v Brady, 316 U.S. 455, be reconsidered?"[1]

The fact that certiorari had been granted meant the Court had decided to accept Gideon's case and to provide a full consideration of the case on its merits. There would be extensive briefing and significant oral arguments over the extent of the right to counsel under the Constitution.

We knew that an attorney would be appointed to represent Gideon but did not learn who they would be until about June 30, when we received notice from the Office of the Clerk that Abe Fortas, an attorney in Washington, D.C., had been appointed in the case.

The granting of certiorari was significant news in our entire office. We knew that *Betts* would likely be overruled and that this could result in the release from confinement of thousands of prison inmates around the United States. We realized that the overruling of *Betts* could lead to a requirement that counsel be appointed for indigent defendants in felony cases and misdemeanors. We weren't sure the states would have sufficient funds to pay so many lawyers. We weren't even sure there were enough experienced criminal defense lawyers in the United States to provide legal representation for all indigent defendants in criminal cases. There were far fewer lawyers in the United States in those days.[2]

Judge Bowen, George Georgieff, and Jim Mahorner gave me good advice. Among other things, they urged me to have a letter signed by Richard Ervin sent to the other 49 state attorneys general, letting them know that *Betts* might be overruled and suggesting that they consider filing amicus curiae (friend of the court) briefs in support of Florida. The letter was sent out in mid-June. Here is what it said:

Dear General:

Enclosed is a photostatic[3] copy of a letter received by me from the United States Supreme Court stating that certiorari has been granted in the case of *Gideon v. Cochran* and advising that the Court desires briefs on the question of whether the holding of *Betts v. Brady*, 316 U.S. 455, should be reconsidered. Four members of the present Court have expressed the view, at one time or another, that *Betts* should be overruled and that the concept of the right to counsel under the Sixth Amendment should be embraced within the due process clause of the Fourteenth Amendment. If the minority can obtain one more vote, *Betts* will be overruled, and the States will, in effect, be mandatorily required to appoint counsel in all felony cases. Such a decision would infringe on the right of the states to determine their own rules of criminal procedure.

Because of the importance of the question, I am hereby inviting the attorneys general of all states to submit amicus briefs in the *Gideon* case. Also, I would appreciate any advice or aid you can offer, including any statistics or information which you believe would be helpful to us in preparing the main brief.[4]

An amicus brief is filed not by one of the parties in the case but by someone or some entity interested in the outcome of that litigation. Our letter did not receive much response, but George D. Mentz, Assistant Attorney General of Alabama, wrote and filed an amicus brief on our behalf. His brief was joined by the Attorney General of North Carolina. It was only two states, but it was good to have some support. George Mentz also helped us by orally arguing the case, at my request, for 30 of the 90 minutes allotted to us by the Court for the arguments in January 1963. I reserved 60 minutes for my argument.

Richard Ervin's letter to the attorneys general of other states resulted in an amicus brief being filed on Gideon's behalf by 22 states, including two— Hawaii and Maine—that had no statute or court rule requiring appointment of counsel in noncapital felony cases. The effort to produce that brief appeared to be spearheaded by Walter Mondale, who then was the Attorney General of Minnesota, and who later became vice president of the United States.[5]

Also, we gave our permission to allow the American Civil Liberties Union (ACLU) to file an amicus brief and to take part in the oral arguments in the case, arguing on behalf of the petitioner that *Betts* should be overruled. And on January 15, 1963, J. Lee Rankin, former Solicitor General of the United States, participated in the oral arguments as the attorney for the ACLU.

I have been criticized for sending the letter to other states' attorneys general asking them to consider submitting amicus briefs in our behalf, because it resulted in the amicus brief being filed against us by 22 other states. These critics have said that sending the letter was not a good "strategy" on our part.

Our office lost a civil case in the United States Supreme Court two or three years earlier. After sustaining the loss, our office was criticized by the attorney general of another state for not letting the other states know that the issue, in that case, was before the Supreme Court. That attorney general would have written and filed an amicus brief if our office had notified him that the Court was considering that issue. Because of this experience, it was important for us to let the other states know that *Betts* might be overruled and that they should consider filing briefs on our behalf if they did not want to be required by the Court to provide counsel automatically to indigents in all felony cases. And, although *Gideon* involved the right to counsel in felonies, we knew that a decision in the *Gideon* case overruling *Betts* probably would lead to a requirement that counsel be provided in all misdemeanors involving indigent defendants. The cost and the practical problems involved in providing free legal assistance on such a broad scale certainly concerned us, and I was sure that at least some of those in other states were just as concerned.

My goal in asking Attorney General Ervin to send the letter was to make sure that the other states knew what was happening and what was at stake in *Gideon* and that they were provided an opportunity to become involved if they wished to do so. In my view, "strategy" had no place before the Supreme Court in a case as important as *Gideon*. The issues in the case were of such enormous importance that the Court deserved the most straightforward presentations possible by both sides. In my view, a lawyer's job in such a case is not to try to prevail through strategy but to prepare the case honestly and thoroughly, to help the Court reach the best result, under the Constitution, for our legal system.

The fact that 22 states joined in a brief urging the overruling of *Betts v. Brady* was not very persuasive to at least one of the Justices. During the oral arguments on January 15, 1963, Justice John Marshall Harlan II questioned why only 22 states had joined that brief. The implication was that if not even half of the states thought *Betts* should be overruled, perhaps overruling that case was not such a good idea.

Shortly after we learned that certiorari had been granted in the case, I asked the Division of Corrections to do a study in their records to tell us what percentage of the Florida inmates had been convicted without the benefit of counsel. Initially, I wasn't sure how I would use this information. There is a basic rule of appellate practice that a reviewing court—in looking at factual information in an appellate case—should only consider information found in the "record." The record in our case consisted only of the petition for writ of habeas corpus filed in the Florida Supreme Court; that court's very brief order denying relief; the petition for writ of certiorari to the Supreme Court of the United States; and the order of the Court granting certiorari. Because the Division of Corrections study was outside the record, I wasn't sure whether it would be appropriate to include those results in our brief. But it seemed to me that members of the Court would want to know the information I was asking the Division of Corrections to provide. During the oral arguments, one of the Justices might ask me how many indigent Florida inmates had not been provided with court-appointed attorneys, so I needed this information even if I could not use it in our brief.

From mid-March until Christmas Eve of 1962, almost every spare moment of my time, and a great deal of my thinking, was devoted to preparing our case. At the Attorney General's Office I continued working on my other cases but also spent many hours researching for *Gideon,* and spending time with Judge Bowen, discussing what arguments I should make and what should be included in our brief.

I decided to research the constitutions, statutes, court rules, and case law of each of the 50 states regarding the right to counsel. I did this detailed research in our library, across the hall from my office, often late into the night, and in the Florida Supreme Court's library across the street a block to the west of the Capitol. I wrote the products of my research onto four-by-six-inch index cards. In our "Brief for the Respondent," filed in December, this data was provided to the Court in 12 printed pages of appendices at the end of our brief.

Around the end of June 1962, we received word that Abe Fortas had been appointed as the lawyer to represent Gideon before the Supreme Court in our case, which then was known as *Gideon v. Cochran,* because H. G. Cochran was the head of the Florida Division of Corrections. Fortas was from Mem-

Justice Abe Fortas. Photo by Martin S. Trisosko/ALAMY.

phis, Tennessee. He had graduated from Southwestern College (now Rhodes College) in Memphis, Tennessee, and Yale Law School. At Yale, he had been the editor in chief of the *Yale Law Journal*. After graduation, he served as a faculty member at Yale. Then he went to work for the federal government during the New Deal. In 1946, he was a founding partner in Arnold, Fortas and Porter. Today, that firm is known as Arnold and Porter. It is now one of the largest firms in the United States, but I recollect that it had only 20 or so lawyers in 1962. Fortas's name was dropped from the firm's name when he was appointed as an Associate Justice of the Supreme Court in 1965.

Fortas was the personal attorney for, and a close friend of, Lyndon B. Johnson while Johnson was a member of Congress, a United States senator from Texas, the vice president of the United States, and later president of the United States. It was Johnson who appointed Fortas to the Supreme Court a couple of years after he was involved in the *Gideon* case.

At about the time I learned that Fortas had been appointed to our case, an older lawyer in Tallahassee who was a friend of mine told me the Holland law firm in Bartow, Florida, was hiring young lawyers and that members of that law firm were interested in interviewing me for a position. My goal when

I went to work at the Attorney General's Office was to gain several years of experience there and then move back to my hometown of Sarasota and go into private law practice. But the Holland firm was acknowledged by many to be the best law firm in Florida. It is named for Spessard Holland, a former governor of Florida and, in 1962, a United States senator.[6] Bartow was not a large town, having about 13,000 residents, but it is situated in the middle of an unusually healthy economic area of Florida. Within a short distance from Bartow, there were phosphate mines, citrus groves, cattle ranches, citrus-packing houses, and canneries. The firm had about 14 lawyers at the time, which was considered a large law firm in those days. It was called the "law factory" by Bartow residents. Even the largest firms in Miami were not much larger.

After an interview, that firm offered me a position as an associate. I was very interested in the Holland firm's offer but wanted time to finish the work I was doing at the Attorney General's Office, especially the *Gideon* case. The Brief for Petitioner in the case would be due 30 days after the printing of the record. Since the record consisted of only a dozen pages or so (petition for habeas, Florida Supreme Court denial of habeas petition, petition for certiorari, and granting of certiorari), I expected the record to be printed by late June or early July. Fortas's brief would be due 30 days later, probably in early August. My brief would be due 30 days after that, probably in early September. All that would be left after that would be the oral arguments in Washington, D.C.

I went to Judge Bowen and Richard Ervin, telling them I had the offer from the Holland firm and that I wanted to accept it, and I asked them if it would be all right if I finished the brief while in the Attorney General's Office and argued the case before the Supreme Court while at the Holland firm. They both said that that would be all right.[7] I spoke with Chesterfield Smith,[8] the head of the Holland firm, and he said that would be fine. After getting these assurances, I accepted the offer. I believe September 15 or 20 was the date I set for leaving the Attorney General's Office and starting at Holland, Bevis and Smith.

I kept researching and putting important ideas and thoughts about the arguments we would make onto index cards. Fortas was to send me a copy of his brief when it was printed, and I expected it by early August. But the brief did not appear. July gave way to early, then mid-August, and I still had not received his brief. Fortas already had to have had the printed record, and his brief was to be completed 30 days later. I could not understand what was delaying the preparation and printing of his brief.

Anthony Lewis explained what was happening. Here is what he says in *Gideon's Trumpet:*

> Fortas decided to get the trial transcript. He telephoned Chief Deputy Clerk Cullinan, who arranges such things for the Supreme Court. Cullinan wrote the Circuit Court of Bay County, Florida, and before long, a transcript of Gideon's trial was typed by the local court reporter from her notes, certified by the clerk of the Circuit Court and mailed to Washington.[9]

This was very disconcerting. In our case, the United States Supreme Court was reviewing the denial of a petition for writ of habeas corpus filed in and denied by the Florida Supreme Court. The habeas case was an independent legal action; it was not an appeal from the trial in Bay County. Because it was not an appeal, a transcript of testimony at the trial before the Bay County Circuit Court was not part of the record before the Florida Supreme Court or the Supreme Court of the United States. However, Fortas obviously wanted it to be included. The accepted way to bring it before the Supreme Court would have been through a motion before that Court to supplement the record, not through an informal approach to Bay County through a deputy clerk. But Fortas must have realized that the Court could have denied a motion to supplement the record.

Finally, in late August, I received Fortas's designation of the record in the case, and that is when I learned that he was trying to include the trial transcript in the record. In August, the transcript was still being typed by the court reporter.

Upon receiving Fortas's designations for printing the record I prepared a motion to strike the paragraphs designating the trial transcript. Our motion was filed at the Supreme Court on August 31. I pointed out that the trial record and transcripts had not been before the Florida Supreme Court and were not a part of the judgment of that court, which was now being reviewed in the Supreme Court of the United States. If this Court believed that the Florida Supreme Court should have obtained and considered the trial transcript in making its decision, the appropriate action was to remand the case to the Florida Supreme Court, with instructions to obtain and review the trial transcript and reconsider its decision in light of the additional information. That court should have been given an opportunity to correct its own mistake if it had made a mistake.

The author (*left*) with Chesterfield H. Smith, taken around 1990. Courtesy of Stetson University College of Law.

These were my arguments in the motion to strike, but in mid-October, just after the court reporter had completed the transcripts, the Supreme Court denied the motion.

Since the Court was flexible about what information should or should not be included in the case, I decided to include the results of the Division of Corrections study in my brief, even though not technically part of the record. Also, I phoned Judge McCrary and asked him what he remembered about Clarence Earl Gideon. He told me that Gideon had been intelligent and capable. I asked if he would send a letter to me to that effect. In his letter, he said it was his opinion that,

> Gideon had both the mental capacity and the experience in the courtroom at previous trials to adequately conduct his defense. This was later borne out at the trial. In my opinion he did as well as most lawyers could have done in handling his case.[10]

I filed this letter with the papers in the *Gideon* case file in the Supreme Court in late October or November. The letter was not technically part of the record in the case, but I had learned that the United States Supreme Court was much less formal than the Florida appellate courts in deciding what could be made part of the record.

My original timetable for finishing the brief in the case was no longer in effect. Now, Fortas's brief would be due in November, and mine would be due after that. I went to Bowen and Ervin and asked if I could not only orally argue the case after leaving the Attorney General's Office but also could work on the brief after leaving my current position. They both told me I could continue with the case. Chesterfield Smith also agreed. I told him I would work on the *Gideon* case at the Holland firm only during nights and weekends. He told me that was not necessary—that I should feel free to work on the case during normal working hours at the Holland firm. But during the fall, I only worked on *Gideon* on nights and weekends except for the final few days in December when I was doing the intensive work of getting the brief ready for the printer.

During the weekend of August 26 and 27, while my fiancée, Ann Wear, and I were driving the 20 miles from Tallahassee to St. Marks on Florida's Gulf Coast, we heard over the car radio that Justice Felix Frankfurter had retired from the Supreme Court. This was bad news for us because Frankfurter was a staunch believer in the concept that determining whether due process had been violated required an after-the-fact review of all the facts and circumstances of a case. He believed that the concept of due process could not be reduced to hard-and-fast rules, such as a rule that due process was automatically violated if an indigent defendant was not provided with an appointed lawyer. He would not vote to overrule *Betts*. Additionally, he was the acknowledged leader of the conservatives on the Court and was known for persuading other Justices to adopt his views. Even before receiving the news of his retirement, the chances the Court would uphold the decision in *Betts v. Brady* had been slim, and now the chances of that happening were even slimmer.

There were four Justices who almost certainly would vote to overturn *Betts*. They were Chief Justice Earl Warren and Justices Hugo Black, William Douglas, and William Brennan. In addition, Justice Tom Clark had just written the opinion for the majority in *Mapp v. Ohio*,[11] making the Fourth Amendment's prohibition against unreasonable searches and seizures, including the exclusionary rule (the rule that evidence unlawfully obtained by police should not be used against the defendant), applicable against the states. Thus, he would likely also vote to make the Sixth Amendment's right to counsel provision for federal courts applicable in state courts.

At the beginning of 1962, there had been three conservative Justices who could have been expected to uphold *Betts*—Felix Frankfurter, John Harlan, and Charles Whittaker. We weren't sure how Potter Stewart, the ninth Justice, would vote.

But, on March 31, 1962, Whittaker resigned from the Court and was replaced by former All-American football halfback and Rhodes scholar Byron "Whizzer" White.[12] White had been deputy attorney general in the Department of Justice for a short while. The Justice Department is the prosecutorial arm of the federal government, and with that background, we thought he might vote to uphold *Betts.*

Frankfurter was replaced on the Court on October 1, 1962, by Arthur Goldberg, an unknown quantity to us. So, by October 1962, there probably were five definite votes for Gideon's position. There was one—Harlan—who might vote to uphold *Betts,* and there were three Justices—Stewart, White, and Goldberg—who could go either way.

# 9

## Marriage, the Holland Firm, and Completion of the Brief

On September 8, 1962, Ann and I were married at the First Methodist Church of Lakeland. We spent four or five days in Jamaica, then flew back to Miami and drove, through Lakeland, to Tallahassee. We had about a week left there before the move to Bartow. This allowed me to finish my work at the Attorney General's Office. During that week, I argued two cases in the Florida Supreme Court on the same day. Also, during the week, we packed our belongings in our cars for the drive south.

My beginning salary at Holland, Bevis and Smith was $6,600 ($69,425 in 2025), and with raises, it reached $7,800 when I left the firm to go to graduate law school and into law teaching about two years later. One of the first differences I learned between working for the state government and a private law firm was that in private practice, lawyers keep detailed records of time spent on each task during the day. We were given small pieces of paper, and for each task we performed, we would write on one of those sheets the amount of time spent in tenths of an hour. So if, for example, I spent about 12 minutes on a phone call for a client, I would write the name of the client at the top of the slip of paper and would write "2," indicating two-tenths of an hour, next to the word "phone," which was one of the tasks described on that sheet.[1] Each evening, our office manager collected, counted, and recorded the information from these time sheets and posted that information into the records pertaining to each client.

The partners used the time records to decide how much to bill each client. But the amount based on hours spent by the lawyers for the client was only a point of beginning in the setting of fees. The partners also used other factors in determining a client's bill. If not much time had been spent on a matter, but the results had been hugely favorable to the client, our firm would charge more than the amount based solely on time spent. And, if our efforts had not been as successful as we wished, the bill would be less than the total value of time spent by the attorneys on that case or matter.

I did a lot of research into federal tax issues for one of the partners. Also, since I had done work on Florida sales and use taxes while in the civil division of the Attorney General's Office, I was our firm's expert on that subject. I drafted contracts, including a complicated joint venture agreement. I represented insurance companies at workers' compensation hearings and also negotiated settlements for our insurance company clients with lawyers for victims in auto accident cases pending in circuit courts. I went to Tampa to represent clients before the federal bankruptcy court. And, since I was the only one in the firm with criminal law experience, I defended a client of ours who was charged with driving while intoxicated. He was tried in a non-jury trial before the municipal court in Bartow and was found guilty of a lesser offense. Each of us had our own clients among the small businesses in the area. One of my clients was the Ford automobile dealership in Bartow.

I will describe some of the cases or matters I still remember from the two years I spent in the Holland firm. First, when the initial phase of the Florida Turnpike was completed, the highway cut right through an enormous cattle ranch, about 30 miles east of Bartow, which a client owned. The road slashed a path for about eight miles through the ranch. The engineers had created two cattle crossings under the highway to enable cattle to move from one side to the other. Still, the road severed the ranch into two parts and made it a less desirable piece of property than before the road's construction.

The state had offered to pay about $45,000 for the land under this four-lane highway running through the ranch. The client was not satisfied with that offer, and the condemnation case went to trial. A young lawyer who had joined the firm about a year before I became an associate was the lawyer for this client, but a couple of weeks before the trial, partners asked me to join him in preparing and presenting the case. On the day of the trial, he and I went to Osceola County to try the case before the circuit court.

Among other things, during the trial, all of us, including the trial judge, lawyers for the state, our client, the two of us, and the jurors, rode on a luxurious, air-conditioned commercial bus to see the ranch buildings, the cattle crossings, and the highway. We rode the entire stretch of the Florida Turnpike that crossed north and south through the ranch.

Back in the courtroom, the jurors awarded the client over twice the amount the state had offered.

Then, one day, the receptionist for the firm came to my office. She said, "You're the only attorney in the office right now, and a man who does not have an appointment just walked in and said he would like to talk with a lawyer. Would you talk with him?" I said, "Sure," and walked to the client waiting room. I met the man and took him back to my office to talk.

He was a civil engineer who was the owner and president of an engineering firm in a northern state. His firm had entered into a contract with the State of Florida, and his company was to do the engineering work for a 12-mile section of the extension of the Florida Turnpike from Orlando to Wildwood.

His firm had just begun to work and then received notice from the state that the contract had been canceled. Apparently, when Florida engineering firms learned that some out-of-state firms had been given contracts to perform parts of the engineering work, they complained to the Legislature. They wanted these contracts to be given only to Florida firms. So the Legislature accommodated them by enacting a statute declaring that only Florida engineering firms would be given these jobs. That statute was the basis for the notice sent to our client telling him that his firm's contract had been canceled.

I was optimistic in my discussions with him because I realized that the action of the Florida Legislature and the cancelation of the contract probably violated a somewhat obscure provision of the United States Constitution—Article I, Section 10, Clause 1—which, among other things, states,

No State shall . . . pass any . . . Law impairing the Obligation of Contracts, . . .

The state had violated this constitutional provision, and our client was entitled to damages. I researched the law of damages and found that our client was entitled to reimbursement for money and labor already expended, plus profit expected from the contract at the time the contract had been entered into. We realized we might have to litigate to obtain the damages, but decided to first write to the state agency involved. We sent a demand letter with a detailed statement of our damages, almost all of which were for lost profits. The total amount was about $92,000. We cited the federal constitutional provision involved. Within about three weeks, we received a check from the state for the $92,000, which would be something like $961,400 in 2025 dollars. We did not have to go to court to collect from the state.

A major New York law firm hired our firm to do some legal work for one of their clients. We were told that the client's identity would not be made known to us, but the client wanted to create a tourist attraction a few miles southwest of Orlando that would consist of an exact replica of the Eiffel

Tower. That tower is almost 1,000 feet high, and the New York firm asked us to give them descriptions of all regulations and restrictions, whether state, federal, or local, they would have to comply with, including federal regulations that might limit the height of such a structure because of interference with air traffic. Several of us did this work. We later learned that the mysterious client was Disney.

This was in 1962 and 1963 when Walt Disney's plans for the theme park in Florida were secret. Construction began in 1967, and Disney World opened in 1971. I'm sure Disney executives never intended to build a replica of the Eiffel Tower, but they wanted to know what legal building restrictions and other hurdles they would face in developing Disney World.

These descriptions should give some idea of what it was like working for Holland, Bevis and Smith when I was preparing the *Gideon* brief. During the last couple of weeks in September, and much of October and November 1962, I would leave the law office at 5:00 or 5:30 and go home for supper. After supper, Ann and I would work in the library in our law office or the old county courthouse library, a block north of our law firm. The librarian had given me the key to the courthouse. We would do research there until about 11:00 p.m. Xerox machines were not yet available in 1962, so Ann would copy excerpts from appellate cases onto four-by-six-inch cards in longhand when I decided those passages should be preserved for use in writing the brief.

On some weekends, we would drive 70 miles west to St. Petersburg to do research in the Stetson University College of Law library. Also, on two of the weekends that fall, we drove to Tallahassee to do research in the Florida Supreme Court's library. That library had historical English materials on the basement level, which I wanted to study. Our system of law is based on the English system. I wanted to learn whatever I could about the right to counsel under English law. The Stetson library was open on weekends, but the library in Tallahassee was not. However, Mrs. Agatha Thursby, the librarian, gave me a key to the Supreme Court building and advised the security guards to allow us to work there on weekends. She was a good friend. Her husband, Dr. Vincent Thursby, a political science professor at Florida State University, had been my faculty adviser six or seven years earlier when I was an undergraduate there. He had invited those of us who were his advisees to his home; thus, I had known them for a long time and liked them both.

As she handed me the key to the Supreme Court building, Mrs. Thursby said, "Bruce, just be sure to lock the front door when you leave." The fact that she allowed Ann and me to enter the Florida Supreme Court building and use the library on our own while the building was closed is astonishing. In

2013 I argued a case there on behalf of a Florida inmate and found that entry by anyone at any time requires passing through an extraordinary amount of security, including walking through X-ray machines manned by court police.

On the weekends in Tallahassee, Ann and I were able to visit Judge Bowen at his home. This made it possible for me to show him drafts of sections of the brief and talk with him about our progress in the case. He advised me on which arguments to stress and on how to organize the brief. I also discussed the case from time to time with lawyers at the Holland firm, especially Warren E. Hall Jr., who was a partner I felt particularly close to. He had been a partner in an Atlanta law firm as a labor lawyer representing unions, including the Teamsters Union. He had worked closely with Jimmy Hoffa, the head of that union. Unfortunately, he had suffered a heart attack, and his doctor advised him to move to a small town where he would have less stress. That is what brought him to Holland, Bevis and Smith. It was a big-city, sophisticated corporate law practice in a small town.

Warren Hall and Reeves Bowen were each what I would call a "lawyer's lawyer." The other lawyers in the Attorney General's Office and all the partners at the Holland firm were excellent, but those two stood out. Each was the kind of lawyer who deserved an uncommon amount of admiration from professional peers for their knowledge, ability, and exceptional skills. They instinctively understood how the law works better than others. A fellow lawyer who needs advice or help in a matter they are working on will seek out the kind of assistance that can be obtained from a "lawyer's lawyer." I was fortunate to have the help of these two friends.

The Cuban Missile Crisis took place during the last two weeks of October 1962 while I was working on the *Gideon* brief. This was during the Cold War, which existed between the United States and its allies versus the Soviet Union and its bloc of Eastern European countries and Cuba. In flying over that island, a United States U-2 spy plane had discovered that the Soviet Union had built nuclear missile launching sites in Cuba, aimed at the United States, which was just 90 miles to the north. This discovery caused an international crisis that could have grown into a full-blown nuclear war.

President John F. Kennedy confronted Nikita Khrushchev of the Soviet Union, making it clear that our nation would not allow offensive nuclear warheads to be delivered to Cuba by the Soviet Union. Instead of a blockade, which would have been an act of war, our government imposed a "quarantine" on all Soviet cargo ships headed for Cuba. Those ships were stopped in mid-ocean by the United States Navy, which inspected each ship to ensure it was not carrying nuclear warheads. After the inspection, if no nuclear materials were found, the ship was allowed to continue on its way to Cuba. No nuclear materials were found during these quarantine inspections.

Finally, after a great deal of tension between the two superpowers, and with the world watching, the two leaders reached an agreement. The Soviet Union would remove the missile sites in Cuba, and the United States would dismantle its missile sites in Turkey, which had posed a threat to the Soviet Union.

During the crisis, I can remember the deafening noise caused by hundreds of military planes flying south over Bartow as they headed for Homestead Air Force Base in the southern part of Florida. These planes would have been used if the crisis had not been solved several weeks after it began. Armed hostilities probably would have broken out between our nation and the Soviet Union if there had been no agreement between Kennedy and Khrushchev.

During the last half of October and all of November we continued doing research, but also I wrote preliminary drafts of sections of our brief, utilizing information from the index cards. As the due date for Fortas's brief, in late November, drew closer we spent less time doing research and more on writing, typing, and rewriting drafts of sections of our brief.

Once we received Fortas's brief, we would have 30 days to complete our brief, mail it to the printer, get it printed, and have 40 copies[2] sent to the Clerk of the Supreme Court. This was a short period of time considering all that we had to do after receiving the Brief for Petitioner. We realized that we better have our brief almost completed by the time we received Fortas's brief. In our draft, before receiving his brief, we would make our arguments and also anticipate and write proposed arguments in response to Fortas's expected arguments. Then, when receiving his brief, we would shift into high gear. First, we would study his brief, looking for arguments we had not anticipated or adequately addressed in our preliminary draft. Second, we probably would have to do further research to respond to his arguments. Third, I would redraft our brief (in longhand), and Ann would retype it. Finally, the brief had to be printed at the Rose Printing Company in Tallahassee[3] and proofread there by me or someone in the Attorney General's Office. In other words, an enormous amount of work had to be done. Sending our final draft to the Rose Printing Company in Tallahassee to be printed, proofread, and then mailed to the Supreme Court and filed there would take at least eight of the 30 days. That left only 22 or so for us to put our brief into final substantive shape after receiving the opposing brief.

Ann and I bought a used typewriter from Holland, Bevis and Smith. It was electric, but it was not a "memory" typewriter like the computers we have today. While I was at the Holland office during the work week, Ann would type my drafts of sections of our brief at home. In the evenings and on weekends, I would edit the typed drafts, and she would retype them. In those days, before computer memory typewriters, each page had to be re-typed and re-edited. Ann typed and retyped every section of the brief many times.

We received Fortas's brief around the end of November. This meant that our brief would have to be completed and sent to the Rose Printing Company before Christmas. We modified our draft to respond to arguments and statements in Fortas's brief, and our efforts became more intense than ever during December.

When we were completely satisfied with our draft, we mailed it to the printing company in Tallahassee. Bartow is over 250 miles from Tallahassee, so I could not do the proofreading. Someone had to go there and proofread the printed version. I phoned A. G. Spicola Jr., an Assistant Attorney General, and asked him if he would perform this task. He was a good friend. He had been a groomsman at our wedding. He readily agreed to do the proofreading, and I added his name to the brief. Richard Ervin's name was on all briefs submitted by our office, so there are three names on the *Gideon* brief—Richard W. Ervin Jr., Bruce R. Jacob, and A. G. Spicola Jr.

Attorney General Richard Ervin participated in the writing of briefs and oral arguments in some civil cases, but he left the work in criminal cases entirely to those of us in the Criminal Appeals section. He was not involved in the *Gideon* case, except to participate in informal discussions with those of us in the office, in morning coffee sessions.

The brief was sent to Tallahassee shortly before Christmas to be printed. I had spent hundreds of hours working on the case since March, and it seemed as if Ann had spent almost as much time helping me. We had been so busy working on the brief during December that I had not had time to buy a Christmas present for Ann until Christmas Eve. I was exhausted from the workload at the Holland firm, plus the finalizing of our brief. All the stores were closed, except drugstores. The gift I bought her that evening was something we needed—a bathroom scale—purchased at a drugstore. It was an awful gift, and I felt very bad about not giving something better, but both of us were exhausted and happy to have completed our work on the *Gideon v. Cochran* case brief.

A couple of years ago, I received an email from a college student asking questions about the *Gideon* case. Among other things, he asked whether I was paid by the Attorney General's Office for my work on the case after I left that office and was at the Holland firm. The answer to the question is no. The Attorney General's Office did reimburse me for expenses while in Washington, D.C., to argue the case (but not Ann's expenses). I never expected or asked for any salary or compensation for work on the case after I left the Florida Attorney General's Office.

# 10

## The Right to Counsel Before *Gideon*

There are two types of the right to counsel—the right to hire or "retain" a lawyer for one's defense in a criminal case and the right of a poor defendant to have counsel appointed for his defense. Under the common law of England, which was transplanted to this country during colonization by the English, a defendant in a felony case was not allowed to have an attorney represent him. Apparently, the thinking at the time was that a guilty defendant in a serious criminal case should not be allowed to obtain an acquittal at trial because of a lawyer's skill.

Only if a legal question or issue arose could a lawyer provide an answer to that question, but that lawyer providing the answer was retained by the defendant or someone in his behalf. Lawyers were not appointed for indigent defendants at government expense. In misdemeanor cases, the rule was different—the defendant could be represented by retained but not appointed counsel.[1]

The framers of our Constitution, in the late eighteenth century, created a "federal" system of government. There is a national or "federal" government and there are 50 state governments, all within the territorial boundaries of the United States. Each state has its own legislature, its own executive branch headed by a governor, and its own judicial system. The federal government likewise has a legislative branch (Congress), an executive (the president), and a "federal" judicial system headed by the Supreme Court. The national, or federal government, was designed to deal with national problems while the states deal with more localized, statewide issues. The federal government maintains offices in every state, and lower federal courts, such as district courts (trial courts), are in every state. The federal courts hear cases involving federal statutory and federal constitutional issues. State courts deal primarily with state issues, but every state judge takes an oath to follow the Constitution and laws of the federal government. If there is a conflict between state and federal law, a state judge must follow federal law. Federal law is supreme in instances of such conflict.

The Constitution was written in 1787. It then had to be ratified by conventions of the people in at least nine states for the new nation, the United States, to be formed.[2] Opponents of the adoption of the United States Constitution during the ratification process that took place during 1787 and 1788 were concerned that a strong central, federal government could become oppressive and arbitrary and would trample the rights of individuals. To obtain enough votes in the state ratification conventions, proponents of the new government promised that a Bill of Rights would be added to the Constitution when the first Congress convened. And in 1788, the Bill of Rights was adopted by Congress, in the form of the first 10 amendments to the Constitution, to protect the people from arbitrary actions by the federal government. It was ratified by the states in 1791.

The First Amendment protects the freedom of speech, press, freedom of religion, freedom of association, and the right to petition the government to redress grievances. The Second Amendment protects the right to bear arms. The Third Amendment prohibits the quartering of soldiers in private homes.

The Seventh Amendment guarantees the right to jury trial in civil cases in the federal courts. The Ninth Amendment provides that "The enumeration in the Constitution, of certain rights, shall not be construed to deny or disparage others retained by the people." And the Tenth Amendment provides that "The powers not delegated to the United States, nor prohibited by it to the people, are reserved to the states respectively, or to the people."

All political power resides in the people, and when the people created a federal government, they carved away certain powers of theirs and granted those powers or delegated them to the federal government. Therefore, the federal or central government is a government of granted powers. It cannot take any action or do anything unless it can base that action on a power granted to it under the Constitution. All political powers and all rights not granted to the federal government remain with the people and the states. This, in essence, is what we are told in the Ninth and Tenth amendments.

You will notice that I have not yet mentioned the Fourth, Fifth, Sixth, and Eighth Amendments. Those are the sections of the Constitution and the Bill of Rights that we will be concerned with most in this book because they are the sections that provide protections for persons being prosecuted for federal crimes in the federal courts.

The Fourth Amendment, for example, provides protection against unreasonable searches and seizures of evidence. The Fifth Amendment states, among other things, that no person shall be required to answer for a federal crime except upon presentment or indictment by a federal grand jury. A grand jury consists of between 16 and 23 persons impaneled to hear evidence. At least 12 must vote to indict. If they do this with the help of a United States attorney, who draws up a "bill of indictment" and presents evidence to them to support that bill, the charge voted upon by the grand jurors is called an "indictment." If the grand jury conducts an investigation on its own initiative and makes its report on the results of that investigation the report is called a "presentment."

The Fifth Amendment also contains prohibitions against "double jeopardy" (trying a person twice for the same offense) and self-incrimination (being compelled to testify—confess—against oneself). Further, it contains a due process clause—guaranteeing that no person shall be deprived of life, liberty, or property without due process of law. This is one of the two due process clauses. The Fifth Amendment's Due Process Clause protects individuals against arbitrary actions by the federal government. In contrast, the Due Process Clause of the Fourteenth protects them from arbitrary actions by state or local governments.

Finally, the Fifth prohibits taking private property for public use without just compensation.

The Sixth Amendment guarantees rights to defendants in criminal cases in federal courts, such as the right to a speedy trial; the right to an impartial jury in the district where the crime has been committed; the right to be informed of the nature and cause of the accusation; the right to be confronted by the witnesses against the defendant; and to have compulsory process for obtaining witnesses in the defendant's favor. The Sixth also contains a right to counsel provision.

The last part of the Bill of Rights, which we will mention at this point, is the Eighth Amendment. It states that "Excessive bail shall not be required, nor excessive fines imposed, nor cruel and unusual punishments inflicted."

For our purposes in this book, the most important right I have mentioned is the Sixth Amendment's right to counsel provision. It states, "In all criminal prosecutions [in federal courts] the accused shall . . . have the Assistance of Counsel for his defence."[3] Its purpose, when adopted, was to ensure that the ancient English common law prohibition against retained counsel, except on issues of law, would not prevail in criminal cases brought by the federal government. The Sixth Amendment was meant to secure the right of defendants in federal criminal cases to appear with retained counsel. It did not mean that counsel had to be appointed if the defendant was indigent.

When the Sixth Amendment's right to counsel provision was adopted as part of the Bill of Rights, there was no comment and no controversy, no debate among the members of Congress as to its meaning.[4] But, while the Sixth Amendment provision was in the process of ratification, the same Congress that had enacted the Bill of Rights, including the Sixth Amendment, enacted a statute in 1790 requiring appointment of counsel in federal courts in cases of "treason or other capital crime."[5]

In his classic book on the right to counsel, William Beaney asks:

> If the proposed Sixth Amendment counsel provision includes a guaranty of appointment in all felony cases, why did Congress pass this halfway measure?[6]

Beaney answers that the Sixth Amendment's right to counsel provision only included the right to be represented by retained counsel, not a right to have counsel appointed.[7] He also points out that Justice Joseph Story, one of the early Justices of the Supreme Court, described the right as "the right to have counsel employed for the prisoner."[8] Beaney concludes by saying, "There was no general understanding that federal courts were required by the Sixth Amendment to appoint counsel in other than capital cases, which were covered by the 1790 act."[9] Clearly, appointment of counsel was not a constitutional requirement under the Sixth Amendment.

But 147 years later, in 1938, the Supreme Court, in the case of *Johnson v. Zerbst*,[10] ruled that the Sixth Amendment right to counsel guarantee required the appointment of counsel for all indigent defendants in federal criminal cases.

Providing free counsel to indigent defendants in criminal proceedings in 1938 was not a difficult requirement for federal trial courts to comply with. For one thing, before the national "War on Drugs," which began during the Nixon administration in the 1970s, the federal courts handled relatively few criminal cases. In 1940, only 31,823 criminal cases were prosecuted in all the federal districts throughout the United States. By comparison, 14 years earlier, in 1926, 31,439 cases were commenced in the four largest cities in one state—Pennsylvania.[11] The great mass of crimes, such as larcenies, robberies, burglaries, and assaults, are state crimes. Federal crimes include such offenses as robbery of a federally insured bank, mail fraud, and smuggling an illegal alien into our country. They are not as common or nearly as numerous as state crimes.

Another reason why providing counsel for indigents in federal cases was not difficult is that lawyers who apply to become licensed to practice in the federal courts can readily be imposed upon by federal trial judges to represent indigent defendants and to do so without expectation of a fee.

Justice Hugo Black wrote the opinion for the Court in *Johnson v. Zerbst*. He did not discuss the history of the right to counsel provision. Beaney says this about that opinion:

> Black's opinion is . . . notable for . . . its indifference to the histori-
> cal aspects of the right to counsel. The probable intentions of propo-
> nents or ratifiers of the Sixth Amendment were ignored.[12]

He describes this as "rather cavalier treatment"[13] of the history of the Sixth Amendment when Justice Black was interpreting the meaning of that amendment in the *Johnson* case.

In 1932 the Court decided *Powell v. Alabama*,[14] another important right to counsel case. It was decided during the Great Depression when men and women seeking jobs would "ride the rails" to get to places where they might find work. In 1931, nine African American boys, aged 13 to 19, were riding on a freight train from Chattanooga to Memphis, passing through northern Alabama. Also on this train were seven white boys and two white girls, Ruby Bates, aged 17, and Victoria Price, aged 21. The black boys and white boys got into an argument, and the blacks threw all except one of the white boys off the train. The six white boys went to a nearby police station, claiming that the blacks were raping the white girls. The police telegraphed ahead to have the train stopped, and the train was stopped at Scottsboro, Alabama. The black boys were placed in jail and charged with the capital crime of rape.

At the first trial of the "Scottsboro boys," the two girls testified that they had been raped. The details were hazy, but all defendants were implicated. A couple of years later, Ruby Bates repudiated her testimony. The lone white boy who was left on the train testified as a rebuttal witness for the defendants. Looking back from today's vantage point, it is clear that rapes did not occur. But this was the South in 1931. There almost seemed to be an assumption that if black boys and white girls were in proximity, rapes must have occurred.

The trial began shortly after the arrests, and the defendants had very little time to obtain counsel, even though there were private groups willing to provide counsel for them. The convictions were upheld by the Alabama Supreme Court, but the United States Supreme Court found the defendants had been denied both the right to be represented by retained counsel and their right to effective appointment of counsel to represent them, in view of the fact they were indigent. The constitutional right to retained counsel had been denied because they had not been afforded enough time to obtain their own attorneys.[15] This violated the Due Process Clause of the Fourteenth Amendment, which applies in state courts.

An Alabama statute required that an indigent defendant in a capital case be provided with counsel at state expense. So the defendants had a state statutory right to have appointed counsel. In addition, the United States Supreme Court held that the defendants, being indigent, had been denied the right to appointed counsel under the Due Process Clause of the Fourteenth Amendment to the United States Constitution. The trial judge had designated "all the lawyers of the bar"[16] of the county to represent the nine defendants, but it was not an effective appointment. The appointment was vague and indefinite, with no lawyer specifically assigned to provide the defense for any particular defendant. This made it easy for the lawyers to do very little under the circumstances, and none of the lawyers took responsibility for providing more than a token defense.[17] The Supreme Court reversed the defendants' convictions.

The Court did not lay down an absolute, flat rule as a matter of due process that counsel must be appointed for every indigent defendant in every state capital case. Instead, if the facts and circumstances of the case were such that counsel was necessary to ensure that the defendants would receive a fair trial, the Due Process Clause of the Fourteenth Amendment required appointment. In *Powell*, the defendants were extremely young, illiterate, and strangers in the place of the trial. The Court said that "[W]here the defendant . . . is incapable of making his own defense because of ignorance, feeble mindedness, illiteracy or the like, it is the duty of the Court . . . to assign counsel for him as a necessary requisite of due process."[18]

So the *Powell* decision was based on the facts and circumstances of that case. But over time, the decision took on a larger meaning. It began to be cited incorrectly for a principle that the Due Process Clause required the appointment of counsel in every capital case in which the defendant was indigent. This was in part because every state that allowed capital punishment had a statute requiring appointment of counsel in capital cases. Some lawyers mistakenly assumed that states had passed those laws because they had been required to do so by the *Powell* decision.

The eight older boys in *Powell* had been sentenced to death, and the 13-year-old was sentenced to life in prison. After their victory in the Supreme Court, their case was sent back to Alabama for a new trial. By this time, Ruby

Bates had changed her testimony, but the defendants again were convicted. In 1933, the Supreme Court overturned their convictions a second time for the failure of the trial court to allow black persons to serve on the jury. There was a third trial, at which four of the boys were acquitted. None of the nine suffered the death penalty, but all served time in prison. In 2013, the Alabama Board of Pardons and Paroles posthumously issued pardons. By that time, it was accepted by virtually everyone that no rapes had taken place.

The *Powell* decision applied in state courts when death was the possible sentence, while *Johnson v. Zerbst* applied in noncapital cases but was relevant only in federal criminal trials. An unanswered question was whether indigent state defendants in noncapital cases were entitled to have counsel appointed for them. This question was answered by the Supreme Court in 1942 in *Betts v. Brady.*[19]

In that case the defendant, Betts, had been convicted of robbery in a state court in Maryland without being provided an attorney, even though he had asked for one. It was a noncapital case. When the case reached the United States Supreme Court, the Court extended the *Powell* decision's rationale to cover noncapital cases in state courts.

Justice Owen Roberts wrote the majority opinion in a six-to-three decision. He said in some cases involving indigent defendants, there are one or more "special circumstances" present that require the state trial court to provide counsel at public expense because it would be unfair and would violate the Due Process Clause of the Fourteenth Amendment to require defendants to handle the case themselves, without the assistance of counsel.[20] This was consistent with the holding in *Powell,* where that Court had said that counsel must be provided in a state capital case if the defendant was extremely young, ignorant, feeble-minded, illiterate, or a stranger in the place of trial. *Betts* applied in noncapital state trials where such special circumstances were present. It would be unfair, for example, to require a 17-year-old, not well-educated defendant without previous experience in court proceedings to represent himself in a felony case. But requiring a 40-year-old man with previous experience in the court system in a case that does not involve complex issues to go to trial without counsel might not violate due process. In *Betts,* the defendant was a 43-year-old man who had had previous experience as a defendant in other criminal cases. The issues in his robbery case were not complex.[21] There was no special circumstance present that would have entitled him to the appointment of counsel, and as a result, his conviction was upheld by the Supreme Court.

Also, the majority of the states at the time, 1942, were not automatically appointing counsel for indigent defendants in all noncapital felony cases. This meant that the states did not consider appointment a fundamental right.

Between 1942, the date of the *Betts* decision, and 1961, when Clarence Gideon asked Judge McCrary for counsel, the Supreme Court reversed several convictions of state inmates who claimed they had been denied the appointment of counsel by state courts even though there had been special circumstances in their cases. Extreme youth, ignorance, illiteracy, feeble-mindedness, unfamiliarity with court procedure, being tried in a place where the defendant was a stranger, and complexity of the charges against the defendant were special circumstances, based on *Powell* and *Betts,* and the Court added several more: lack of education,[22] insanity,[23] the inability of the defendant to understand the English language,[24] and prejudicial conduct by the trial judge, prosecuting attorney, or public defender.[25]

There were no special circumstances in Gideon's case. He was about 50 years old. He had previous experience as a defendant in criminal cases and, therefore, was familiar with court procedures. Accordingly, under the principles of *Betts v. Brady,* he was not entitled to the appointment of counsel.

Even so, in his colloquy with Judge McCrary, Gideon seemed certain he was entitled to counsel. What led him to erroneously believe that under Supreme Court precedent Judge McCrary should have appointed an attorney for him? One reason might have been that, because he had previously been tried and convicted in 1934 in a federal court and served time in federal prison during the 1930s, he likely was familiar with the decision in *Johnson v. Zerbst,* which was decided in 1938. He may have thought that that decision and the widespread federal court practice of appointing counsel for indigent defendants applied in state as well as federal courts. Furthermore, Gideon previously had been convicted of crimes in Missouri. Missouri had a statute requiring appointment of counsel for indigent defendants in felony cases,[26] and Gideon could have mistakenly believed that the law in Missouri was the law in every state.

# 11

## The Brief for the Petitioner

The brief for Clarence Earl Gideon was signed by Abe Fortas and by two other members of his law firm—Abe Krash and Ralph Temple. It began with the simplest and most significant argument for the petitioner—that a person accused of a serious crime cannot effectively represent himself. Fortas explains:

> Without counsel, the accused cannot possibly evaluate the lawfulness of his arrest, the validity of the indictment or information, whether preliminary motions should be filed, whether a search or seizure has been lawful, whether a "confession" is admissible, etc. He cannot determine whether he is responsible for the crime as charged or a lesser offense. He cannot discuss the possibilities of pleading to a lesser offense. He cannot evaluate the grand or petit jury. At the trial he cannot interpose objections to evidence or cross examine witnesses, etc. He is at a loss in the sentencing procedure. An indigent is almost always in jail, unable to make bail. He cannot prepare his defense.[1]

These are handicaps that every indigent defendant without counsel is under, regardless of the existence of a "special circumstance" in his case. As Fortas states, "The necessity for counsel in a criminal case is too plain for argument."[2]

He discussed the importance of *Johnson v. Zerbst*.[3] That case was based on Justice Black's opinion for the Court, in which he said,

> [T]he obvious truth [is] that the average defendant does not have the professional legal skill to protect himself when brought before a tribunal with power to take his life or liberty, wherein the prosecution is represented by experienced and learned Counsel.[4]

Fortas next argued that, contrary to the thinking of some in the legal profession, a person cannot act as both trial judge and defense counsel.[5]

He [the judge] cannot investigate the facts, advise and direct the defense, or participate in those necessary conferences between counsel and accused which sometimes partake of the inviolable character of the confessional.[6]

By 1962, all states that utilized the death penalty as punishment for the most serious crimes had statutes requiring an appointment of counsel for indigent defendants in those cases. Also, in *Powell v. Alabama,* the defendants were charged with capital crimes, and the Court ruled that they were entitled to counsel, but in *Betts v. Brady,* the charge had been a noncapital crime, and the Court had denied the right to counsel. Fortas mentioned this difference and said:

We do not believe [the] distinction between capital and noncapital offenses furnishes an appropriate or constitutionally valid basis for determining when counsel must be appointed. The due process clause protects against deprivation of "liberty" and "property" as well as against deprivation of "life."[7]

In the brief, Abe Fortas recognized the importance of *Griffin v. Illinois*[8] in determining the outcome in *Gideon.* That decision was based on both the Due Process Clause and the Equal Protection Clause of the Fourteenth Amendment. At one point, the Court, in *Griffin,* said, "There can be no equal justice where the kind of trial a man gets depends on the amount of money he has."[9]

Fortas argued that allegations by prisoners of violations of the special circumstances rule of *Betts v. Brady* had given rise to a "flood of habeas corpus petitions in the federal courts which create state-federal friction."[10] As Fortas put it, the special circumstances rule "increases the problem of federalism."[11] As of the time of his brief, 37 states required the appointment of counsel in all felony cases.[12] Thus, 13 states did not require appointment in all felony cases for indigent defendants.[13] Prison inmates in those 13 states were challenging their convictions by arguing that they were denied counsel but should have been given counsel under the *Betts* special circumstances test. These cases were winding up in federal courts. Federal courts, thus, were exercising supervisory scrutiny over state court decisions, causing friction between federal and state courts, according to Fortas. The idea for this argument probably came from Justice Potter Stewart's comment in *Elkins v. United States,* where he said, "The very essence of a healthy federalism depends upon the avoidance of needless conflict between state and federal courts."[14] Fortas argued that getting rid of the special circumstances test and imposing an absolute rule requiring counsel would end this friction between federal and state courts.

He also argued that the *Betts* test was vague and difficult for trial courts to apply. In addition, the Supreme Court had applied it in ways that seemed contradictory. As one example, in *DeMeerleer v. Michigan*,[15] the Court reversed a conviction because the defendant had been a youth of 17. In *Gayes v. New York*,[16] however, the conviction was not set aside even though the defendant had been 16 when convicted.

Finally, Fortas urged the Court to overrule *Betts*, although by overruling that case many prisoners in some states would be released.[17] The need for counsel, when charged with a serious crime, was so great, he argued, that the fact that there would be practical consequences of a decision overruling *Betts* "should not frustrate vindication of [the] constitutional principle [of the right to counsel]."[18]

# 12

## The Brief for the Respondent

The two most basic questions we discussed in our brief were as follows: (1) Was Gideon entitled to relief under the *Betts v. Brady* decision, and (2) should the doctrine of *Betts v. Brady* be reconsidered? By using the word "reconsidered," the Court was asking whether *Betts* should be overruled and the "special circumstances" test replaced by a rule requiring the appointment of counsel for indigent defendants in all felony cases.

It was easy to answer the first question. I used my argument on this issue from my typewritten response to the Court from early April 1962. As to the second question, I think everyone (including me) believed that providing counsel to indigent defendants in all serious criminal cases was a good idea. But whether it was a good idea was not the question before the Court. The issue was whether the United States Constitution required the states to automatically appoint counsel in every case.

There were four very important past decisions, in particular, by the Supreme Court that had to be closely analyzed to respond to the question of whether *Betts* and the special circumstances rule should be abandoned. In order of the dates when the cases were decided, those decisions were *Powell v. Alabama*,[1] *Johnson v. Zerbst*,[2] *Betts v. Brady*,[3] and *Griffin v. Illinois*.[4]

There also were four amendments to the United States Constitution that had to be analyzed and fully and correctly understood in order to provide the Court with the knowledge it needed to decide our case. They were the right to counsel provision of the Sixth Amendment, the Tenth Amendment, the Due Process Clause of the Fourteenth Amendment,[5] and the Equal Protection Clause of the Fourteenth Amendment.

In 1791, Congress fulfilled the promise made during the ratification of the Constitution that it would adopt a Bill of Rights to protect individuals against the new national government if it engaged in arbitrary, oppressive actions harmful to citizens. There were 10 amendments in the Bill of Rights, with the first eight providing protections to individuals. However, these were protections only against federal government actions. They did not protect against wrongdoing by state or local governments.

But following the Civil War, the Thirteenth, Fourteenth, and Fifteenth Amendments were adopted to protect individuals against arbitrary, oppressive, illegal actions by state and local governments and their agents or employees. The Fourteenth contained a Due Process Clause, an Equal Protection Clause, and a Privileges and Immunities Clause. So now we had the two due process clauses—one in the Fifth Amendment, which protects against federal government actions, and the other in the Fourteenth, which protects against state or local government wrongdoing. Presumably, these two clauses have the same meaning.

So, the first eight amendments did not apply as protections against state or local wrongful actions. Instead, it was the Fourteenth that protected individuals from wrongful state action. But were some or all the explicit protections of the first eight amendments applicable against the states and federal government? And, if so, by what method? Could they be made applicable to the states, including state judicial systems, by somehow being assimilated and made a part of one of the three essential provisions of the Fourteenth Amendment?

Our arguments centered on the meaning of "due process." The decisions in *Powell v. Alabama* and *Betts v. Brady,* two cases of the four just mentioned that dealt with the right to counsel in state courts, were based on the Due Process Clause of the Fourteenth Amendment. If the Court were to now announce an absolute rule that counsel must be provided in every case, that requirement most likely would be imposed on the states through the Court's interpretation of the concept of due process. But was the concept of due process in the Fourteenth Amendment amenable to such an interpretation? Could the concept of due process include a black-and-white, absolute requirement that counsel must be appointed in every case, regardless of the facts and circumstances involved?

Our answer was no. The Court in *Johnson v. Zerbst* had created a hard-and-fast, black-and-white, absolute rule requiring the automatic appointment of counsel. Still, that decision applied only in federal courts and was based on the language of the Sixth Amendment, not on the requirements of the Due Process Clause. Justice Owen Roberts had said, in *Betts:*

> The phrase [due process] formulates a concept less rigid and more fluid than those envisaged in other specific and particular provisions

of the Bill of Rights [such as the Sixth Amendment's right to counsel provision.] Its application is less a matter of rule. Asserted denial is to be tested by an appraisal of facts in a given case. . . .[6]

In other words, the Supreme Court should not inject the automatic right to counsel rule of the Sixth Amendment into the Due Process Clause because the two provisions were incompatible. The Due Process Clause of the Fourteenth Amendment was a broad, inexplicit provision that was not susceptible to being reduced to a mechanical or fixed formula. Determining whether due process had been violated involved a flexible, case-by-case, fact-based approach, not a hard-and-fast rule that applied the same exact way in every case. Due process requires fairness, but what constitutes fairness depends upon the circumstances of a particular case. The absence of counsel violates due process only if that deficiency results in a lack of fairness under the facts of a specific case. The case-by-case approach under the *Betts* decision was the only approach consistent with the meaning of due process.[7]

These were the conclusions of many of those who have sat as Justices of the Supreme Court. For instance, Justice Benjamin Cardozo said this, in *Snyder v. Massachusetts*:

[F]airness is a relative, not an absolute, concept. It is fairness with reference to particular conditions or particular results. The due process clause does not impose upon the States a duty to establish ideal systems for the administration of justice, . . .[8]

Cardozo also provided us with a definition, a meaning, of "due process," in his opinion in *Palko v. Connecticut.* The freedoms or protections that are included within the concept of due process are those which have been found to be "implicit in the concept of ordered liberty."[9] The term "due process," as used in the Fourteenth Amendment, was not meant as a mere shorthand description of the protections of the first eight amendments to the United States Constitution, the provisions that protect the rights of individuals against wrongdoing by the federal government.

Many Justices of the Supreme Court had expressed the view that due process included protections or freedoms that were "implicit in the concept of ordered liberty." Included in this group, in addition to Benjamin Cardozo, were Chief Justice Charles Evans Hughes, Justice Louis Brandeis, Justice Oliver Wendell Holmes, Chief Justice Harlan Stone, Justice Felix Frankfurter, and Justice John Harlan II.[10] I will refer to this group as advocates of what I will call the "ordered liberty concept"[11] of due process.

There was a contrary view, one advocated by Justice Hugo Black. He had written the majority opinion in *Johnson v. Zerbst* in 1938 and a dissent in *Betts v. Brady* in 1942.

In *Johnson,* the Court had interpreted the Sixth Amendment's language to require an absolute right to counsel for indigent defendants in federal court criminal cases. In *Betts,* in his dissent, which Justices Douglas and Murphy joined, he said that to him, the right to counsel was "fundamental"[12] and that "the Fourteenth Amendment made the Sixth applicable to the states."[13] In other words, the Sixth Amendment, and the interpretation of that Amendment by the Court in *Johnson v. Zerbst,* should be incorporated into and become part of Due Process of he Fourteenth. There it would operate as a protection for defendants in state judicial systems. This was the "incorporation" concept or doctrine.

Justice Black gave us his reasons for favoring the incorporation approach in such opinions as his concurring opinion in *Coleman v. Alabama.* Here is what he said:

> I can have no part in the unauthorized judicial toying with the carefully selected language of our Constitution, which I think is the wisest and best charter of government in existence. It declares a man charged with a crime shall be afforded a lawyer to defend him even though all the judges throughout the United States should declare, "It is only when we think fairness requires it that an accused shall have the assistance of counsel for his defense." For one, I still prefer to trust the liberty of the citizen to the plain language of the Constitution rather than to the sense of fairness of a particular judge.[14]

In 1947, in *Adamson v. California,*[15] four dissenting Justices advocated for a doctrine requiring "total incorporation" of every one of the provisions of the first eight amendments, plus federal case law interpreting those amendments, into the Fourteenth Amendment's Due Process Clause. But, of course, the Fifth Amendment's due process provision would not need to become part of the Fourteenth because the two provisions are identical. Justice Black was the leader of this group,[16] which included Justices William Douglas, Frank Murphy, and Wiley Rutledge. Justice Murphy wrote his dissent separately from that of Justice Black, differing from Black's approach in an important respect. He said:

> I agree that the specific guarantees of the Bill of Rights should be carried over intact into the first section of the Fourteenth Amend-

ment. But I am not prepared to say that the latter is entirely and necessarily limited by the Bill of Rights. Occasions may arise where a proceeding falls so far short of conforming to fundamental standards of procedure as to warrant constitutional condemnation in terms of a lack of due process despite the absence of a specific provision in the Bill of Rights.[17]

Justice Rutledge joined Justice Murphy in this dissent.

To Justice Black, it was the original purpose of the Fourteenth Amendment "to extend to all the people of the nation the complete protection of the Bill of Rights."[18] But if the choice was to apply none of the Bill of Rights provisions against the states or some of them selectively, he said he would choose the selective method.[19]

In *Weeks v. United States*,[20] the Supreme Court held that in federal prosecutions, evidence obtained in violation of the Fourth Amendment should be excluded from use by prosecutors. At the time, it was unclear whether this "exclusionary rule" was required by the Fourth Amendment or was an evidentiary rule imposed by the Court under its supervisory powers over the lower federal courts. The purpose of this rule was to deter violations of the Fourth Amendment by police. In 1949, in *Wolf v. Colorado*,[21] the Court, through the majority's opinion by Justice Felix Frankfurter, rejected the idea of making the exclusionary rule applicable in state court proceedings through the Due Process Clause of the Fourteenth Amendment.

Frankfurter said that the security of the privacy of individuals from arbitrary intrusion by police was at the "core" of the Fourth Amendment and that this core right to privacy also exists in the Due Process Clause of the Fourteenth. I do not think he meant that the Fourth Amendment was being incorporated into the Fourteenth. Felix Frankfurter believed in the ordered liberty concept, not the incorporation approach, and the statement was dicta,[22] meaning that statement was not necessary to the holding of the case—the holding that the exclusionary rule was not applicable to the states. I believe that what Frankfurter was doing was recognizing that the concept of personal privacy was at the core of the Fourth, but this right was also implicit in the concept of ordered liberty. This same right or liberty existed in both sections of the Constitution, and there was no reason to "incorporate" that aspect of the Fourth into the Fourteenth.

When *Mapp v. Ohio*[23] was decided in 1961, many of us practicing criminal law at the time were not exactly sure what the Court had done. Looking back from today's vantage point, we realize that in that case, the Court incorporated the Fourth Amendment, including the exclusionary rule into Due Process of the Fourteenth Amendment and recognized that the exclusionary rule is constitutionally based, not merely an evidentiary rule. The exclusionary rule was now part of the Fourth Amendment and the Due Process Clause of the Fourteenth. It had been "incorporated" into that clause.

*Mapp* was decided a year before Fortas and I wrote our briefs in *Gideon*. Today, almost every judge, lawyer, and law student knows what the word "incorporation" means when used in the constitutional law context. But that wasn't true in 1961 and 1962, when many were not familiar with the incorporation theory. And during that time, those who had heard about the concept of incorporation were not even sure that was the best word to describe Justice Black's doctrine. During the oral arguments in *Gideon* in January 1963, Justice Arthur Goldberg asked whether the word "absorption" would be a better description of Black's theory than the word "incorporation."

In Justice Tom Clark's majority opinion in *Mapp*, he does not use the term "incorporation" or the term "selective incorporation."[24] In *Mapp*, the Court overruled *Wolf v. Colorado* when it made the exclusionary rule applicable in the states.

There was a vehement dissenting opinion in *Mapp* by Justice John Harlan, joined by Justices Felix Frankfurter and Charles Whittaker. They recognized that the Justices in the majority were incorporating the Fourth, including the exclusionary rule, into the Fourteenth and argued that because of the "flexible contours of the Due Process Clause"[25] (an affirmation of the "ordered liberty concept"), the Due Process Clause of the Fourteenth could not and should not be used by the Court to make the Fourth Amendment and the exclusionary rule applicable in state courts. Harlan noted that the Fourth Amendment, "together with its configurations,"[26] did not fit into the Due Process Clause.

In our brief, we argued that the ordered liberty conception of the meaning of due process was the proper view. But, in the *Gideon* decision in March 1963, Justice Black's viewpoint prevailed. In 1961 and 1962, we were not quite sure what the Court had done in *Mapp*. But when *Gideon* was decided, we knew that the selective incorporation method of determining that certain provisions in the first eight amendments were applicable to the states had been approved and adopted by a majority of the members of the Court. Justice Black had won. The concept of due process was no longer the same.

Two more of our arguments were based on Justice Roberts's reasons in *Betts* for not imposing an absolute rule requiring counsel for every indigent defendant in a felony case. One was that the Sixth Amendment states, "*In all criminal prosecutions* the accused shall . . . have the Assistance of Counsel for his defence" (emphasis supplied). The words I have italicized contemplate misdemeanor as well as felony cases. So, if the Sixth Amendment were incorporated into the Fourteenth Amendment, counsel would have to be appointed for all indigents in misdemeanors and felonies. This requirement would include some traffic offenses because some are considered criminal. This would impose an enormous burden on members of the bar, who would be called upon to defend against those charges, or upon the state, which would have to provide funds for the defense of those defendants.[27]

Fortas, in his brief, had argued that there could be no distinction between capital and noncapital felonies when deciding whether free counsel should be provided.[28] We made the point that if there could be no distinction between capital and noncapital felonies, by the same token there should be no differentiation between felonies and misdemeanors.[29] If counsel was necessary for one of these categories, it also was necessary for the other. This would place an enormous financial and practical burden on the states.

Fortas also argued that *Powell v. Alabama* had required counsel in all capital cases and that it made little sense to have one rule for capital cases and another for noncapital cases. But, of course, he was wrong in his reading of the *Powell* decision. *Powell* did not require automatic appointment in all capital cases. It was meticulously limited to its own facts. *Betts v. Brady* was an extension of *Powell* to felony cases less than capital.

Justice Owen Roberts had pointed out in *Betts* that

[A]s the Fourteenth Amendment extends the protection of due process to property as well as to life and liberty, if we hold with the petitioner, logic would require the furnishing of counsel in civil cases involving property.[30]

Since the Due Process Clause speaks of life, liberty, and property, we argued that an inflexible counsel appointment rule promulgated by the Court would have to apply in civil cases involving property.[31] Extending the right to counsel to all indigents in civil proceedings, a logical requirement if the Sixth were incorporated into the Fourteenth, would have been such an outlandish consequence in 1942 when Justice Owen Roberts was writing the *Betts* majority opinion that he had little difficulty in rejecting the incorporation theory.

Because the *Johnson v. Zerbst* decision was such an essential part of Fortas's case, I wanted to minimize, to the extent possible, the impact of that case in our discussions in *Gideon*. I made this argument:

In *Johnson v. Zerbst*, . . . this Court construed the Sixth Amendment as requiring the automatic appointment of counsel in all federal criminal cases. The decision was an outgrowth of the practice which had developed in the federal court system. . . . The construction given the Sixth Amendment counsel provision in *Johnson v. Zerbst* constituted, to some extent, an exercise by this Court, of its supervisory and rule-making power over federal criminal procedure.[32]

The Supreme Court has supervisory and rulemaking powers over the lower federal courts, which meant that it had this power and authority to impose a rule requiring automatic appointment of counsel in all federal criminal proceedings in United States district courts. In *Johnson v. Zerbst*, the Court based its decision on the language of the Sixth Amendment. But my point in our brief was that the Court could have imposed that same requirement through its supervisory, rulemaking powers over the federal trial courts. Therefore, it had two sources of power for its decision, making it very easy for the Court to reach the result it did in *Johnson*. Imposing an automatic rule on the states was an entirely different matter. The Court had less authority and power in contemplating whether to impose that requirement on the states' courts. In my argument, I tried to downplay the importance of the *Johnson* decision and its relevance to our case.

In *Johnson v. Zerbst*, in the opinion for the Court by Justice Hugo Black, the Sixth Amendment's right to counsel provision was interpreted to require an automatic right of indigent criminal defendants in the federal courts to have counsel appointed for them. Four other Justices joined that opinion. One Justice, Benjamin Cardozo, did not participate in the case, and Justice Pierce Butler believed that Johnson had waived the right to counsel. Justice Stanley Reed concurred with no opinion, apparently agreeing with the result but not necessarily the reasoning of Black's opinion. And Justice James Clark McReynolds dissented.

The right to counsel provision of the Sixth was adopted as part of the Bill of Rights to ensure that the English common law rule of not allowing lawyers for defendants in serious criminal cases would not be followed in our federal courts. But, as pointed out in chapter 10, that provision was not meant as a requirement for the appointment of counsel for indigent defendants. It was a right to retain counsel, not a right to the appointment of counsel.

Justice Black ignored this history. One explanation for not discussing this history is that Black was a literalist who carried a small copy of the Constitution around with him. If someone claimed that a particular right existed in the Constitution, he would hand the Constitution to that person and ask him to show him the words describing that right. If the exact language was not found, there would be no such right. Black may have believed seriously that the language of the Sixth Amendment alone required appointment of counsel for all indigent defendants. He could have believed that he could ignore the history behind that provision.

There were other possible reasons for the Court's opinion in *Johnson v. Zerbst*. Lawyers admitted to practice in the federal courts could be expected to accept appointments to represent indigent defendants without expecting a fee because doing so was required as part of their privilege of practicing in those courts. Furthermore, there were fewer federal criminal cases in federal courts in the 1930s when the *Johnson* case was decided, so appointing attorneys to handle these cases would not have imposed an enormous burden on the lawyers practicing in the federal courts. Also, a practice had developed in some federal district courts of appointing counsel for indigent defendants.

In my view, another reason why the Court construed the Sixth Amendment to require appointment for indigents was that the Court also had the power to require appointment in all cases under its supervisory authority over the lower federal courts. It could have reached the same result by issuing a rule governing the practice in the federal trial courts. Thus, it had this additional source of power to make the decision it did in the *Johnson* case.

Any court must be able to point to the source, the basis, of its authority, to make its decisions. In this instance, the Court had two: (1) the language of the Sixth Amendment; and (2) its supervisory powers over the federal trial courts. Having this additional source of power made it easier for the Court to reach its result in *Johnson*.

Would the Court have reached the same result, changing the meaning of the right to counsel in the Sixth—from only the right to retain counsel to the additional right to appointment of counsel—if it had not had this second source of power to reach that result? Maybe, but Justice Black and the other Justices who reached their result were certainly strongly supported in their decision because they had this additional source of power to reach that result. The Court made a momentous decision, changing the meaning of the Sixth Amendment. The fact that it could have reached the same result using its supervisory powers over the federal trial courts helped to enable it to make its decision in *Johnson*. Thus, I did not think that *Johnson* was as persuasive a right to counsel decision as *Betts v. Brady*.

Under the Tenth Amendment, powers not granted to the central government were reserved for the states. One of these was the power to provide their own rules of criminal procedure. We argued in our brief that a Supreme Court decision requiring appointment of counsel for all indigent defendants would infringe upon this historic constitutional provision that protects the states.[33] There were many Supreme Court cases in 1962 in which the Court held that the states should have control over the procedures in their courts. Since the *Gideon* decision and cases that followed *Gideon,* incorporating many of the specific protections of the first eight amendments into the Fourteenth Amendment, the pre-1963 Supreme Court decisions giving states control over their own rules of procedure in criminal cases now are of little consequence. There has been what I call a "federalization" of criminal procedure since the *Gideon* decision. The states have much less latitude than they once had to develop their own procedural rules.

*Griffin v. Illinois*[34] was a case that, if broadly interpreted and applied, could have required complete equality of treatment for all persons in the criminal justice system, rich or poor. Illinois, in that case, had made it very difficult for an indigent convicted defendant to obtain appellate review of their conviction. A transcript was necessary for an appeal, and indigent convicted defendants could not afford those transcripts.

The Court decided in favor of the convicted defendant seeking review of his conviction. In our brief in *Gideon,* we quoted from Justice Black's opinion for the majority when he said:

> We do not hold . . . that Illinois must purchase a stenographer's transcript in every case where a defendant cannot buy it. The Supreme Court [of Illinois] may find other means of affording adequate and effective appellate review to indigent defendants. For example, it may be that bystanders' bills of exception or other methods of reporting could be used in some cases. . . . We are confident the State will provide corrective rules to meet the problem which this case lays bare.[35]

In other words, the Equal Protection Clause of the Fourteenth Amendment did not require the states to provide indigent defendants with the exact same advantages in criminal appeals which were available to defendants with money. The state could develop other methods of providing adequate review for indigent convicted defendants.

To answer arguments for the petitioner based on the *Griffin* decision, we said this in our brief:

> If automatic appointment of counsel . . . should be required by this Court under the equal protection clause . . . such requirement

would open a veritable "Pandora's Box." . . . For instance, if the state can be required to provide counsel in every criminal trial, under that clause, it can just as logically be argued that a state should provide counsel in appeals and in post-conviction proceedings. Also, . . . states would logically be required to provide an indigent with bail, with the services of investigators, psychiatrists, etc., in criminal proceedings since those things are available to the rich man.[36]

We did not want the Equal Protection Clause to be used as the basis for a decision in our case because of the practical and financial implications that would flow from such a decision.

Those implications could seriously and adversely impact the states from a practical and financial standpoint.

In our brief, we reported the results of the survey done by our Division of Corrections during the summer of 1962. Here are those findings:

1. As of June 30, the Division had 8,000 prisoners in custody.
2. Of this group, 4,065 entered pleas of guilty with no counsel.
3. Of this group, 1,504 entered pleas of guilty and were represented by counsel when they entered their pleas.
4. 477 of this group entered pleas of not guilty and were not represented by counsel.
5. 975 entered pleas of not guilty and were represented by counsel.
6. As to the remaining 979, the records were so old that the information needed was not contained in them, or for some other reason, the Division could not determine whether those inmates had been represented by counsel.[37]

These figures showed that approximately 65 percent of Florida inmates had not been represented by counsel in the proceedings that resulted in their convictions. (Of the 7,021 inmates for whom records were available, 4,542, or 64.69 percent, had been indigent and unrepresented.) On November 30, 1962, as we were writing our brief, the Division had 7,836 prisoners in custody. Applying the 65 percent figure, approximately 5,093 prisoners who had not been represented by counsel were in custody as of that day. I argued that if *Betts* were to be overruled and the new rule applied retroactively, as many as 5,093 prisoners could be eligible for release "in one mass exodus in Florida alone,"[38] not to mention those in the other twelve states that were not automatically providing counsel in every noncapital felony case. Some of these individuals could be retried with counsel, but I pointed out that it often is impossible to retry a person because of difficulties in locating witnesses and marshaling evidence when many years have passed since the original conviction. If they could not be retried, they would be freed from custody.

If *Betts* were overruled, I requested that the overruling be accomplished in such a way as to make the new rule operate prospectively from the date of the Court's decision, and I cited judicial opinions that would support such a ruling.[39]

In the Brief for Petitioner, Fortas had argued that *Betts v. Brady* was "not an operable guide." To him, cases under the special circumstances test were not consistent.[40] He had said, for example, that in *DeMeerleer v. Michigan,*[41] the Supreme Court decided that the conviction of the 17-year-old defendant should be reversed, while in *Gayes v. New York,*[42] the Court upheld the conviction even though the defendant had been only 16. In my brief, I countered Fortas's example by pointing out that:

> DeMeerleer was confronted by a complex first-degree murder charge and was arraigned, tried, convicted, and sentenced on the same day. The record showed he had never been advised of his right to counsel and indicated considerable confusion in his mind at the time of arraignment regarding the effect of a guilty plea. No evidence was introduced on his behalf, and no witnesses were cross-examined. Gayes, at the age of sixteen, was charged with burglary in the third degree and petit larceny. He said he didn't want counsel and pleaded not guilty.
>
> At the age of 19, he pleaded guilty to a charge of being a second offender. After serving the first sentence, he sought relief from the second offender sentence, but this Court pointed out that he could not "by a flank attack" challenge the first sentence.[43]

Fortas gave two other examples of what he deemed to be inconsistencies. But as in the first example, a careful reading of the cases being compared showed that the Supreme Court was rationally and consistently applying the special circumstances rule of *Betts v. Brady.*[44]

I summarized my response to this portion of the Brief for Petitioner by saying:

> If it can be said that *Betts* and the cases which have followed are inconsistent and that they do not comprise a workable standard, it can be argued with equal force that the entire common law is inconsistent and that it, likewise, should be rejected. The *Betts* approach is

the common law approach, consisting of the development of a body of law on a case-by-case basis, and lawyers for centuries have thrived on distinguishing one case from another on the basis of factual situations and circumstances.[45]

The common law is derived largely from judicial decisions rather than statutes enacted by the legislature. Our legal system in the United States is essentially based on the common law system derived from centuries of experience in England. It is a legal system and a body of law that has been developing in the courts probably since 1066, the time of the Norman Conquest of England.

In this system, courts make decisions on a case-by-case basis, studying the facts in each case and reaching a commonsense solution to the dispute before them. For example, two neighbors may have quarreled over who owned the apples in a tree that hung over the property line. A judge would have decided that it made common sense for each to have the apples on his side of the boundary. Other courts would follow this decision. Eventually, it could be put into writing and become precedent for other courts in other cases. This is the way the common law developed.

The body of law that emerged in this way sometimes was turned into statutory law by the legislative branch. This entire body of law and this system of case-by-case decision-making was transplanted to the United States early in our history.

France and other European countries have a different type of legal system—the "Civil Law" system. It is derived from the Napoleonic Code and is based much more on statutory law.

The Supreme Court often utilizes the common law method of deciding the cases that come before it for decision. Between the time of *Betts* in 1942 and *Gideon* in 1963, it had used the common law method to develop consistent guidelines for courts to follow in applying the special circumstances test. The Court had proclaimed the following factors or circumstances as guides for determining whether the defendant had been improperly denied the aid of a court-appointed attorney through a failure of the trial court to follow the special circumstances test:

1. Gravity of the offense[46]
2. Complexity of the charges[47]
3. Ignorance[48]
4. Illiteracy or lack of education[49]
5. Extreme youth or lack of experience[50]

6. Unfamiliarity with court procedure[51]
7. Feeble-mindedness or mental illness[52]
8. Inability to understand the English language[53]
9. Prejudicial conduct by the trial judge, prosecuting attorney, or public defender[54]

These cases showed that the Supreme Court had provided a workable set of guidelines for courts to follow in applying the special circumstances test.

Fortas argued that *Betts v. Brady* had caused "friction," or "conflict between the federal and state courts because of the case-by-case review it entails,"[55] and that friction should be avoided. To me, while writing our brief, this was not a convincing argument. Our federal system has been set up in such a way as to make sure that if a state violates a provision of the United States Constitution, that violation can be reviewed by federal courts. It is the way our legal system is supposed to work. Federal law is supreme. When a federal court overturns a state court decision, it is doing its job. It seemed to me that a certain amount of friction is necessary if our federal-state justice system is to work properly.

Furthermore, the Supreme Court, in the years following *Betts,* had not been inundated with cases of inmates arguing that *Betts v. Brady's* special circumstances rule had been violated. I believe that only 25 or so of these cases reached the Supreme Court between the decisions in *Betts* in 1942 and *Gideon* in 1963, not much more than one case per year. This did not seem to be the volume of cases that would cause an inordinate amount of state-federal friction if "friction" could be considered a problem.

I also pointed out that

> [R]eversal of *Betts v. Brady* would create myriad and complex new legal questions regarding the right to counsel in misdemeanor and civil cases. . . . Also, [there is] an increasing trend in right to counsel cases . . . for prisoners to attack their sentences on the grounds of inadequate representation.[56]

And, in the years since *Gideon,* cases of ineffective representation by counsel, retained and appointed, have flooded the state and federal courts. At the time I wrote the *Gideon* brief, I could not foresee any decline in right to counsel cases in our courts. I did not believe that the overruling of *Betts* would result in fewer right to counsel cases and less "friction" between state and federal courts.

There was an argument that I thought about making but decided not to make in our brief and our oral argument. Approximately 90 percent of all criminal prosecutions end in a plea of guilty. We could have argued to the Court that the rule of *Betts v. Brady* should be modified to require automatic appointment of counsel for indigent defendants who plead not guilty and go to trial but continue using the special circumstances test for those who wish to plead guilty.

George Mentz, the Assistant Attorney General of Alabama who wrote the amicus brief supporting us, did suggest that this would be an acceptable outcome in our case. Here is what he said at the outset of his oral argument in *Gideon:*

> [E]ach individual state should have the privilege of exercising its constitutional right under Tenth Amendment of determining when appointment is necessary.
>
> * * * * *
>
> The petitioner in this case has said that 75% to 90% of all state cases are decided on pleas of guilty.
>
> * * * * *
>
> [E]veryone who pleads guilty does so because he knows that the prosecuting authorities can prove his guilt and because he hopes to obtain leniency by dispensing with an unnecessary trial.
>
> And we say that a state should not be burdened with the expense of appointing an attorney who in good conscience could recommend only to his client that he should enter a plea of guilty.[57]

My belief was that if the Court were to require counsel for indigent defendants, there should be no difference in how guilty plea cases should be treated. Before a lawyer allows a defendant to plead guilty, they must investigate and interview witnesses, including police. The lawyer must research whether the charges can be challenged through a motion to dismiss. Understanding the tendencies of the judge assigned to the case is important. A lawyer is best equipped to decide whether pleading guilty is the best option for the defendant. A lawyer is in a position to plea bargain on behalf of the client, and a lawyer's knowledge of sentencing laws and practices is invaluable. These were reasons why I did not argue that if *Betts* should be overruled, only indigent defendants who wish to plead not guilty and stand trial should be entitled to appointed counsel.

Our brief, when printed, was 57 pages long, plus 17 pages of appendices, for a total of 74 printed pages. We cited 109 cases in the body of the brief. Also, in the appendices we cited the 44 state cases we had found in our research concerning the right to counsel.

My personal belief at the time I was working on the brief was that every indigent defendant in a serious criminal case should be entitled to appointed counsel. In Florida, we already had a public defender office in Dade County (Miami). Also, there was an organized appointment-of-counsel program in existence in Duval County (Jacksonville), then our second-largest county. In that program, indigent defendants in felony cases were automatically given assigned counsel. Furthermore, our Legislature had just enacted a statute creating a public defender office in Hillsborough County (Tampa). I hoped that the Florida Legislature would soon see the wisdom of finding a way to provide counsel for all indigent defendants in serious criminal cases throughout our state.

But I was a lawyer, and there were very serious, legitimate, important constitutional and other issues involved in the *Gideon* case. I did not consider my position in the case to be that of a "pure advocate." The case was so momentous, so incredibly significant, that it seemed to me that the roles of the lawyers should be different than the usual roles of advocates in contested cases. It was my job to do my best to provide the Court with what it needed, in the way of information and argument, to enable it to make the best possible decision for the future of our legal system and our country.

# 13

## The Oral Arguments in Washington, D.C.

The Clerk of the Supreme Court set oral arguments in our case for January 14, 1963. The argument would not necessarily take place on that date. Cases were scheduled a day or so in advance, and a lawyer was expected to be there ahead of time, waiting for their case to be called.

To prepare, I carefully reread every one of the cases I thought would come up for discussion during the oral arguments. In those days, we did not yet have xeroxing, and it was not possible to make copies of appellate decisions. We could make a copy of a single sheet of paper, such as a deed, but the only way to take judicial opinions on the trip was to take the books that contained the opinions. I decided to take a number of opinions, so Ann and I took about 30 law books to Washington, crammed into suitcases.

On a legal pad, I put together the notes I expected to use during my oral argument. Today lawyers who are about to argue before an appellate court, especially the United States Supreme Court, will hold a dress rehearsal, arguing from a podium before a group of fellow lawyers. The panel will grill the lawyer with tough questions to prepare them for the actual argument. But in those days, to my knowledge, lawyers did not do this. I presented my argument orally before my wife, Ann, but I did not practice before a panel of fellow lawyers.

I spoke by telephone with Michael Rodak, an assistant clerk at the Supreme Court, to find out what to wear in my appearance before the Justices. Some lawyers arguing before the Court wear formal attire, called "coats and tails." Rodak assured me that a dark suit would be appropriate. I wore a dark blue suit that my parents had purchased for me on my first day of law school, at Stetson Law School, six years earlier. I wore black dress shoes that my paternal grandfather had given me the day I graduated from Sarasota High School in Florida, about nine and one-half years earlier. They were his, and he had planned to wear them, but when he saw that I did not have appropriate shoes for the graduation ceremony he had me try his. They fit perfectly, and he made a gift of them to me.

George Mentz and I met at our hotel and spent several hours discussing our case. We talked about the arguments we expected Fortas to make and how we would respond to them. Mentz, Ann, and I went to dinner together that evening.

The next morning, on Monday, January 14, Ann, George Mentz, and I walked together to the Supreme Court. It was a sunny but chilly morning. This was the first time I had been to the Supreme Court, and my impressions still are vivid in my mind. Before the Justices entered, we noticed that each one had a different-sized chair. For example, Justice White, the former football star, had a very large chair, and Justice Black's was quite small.

We stood as the Justices entered the room. I recalled reading about Justices Black and Douglas while in grade school. Chief Justice Earl Warren had been named to the Court the year I graduated from high school. These were childhood heroes of mine.

The first item of business was the swearing-in of lawyers to be admitted to practice before the Court. We had made arrangements beforehand for me to be admitted. I was 27 years old and had been licensed as a lawyer in Florida for three years as of November 1962. Three years was the minimum required for admission to practice before the Court, so I had met this requirement.

My name was called. George Mentz and I approached the bench. He already was a member of the bar of the Supreme Court, and he orally moved my admission. I took the oath administered by Chief Justice Earl Warren. I was standing before Justice Warren, who, with a vast smile, leaned out over the bench and said to me, "Welcome to the bar of the Supreme Court, Mr. Jacob."

For the remainder of that day, we listened to the reading of their opinions by the Justices. These readings took all that day, meaning our case would not be heard until Tuesday, January 15.

During these readings, Justices would give notes to court pages, and the pages would walk into and out of the area behind the Justices, delivering messages or carrying books that had been requested. Occasionally, a Justice would get up from his chair, walk behind the curtains and later return.

At one point, Justice White whirled around in his chair and faced the curtains behind the bench for what seemed like 10 minutes or more. Justice Potter Stewart looked out into the audience and began combing his hair with his fingers, facing straight ahead at the audience as if looking into a mirror. Justice Douglas wrote feverishly for a while and then began licking envelopes and pounding them shut with his fist. Anthony Lewis, who then

The interior of the U.S. Supreme Court. Photo by CHDB/iStock.

Members of the U.S. Supreme Court, 1963. *Top row, left to right*: Justices White, Brennan, Stewart, Goldberg. *Bottom, left to right*: Justices Clark, Black, Warren, Douglas, and Harlan. Photo by Harris & Ewing, courtesy of the President Harry S. Truman Library.

was the Supreme Court reporter for the *New York Times,* told me later that Justice Douglas frequently wrote letters to friends during court sessions.

The atmosphere was relaxed. It was obvious that the Justices were not concerned about formality or ceremony. This contrasted with the more formal atmosphere that prevailed in Florida appellate courts. All of this changed, however, the next day when the oral arguments began. The informality disappeared, and the atmosphere became businesslike and rather tense.

In the hotel on the morning of January 15, Ann asked whether I was nervous.

I told her it was like giving a violin recital—I would be nervous beforehand, but I would lose my nervousness once I began to play. That was partially true in the argument before the Court that day, but it was the most harrowing experience of my 65 years as a lawyer.

On Tuesday morning, the three of us again walked to the Court together. There was one case scheduled for argument before ours. It was *White Motor Company v. United States.*[1] Mentz and I sat at the "ready" table on the left side of the courtroom as we faced the bench. The ready tables are where lawyers sit while waiting for the case ahead of them to conclude.

The members of the Court had not yet appeared, and lawyers, clerks, and others were milling around inside the bar. I believe this was when I first met Anthony Lewis, the reporter for the *New York Times,* writing articles about the Supreme Court. He was not a lawyer but was allowed to sit at a small table inside the bar, to our left, with his small portable typewriter.

The courtroom was called to order. We stood as the Justices entered the room from behind the curtains and took their seats. Arguments began in the *White Motor Company* case, an antitrust case. The government's lawyer was Archibald Cox, a Harvard law professor who served as Solicitor General of the United States from 1961 to 1965. He was dressed in a coat and tails, was tall, and had a crewcut. His argument was one of the best I have ever heard. I had never before heard a lawyer speak so easily and effortlessly. Six years later, as a graduate student at Harvard Law School, I was able to audit his course on Constitutional Law.

In front of me, arguing for the White Motor Company, was attorney Gerhard A. Gesell. He also was wearing a coat and tails. As Cox argued, Gesell leaned back from his table to my ready table several times to speak with me. He had a great sense of humor, making amusing comments about the proceedings. Once, he whispered to me, "Watch me; I'm going to have to make a jury argument." That is what lawyers say when they do not have the law on their side and have to make a stirring, emotional argument to try to win their case. But years later, I read the Court's opinion in his case and learned that the White Motor Company had won. The law must have been on his side, so I am puzzled as to why he made that comment.

Four years later, Gesell was appointed as a United States District Judge for the District of Columbia, and in that position, he was the judge in some monumental cases. For example, he presided over the trial of Oliver North, the United States Marine Corps Lieutenant Colonel and Vietnam War veteran who, during the 1980s, was serving as a National Security Council staff member. He became involved in the Iran-Contra scandal, which involved the secret illegal sale of weapons to the Islamic Republic of Iran to encourage the release of American hostages. North was responsible for part of this plan, which was to divert proceeds from these sales of arms to buy weapons for right-wing Contra rebel groups in Nicaragua to aid them in their insurgency against the socialist government of that country. Congress had prohibited giving arms to the Contra rebels. North was charged, tried, and convicted on felony charges for being involved in this scheme. However, the convictions were reversed, and the charges against him eventually were dropped.[2]

The "Watergate" scandal of 1973 and 1974 involved the burglary of the Democratic National Committee's headquarters at the Watergate apartment complex in Washington, D.C. Republican President Richard Nixon was running for re-election. The scandal was orchestrated by members of the Committee for the Re-Election of the President, by Richard Nixon himself, his attorney general, John Mitchell, and members of Nixon's White House staff. The break-in's purpose was to photograph Democratic Party documents and install listening devices. The burglars were caught, and Nixon, White House staff, and other friends of the president engaged in a cover-up of their participation in the planning of the burglary. The cover-up eventually led to proceedings for Nixon's impeachment and his resignation from the presidency. As a United States District Court Judge, in 1974, Gerhard Gesell presided over the trials of seven of those charged with felonies for their roles in the scandal. They included John Mitchell; H. R. Haldeman, Nixon's Chief of Staff; John Ehrlichman, Assistant to the President for Domestic Affairs; and Charles Colson, the director of the Office of Public Liaison.[3]

Archibald Cox was appointed to investigate and charge those responsible for the Watergate scandal in 1973 by Elliott Richardson, the newly appointed Attorney General of the United States, to be the special prosecutor for the Watergate scandal. Cox again took leave from his position at Harvard Law School to oversee the Watergate investigation. He only served for five months because when he sought to obtain secret tapes of conversations that had taken place in the Oval Office at the White House, Richard Nixon gave him a direct order to cease trying to obtain those tapes. Nixon argued that Cox, as part of the Justice Department, was in the executive branch of government and that Nixon, as head of the executive branch, should have absolute control over Cox's activities. Of course, this was an unsupportable position because Nixon himself was one of those who were being investigated. When Cox refused to comply, Nixon had him fired in what has become known as the "Saturday Night Massacre."[4]

Cox and Gesell had been adversaries in the *White Motor Company* case, but Judge Gerhard Gesell now took Cox's side. He ruled in a case that the firing of Archibald Cox as special prosecutor had been illegal.[5]

There was no one at the ready table to my right, located behind Archibald Cox. Fortas was waiting until the last minute to appear. He must have been relaxing at the Office of the Clerk.

As the previous case ended, Chief Justice Warren called our case, saying, "the next case is Clarence Earl Gideon v H.G. Cochran, director, Division of Corrections." Fortas had just entered the room and was briefly seated at his ready table. He was by himself. As Chief Justice Warren called our case, George Mentz and I moved to the table ahead of us while Fortas and his briefcase made their way to the table to our right previously occupied by Archibald Cox. He stood, approached the podium, and began to speak.

He appeared to be in his early fifties. He was of medium height and build. He wore a dark brown suit and had a slow, deliberate, deep voice.

Early in his argument Fortas referred to the trial transcript in our case and said:

[I]f you will look at this transcript of the record, perhaps you will share my feeling, which is a feeling of despondency. The record is not—does not indicate that Clarence Earl Gideon is a man of inferior natural talents. This record does not reflect that Clarence Earl Gideon is a moron or a person of low intelligence. This record does not indicate that the judge of the trial court in the state of Florida or that the prosecuting attorney in the state of Florida was derelict in his duty. . . . On the contrary, it indicates that they tried to help Gideon. But to me, if the Court pleases, this record indicates the basic difficulty with Betts against Brady. And the basic difficulty with Betts against Brady is that no man, certainly no layman, can conduct a trial in his own defense so that the trial is a fair trial.[6]

\* \* \* \* \*

Indeed, I believe the right way to look at this . . . is that a court, a criminal court is not properly constituted—under our adversary system, unless there is a judge, and unless there is a counsel for the prosecution, and unless there is a counsel for the defense.[7]

After about 30 minutes of his argument, it was noon, and the Chief Justice announced that we would recess for lunch. Fortas and I were led by a clerk to a stairway far to my right as I faced the bench. It was in the corner of the courtroom. We were led down the stairs into a small room one floor below the level of the courtroom. We shook hands, introduced ourselves, and sat at a small table, facing each other. We were the only people in the room, except for the waiter who entered only to bring us our food. (We had given our orders from the menu earlier to an assistant clerk.) George Mentz had decided to eat lunch in the Court's cafeteria with a friend of his.

Abe Fortas began with an apology. *Gideon* was one of four companion cases set together for argument, one after the other, beginning with our case. The others were *Douglas v. California*,[8] regarding the right to counsel for the first appeal of right from a felony conviction; *Draper v. Washington*,[9] on the right to a transcript for appeal where the trial judge could deny a request on the ground that the appeal was frivolous; and *Lane v. Brown*,[10] involving the right to a transcript for an appeal where, under state law, only the public defender could procure a free transcript and the public defender, in that case, had refused to obtain a transcript. Fortas told me he had sent invitations to the lawyers in all these cases for a dinner party at his home on Sunday evening before the cases were set for argument. Unfortunately, the invitations had been sent a short time before the dinner took place. Apparently, mine had gone to Tallahassee, not Bartow, so I had not received it in time to attend the party.

This was the first I had heard about the party. He was very apologetic, but I explained that he could not have known that I was working in Bartow, not Tallahassee, and therefore it was not his fault that the invitation had not reached me in time. I thanked him for the invite and told him I regretted missing out on the dinner at his home.

During our lunch, Fortas talked admiringly about Justice Black and a case in which he appeared before Black in chambers. Fortas had represented Lyndon Baines Johnson, vice president in 1963 and later president of the United States, in a lawsuit over a Texas election some years earlier when Johnson was running for the first time for the office of United States senator. I didn't fully understand the case he was talking about but later learned more details.

The Democratic run-off for a vacant Senate seat in August 1948 was between Johnson and former Governor of Texas, Coke Stevenson. Johnson won by 87 votes, but the outcome was in doubt. A ballot box in one county contained 202 votes for Johnson, all in the same ink and the same handwriting. And, when the election supervisors opened the box, it was empty.

Nevertheless, the Democratic Party executive committee certified Johnson as the winner. Stevenson filed an action alleging fraud in federal court before a friend of his, United States District Judge Whitfield Davidson. Davidson invalidated the election results. Johnson was now off the ballot for the general election, which in those days in Texas was always won by the Democratic candidate.

Fortas entered the case at that point. He argued Johnson's cause before Judge J. C. Hutcheson of the United States Court of Appeals for the Fifth Circuit, but Hutcheson decided to wait until later in the fall when the entire court could hear the case. Fortas then took the case to the Supreme Court, to Justice Hugo Black, serving as circuit justice for the Fifth Circuit. Each circuit has one Supreme Court Justice assigned to oversee that circuit, and Black was that Justice for the Fifth Circuit. Fortas's position was that a federal judge should not enjoin a state-run primary election. Arguments occurred in Justice Black's chambers in the Supreme Court building for four hours. Fortas argued that state law controlled and that the federal district court did not have jurisdiction over the case. He also argued that delay in obtaining judicial relief would bar Johnson from running in the general election. Justice Black ruled with Fortas. Johnson was certified as the Democratic candidate, and he won election to the Senate in November 1948.[11]

From our lunch conversation, I learned that he and Justice Hugo Black knew each other well. And, though I did not realize this until later, Fortas and Justice William Douglas had been at Yale Law School at the same time; Douglas as a professor and Fortas as one of his students.

After our lunch, Abe Fortas and I walked back up the stairs to the courtroom. He went to his counsel's table, and I went to mine, where George Mentz was already seated. Very few people were in the audience, unlike the packed room the day before.

We rose from our seats as the members of the Court filed into the room. Abe Fortas finished his argument, and J. Lee Rankin spoke for 15 or 20 minutes. He was the lawyer for the ACLU, which had filed an amicus brief. Rankin argued that *Betts v. Brady* should be overruled.

When Rankin finished, Chief Justice Warren said, "Mr. Jacob." My best estimate is that it was around 2:15 p.m. I walked to the podium. From left

Justice Hugo L. Black. Photo by Harris & Ewing, courtesy of the Collection of the Supreme Court of the United States.

to right, the Justices before me were Justices White, Brennan, Clark, Black, Warren, Douglas, Harlan, Stewart, and Goldberg.

My first impression was a feeling that I was at the bottom of a pit, looking up to the Justices, who were high above me. The speaker's podium was very close to the bench, and the Justices were spread out far to my left and right. This was different from Florida appellate courts, where I previously had argued, where the speaker was farther from the bench and the judges sat closer together.

The podium had lights on it. There was a green light to let speakers know there was time left for their remarks and a red light as a signal to stop talking.

I began to make my prepared argument, but there were questions immediately. In the Florida courts, judges asked very few questions, but here the questioning was extremely intense. I have read the transcript, and it shows that all nine Justices were involved in the questioning. A total of 92 questions, comments, and interruptions occurred during my one-hour argument, most of which came within the first half hour.

Never in the cases I previously had argued in the Florida appellate courts had I encountered anything like the emotion and zeal that emerged in the questioning. I felt as if I was in a cross fire. It was difficult to know which question to take next, with questions coming from different directions. Two Justices would ask questions simultaneously while there was still a previous question from another Justice that I had not completely answered. It was difficult to remember questions that often were coming at me at the same time. I should have had, but did not have, a pad and pencil on the podium to write brief notes to myself. I would have written the name or initial of the Justice, in the order the questions were asked, and a couple of words by each name to remind me of that Justice's question so I could have responded more fully, in the order in which the questions were asked. The questioning was relentless.

During the questioning, I got the impression that some of the questions were being asked not for the purpose of trying to elicit an answer from me, but instead to persuade a fellow Justice to agree on an issue in the case. Immediately after asking a question, a Justice would look toward one of the other Justices down the bench as if to say, "You should consider the point I am making by this question in making your decision in this case."

Here is one of the first exchanges that took place:

John M. Harlan II: Could I ask you a question about—
Bruce R. Jacob: Yes, sir.

John M. Harlan II:—the operation of your Florida statute. The judge said that he couldn't, under the law, appoint counsel to this man. Does that mean he couldn't appoint counsel that would be compensated by the State, or does it mean that if he chose as a judge of the court to say, "You, Mr. X, a member of the bar, will serve this man without compensation," that he couldn't have done that?

Bruce R. Jacob: Right. He could have—

John M. Harlan II: But there's nothing in your law that prevents the judge from appointing counsel without compensation?

Bruce R. Jacob: That's right, Your Honor. Our state, the judges in our state, have discretion, and they can appoint counsel when special circumstances—

John M. Harlan II: Are there some that do?

Bruce R. Jacob: Yes, Your Honor. In fact, there are some judges who appoint counsel in all cases.

John M. Harlan II: All cases.

Bruce R. Jacob: And generally, that is in the more urban areas. In the rural areas where there are fewer lawyers, and especially fewer criminal lawyers available, the courts have many times not appointed counsel as often as they do in urban areas.[12]

Chief Justice Warren commented on the study by the Florida Division of Corrections, set out in our brief: "[O]n page 56 of your brief, are as follows, that there are 65% of all of your prisoners now in jail were not represented by counsel, 65%."

Bruce R. Jacob: Yes, Your Honor.

Earl Warren: And you had 8,000 prisoners; therefore, 5,200 prisoners have not been represented by counsel in the trial court.[13]

I believe Chief Justice Warren's point was that Florida courts often do not find special circumstances. So part of my response was as follows:

[M]any trial courts appoint counsel when they see special circumstances. This trial—this particular trial judge, in this case, misquoted the law. . . . He said, "Sorry, Mr. Gideon, I cannot appoint counsel for you except in a capital case."

Now, on its face, that appears to be a misstatement of the law because Florida does follow Betts v Brady, and in Florida, a man is entitled to counsel if he is indigent and also he is ignorant, illiterate, or incompetent in some way.[14]

Judge Hugo Black believed that *Betts v. Brady* did not provide clear enough guidelines for the states to follow. He said:

> [The State is] entitled to know with some degree of certainty what they can do to comply with what this Court says the Constitution requires.
>
> Bruce R. Jacob: Your Honor, I don't think *Betts v Brady* is that unclear. I think it's inconsistent in the same way that the entire common law is inconsistent.
>
> Hugo L. Black: You think it's clear?
>
> Bruce R. Jacob: Yes, Your Honor ...
>
> Hugo L. Black: Well, how come most states don't know what circumstances will be held sufficient after we review them several years after your states view them?
>
> Bruce R. Jacob: Each time this Court decides a case, that adds a new special circumstance which we must consider in determining whether the defendant is entitled to counsel.

\* \* \* \* \*

> Bruce R. Jacob: We contend that it would be better for this Court to review [state decisions regarding the special circumstances test] on a case-by-case basis. It still allows us some freedom to impose our own criminal procedure rules.[15]

Chief Justice Warren asked further questions about our Division of Corrections study.

> Earl Warren: Mr. Jacob, I suppose that out of those 5,200 prisoners now in your jails who are not represented by counsel, that a vast majority of them are not only poor but are illiterate. Would that be a fair observation?
>
> Bruce R. Jacob: Your Honor, I don't know.
>
> Earl Warren: Well, what's your observation?
>
> Bruce R. Jacob: My observation is that it—in all honesty, my observation is that there are some—
>
> Earl Warren: Some—
>
> Bruce R. Jacob:—but I have no idea how many.[16]

When enacted, the Sixth Amendment only gave a federal defendant the right to be defended by retained counsel. The meaning of this provision was changed by the Court in 1938, in *Johnson v. Zerbst,* to require appointment of counsel for indigent defendants in federal criminal cases.

Government entities, such as the Supreme Court, have greater powers in some situations than others. The Court had two sources of power in *Johnson v. Zerbst* in deciding that counsel should be appointed for indigent federal defendants: (1) the power to interpret the meaning of the language of the Sixth Amendment; and (2) its supervisory power over the lower federal courts. If it had had only the language of the Sixth Amendment as its source of power to make that decision, that source alone, we speculated, might not have been sufficient for each of the Justices in the majority to reach the decision they did in *Johnson.*

This issue of whether the supervisory authority of the Supreme Court over lower federal courts was at least a partial underlying reason for the result in that case came up during the oral arguments in *Gideon.* Here is an excerpt from my argument on this point:

Bruce R. Jacob: In Johnson versus Zerbst, this Court decided that in the federal court system, every man was entitled to counsel unless he waives that right.

And we take the position that in *Johnson v Zerbst,* this Court, although it proceeded by construing the Sixth Amendment, we take the position that this Court had in mind, at least to some extent, the supervisory powers of this Court over the federal—the inferior courts in the federal system.

Hugo L. Black: It wasn't put on that basis, was it?

Bruce R. Jacob: It wasn't put on that basis, Your Honor, but we can—

Hugo L. Black: Is there any intimation that it was on that basis, either in the argument or the Court's opinion?

Bruce R. Jacob: No, Your Honor, it wasn't, but generally, when a court construes the Constitution, they go into history and the intention of the Framers.

In that case, the Court did not go into the history of the provision; it did not go into the intention of the Framers, so we feel that at least this Court took cognizance of its supervisory powers and knew that it could impose—

Hugo L. Black: Well, I assure you, that's the first time I ever thought about it in that way.[17]

My comments had angered Justice Black. His face was red as he said those words.

Justice Black and I were not talking about the same thing. He was referring to the fact that he had based his opinion in *Johnson v. Zerbst* only on the language of the Sixth Amendment's right to counsel provision. I was talking about the history of the Sixth Amendment's right to counsel provision and the sources of power the Court had in reaching the result in that case.

Normally, if the Court decides to change the meaning of a section of the Constitution, it would discuss the history and explain why it believes that that history should no longer be controlling. The Court had not done that in the *Johnson* opinion. To my mind, Justice Black had been enabled to disregard this history because he and the Court could have reached the same result using its other source of power for making the decision—its supervisory power over the federal district courts.

Florida already had or was about to have a public defender or attorney assignment system in its larger counties. Justice Stewart wanted to know how many in the state population were in those areas.

> Potter Stewart: Do you know offhand how much of the population of Florida is in those four counties? Half of it?
>
> Bruce R. Jacob: Just about, Your Honor.
>
> Dade County alone has a million people, and the state has between four and five million, I believe.
>
> So Dade alone has, I believe, about 25% of the population.[18]

In my argument, thinking in terms of minor criminal cases, I made this statement:

> A state should be free to adopt any system it wants. If it wants, it should be able to do away with the need for a prosecutor.
>
> Perhaps a judge could handle the whole trial.
>
> I'm not urging this, but I'm saying that the Court—that the states have the right to do this.[19]

Justice Harlan, the Justice most favorably inclined to our position, said, in response to this comment by me, "Careful, now, don't go too far."[20] He was trying to help me.

I argued that if the Sixth Amendment were incorporated into the Due Process Clause, the absolute rule requiring counsel for all indigents would have to apply in misdemeanor cases, placing an enormous practical and financial burden on the states.

Justice John Marshall Harlan II. Photo by Abdon David Ackad, courtesy of the Collection of the Supreme Court of the United States.

Bruce R. Jacob: [I]f the Sixth Amendment, as it's presently construed in Johnson versus Zerbst, is to be incorporated or absorbed into the Fourteenth Amendment, the rule would have to extend to all misdemeanors because the Sixth Amendment just says in all criminal prosecutions the defendant is entitled to counsel.

And, of course, misdemeanors are crimes.

I don't see how the Court could draw a distinction; they'd have to provide lawyers in all crimes, no matter how minute or how small they are.

This would place a tremendous burden on the taxpayers of every state.

Hugo L. Black: What do you understand Johnson and Zerbst held with reference to that right?

Bruce R. Jacob: Johnson versus Zerbst held that the Sixth Amendment meant you are entitled to counsel in every single case.

Hugo L. Black: Without exception?

Bruce R. Jacob: Without exception, because the Sixth Amendment doesn't make any differentiation between different types of crimes.[21]

I also argued that if *Betts* were overruled based on the Equal Protection Clause, the states would have to provide counsel for indigents in civil and criminal cases.

Bruce R. Jacob: If this rule is imposed under the Equal Protection Clause, I think it would result in a number of absurd situations.

For instance . . . the states would also be required to appoint counsel in civil cases because a man who has money can be represented by a lawyer in civil cases.

The court would have to see to it that a man is given investigators, that he's given psychiatrists and expert witnesses, if he wants them, because those things are available to the man who has money.

This Court would have to see to it that every man is equally entitled to bail, that the state would have to give him money for bail if he couldn't afford it.[22]

One of the arguments made by the petitioner was that automatic appointment was required for indigent defendants in capital cases and that there should be no distinction made between capital and noncapital cases when it comes to the need for an absolute rule regarding appointment of counsel.

This argument had begun with *Powell v. Alabama*. By 1962 and 1963, *Powell* was being cited incorrectly by lawyers and courts for the proposition that appointment of counsel was required in all capital cases under the Due Process Clause of the Fourteenth Amendment. But, of course, that is not what the Court had held in *Powell*. The right to counsel in that case depended on the facts and circumstances of the case.

Here are some of my comments and those of the Justices on this issue:

Bruce R. Jacob: Powell versus Alabama was decided on the circumstances of that case. It did not lay down an inflexible rule in all capital cases.

* * * * *

Earl Warren: We said in *Betts v Brady* that they must furnish counsel in all capital cases, didn't we?

Bruce R. Jacob: In Betts versus Brady, no mention was made, no distinction was made between capital and non-capital cases, your Honor.

I realize since that case, legal writers and judges have cited Betts versus Brady for the proposition that an inflexible rule exists in capital cases and not in non-capital cases. But in reading Betts versus Brady, not in one place is there the word "capital" . . . as opposed to "non-capital."

William J. Brennan, Jr.: What about Powell versus Alabama?

Bruce R. Jacob: Powell versus Alabama was decided on the circumstances of that case, Your Honor.

There the Court held that in a capital case where a man can show that he is illiterate, ignorant, or incapable of handling his own defense, he should have counsel appointed for him.

John M. Harlan II: Well, that's quite true, but you've got to recognize that in substantive [subsequent] cases in this Court, we have laid down an absolute rule in capital cases.

Hamilton versus Alabama is the latest expression of it, and of course, we can't argue that.

Bruce R. Jacob: I'm not sure that Hamilton versus Alabama does say that, Your Honor.

In that case, there was a state court finding that the man was entitled to counsel because the state court appointed counsel for the man, and he was arraigned on a charge of burglary.

That charge was dropped, and then he was arraigned on a capital charge, and the counsel was not present.

And two days later, the same counsel who had been previously appointed was appointed for him on that capital charge.

And we take the position that Hamilton merely says that when the state court has already determined that a man is entitled to counsel in a state court procedure, an arraignment is very difficult and very complex.

The man should have had counsel at the arraignment stage.[23]

My recollection, from reading *Hamilton,* was that the arraignment in Alabama, in capital cases, was complex, and counsel, therefore, was necessary at that arraignment. Complexity of the proceedings was one of the circumstances in *Powell* and *Betts* that required appointment of counsel.[24] The Court in *Hamilton* had made comments assuming that there was an absolute right to counsel in capital cases, but that was dicta. To my mind, the holding was based on the complexity of the arraignment in Alabama in that case.

A low point, for me, came in this part of the argument:

> Potter Stewart: Florida wouldn't permit Gideon or any other layman to defend anyone else in the state on trial, would it?
>
> Bruce R. Jacob: Gideon could—if a man came into court and said, I want to be defended by Gideon, then certainly the court would not object.
>
> Hugo L. Black: It wouldn't?
>
> Potter Stewart: Wouldn't Gideon maybe get in trouble for practicing law without a license?
>
> Hugo L. Black: With the local bar association.

When Justices Stewart and Black made these comments, my immediate thought was that they were right—the state bar association and the courts would never allow a layperson to represent anyone, and I said:

> Bruce R. Jacob: I'm sorry, Your Honor; that was a stupid answer.[25]

I am not sure why I said the word "stupid." That word just popped out of my mouth. I certainly meant to be completely truthful and honest with the Court in answering their questions, but in this instance I carried my honesty to an extreme.

Within the next three years, I was involved in federal litigation that established the principle that a layman could represent another in some types of litigation despite possible objections by the bar association. My answer to Justices Stewart and Black had not been wrong as I had thought during the oral arguments in *Gideon.*

In the fall of 1965, two years after the Gideon argument, I began my law school teaching career as an assistant professor at the Emory University School of Law. About a week after I had started at Emory, I received a phone call from Frank Hooper, one of the two United States district judges in Atlanta, asking me to come to see him at his office in downtown Atlanta. He told me that the United States Penitentiary, on the southern edge of the city of Atlanta, had rules preventing one inmate from doing legal work for another inmate. However, a knowledgeable inmate named Robert Joyner White was willing to provide legal assistance to three other inmates, and those inmates wanted his help. Because all four were afraid of being punished under prison rules if White provided this assistance, White filed a civil suit in the district court asking for declaratory and injunctive relief in his own behalf and behalf of the other three inmates, asking the court to rule that the applicable prison rules were unconstitutional. White was representing himself, and Judge Hooper wanted me to represent the other three inmates.

I told the judge that I was admitted to practice in the United States District Courts in Florida but not the Northern District of Georgia. He said, "That's no problem. Raise your right hand." There, in his office, I stood and was sworn in by Judge Hooper as a member of the bar of his court.

During the next several months, I interviewed my clients and met with White. I engaged in extensive discovery. I interviewed and took notarized statements of many inmates at the Atlanta Penitentiary who wanted help from jailhouse lawyers. I made demands for admissions of facts from prison officials. I did a lot of legal research, preparing for the trial.

In the spring of 1966, the trial in our case took place before Judge Hooper in the federal courthouse in Atlanta. For three days, White and I and the assistant United States attorney examined and cross-examined witnesses, introduced documents, including affidavits of many inmates (the court allowed the affidavits), and made our arguments concerning the legal issues involved.

Judge Hooper ruled with us. My three clients had to be allowed to seek legal assistance from White, and White had to be allowed to provide that legal help. Prison rules previously preventing this were found to be unconstitutional. The name of the case is *White v. Blackwell*.[26]

A case involving virtually the same issues had been decided differently by the United States Court of Appeals for the Sixth Circuit in Tennessee.[27] The lawyers for the inmates in that case were considering seeking review through a petition for certiorari to the Supreme Court. They had heard about our case and contacted me to ask for assistance. I made copies of the papers in my file and the file of Robert Joyner White, including our research and legal arguments, and sent all of them to the lawyers in Nashville. Certiorari was granted, and the lawyers won their case, *Johnson v. Avery*,[28] in the Supreme Court. The Court held that in the absence of an alternative, such as a public defender office or an assigned counsel system for inmates seeking legal help with their post-conviction petitions and appeals, prison authorities could not be allowed to prohibit jailhouse lawyers from providing legal assistance to other, less knowledgeable inmates wanting their help. One of our most important rights is the right of access to the courts, and the prison rules were blocking inmates from gaining this access. The author of the opinion in this case was Justice Abe Fortas.

In 1966, with Judge Hooper's assistance, I obtained a grant from the National Defender Project, which the Ford Foundation funded, to establish the Legal Assistance for Inmates Program at the Emory Law School. And with the help of John Cleary, deputy director of the National Defender Project, I was able to hire Robert Joyner White and Benjamin Rayburn, another competent jailhouse lawyer at the Atlanta Penitentiary, to assist a staff attorney and me in the supervision of law students. We obtained their release on parole to allow them to work with our students at the law school in our program, providing legal help to inmates at the Atlanta Penitentiary.[29]

Getting back to the questions or comments by Justices Stewart and Black, after my experiences with jailhouse lawyers, I realized that my answer to those Justices was not "stupid." There are situations where an intelligent, knowledgeable layperson can be quite capable of representing another in a legal matter, including involvement in judicial proceedings. I have learned through the years that a person does not have to be a licensed attorney to be competent at providing legal services. I believe that even in a criminal prosecution if the defendant wants a very knowledgeable layperson, perhaps a friend, to represent him, the trial judge might allow that person to act as the defendant's counsel. The judge should have control over their courtroom. The judge should probably interview the proposed non-licensed defender to ensure they can provide a competent defense. However, I do not think this unlicensed person would or should be allowed to collect a fee.

When I finished my argument before the Supreme Court, George Mentz took the podium. Among other things, he argued that, even if *Betts* were to be overruled by the Court, the states should not have to appoint counsel for the 90 percent or so of defendants who wish to plead guilty to the charges against them.

Near the end of his argument, one of the Justices said, "You don't really expect to win this case, do you?" Mentz answered, "Your Honor, hope springs eternal." This drew laughs from the members of the Court.

During most of my argument and that of George Mentz, there was only one person in the audience: my wife, Ann. It was strange that the courtroom was almost empty for the arguments in what would become one of the great cases in American legal history.

When Mentz's argument ended, I thanked him for his assistance in the case, and then Ann and I left the courtroom. In a hallway outside the courtroom, Abe Fortas sat on a bench, alone, organizing his papers in his briefcase. I introduced Ann to him, and he stood to talk with us. He apologized profusely to Ann for not getting the invitation to us in time for us to attend the dinner party at his home, but I again assured him that it was not his fault for our failure to receive the invitation in time.

He probably sensed that I was sad after being battered by the Court's questioning, and to make me feel better, he said, "You know, you have a wonderful way before the Court." I often have wondered what he meant by that comment. My best guess is that he appreciated my honesty in answering the Justices' questions.

In mid-February 1963, while sitting in my office in Bartow, I received a phone call from Anthony Lewis. The *New York Times* had shut down because of a strike. As a result, he was temporarily out of work. To fill his time, he decided to write a book about the *Gideon* case. He asked if he could interview me, and I said yes. He flew to Tampa, and Ann and I met him at the Hawaiian Village Motel near the old Tampa Airport. We had brought all our files regarding the case with us. He had his portable typewriter and typed our answers to his questions. Also, he went through our files and told us what items would be helpful to him in writing the book.

I still have clear memories of that meeting with Anthony Lewis. He asked whether the Attorney General's Office had considered the possibility of confessing error in the case—in other words, telling the Court we should lose. In a previous Supreme Court case, our office had confessed error, and we were embarrassed when the Court rejected that confession. If we had confessed error in the *Gideon* case, I believe the same thing would have happened.

The main question in the case was whether counsel should automatically be provided for all indigent defendants in state noncapital felony cases. A poll of the American people at the time probably would have shown that the vast majority liked providing counsel to all. That would have been the popular response in such a survey. But cases involving constitutional issues are not decided through popularity polls. They are decided through a careful examination of the constitutional provisions involved, and many difficult constitutional and other issues had to be resolved by the Court in *Gideon*. Was the history regarding the appointment of counsel relevant? Was "fairness" a good enough standard for determining whether counsel should be provided in a given case? Historically what was the meaning of due process? If the Court were to overrule *Betts v. Brady* should the new decision be based on the Equal Protection Clause or the Due Process Clause? Should counsel be provided in misdemeanor cases? If *Betts* were overruled, should the new decision operate retroactively? Should the states be allowed to make decisions regarding their rules of procedure as a matter of policy rather than having the decisions made through an interpretation of the Constitution by the Supreme Court? These and more issues needed to be briefed and argued, and I told Lewis that it would have been wrong, in my view, for us to confess error.

As he was interviewing us, he very suddenly, unexpectedly blurted out the words, "Oh good, now I have my theme." I said, "What do you mean? I thought this is a nonfiction book. Why would you need a theme?" He explained that even a nonfiction book must have a theme. He said, "The book would never sell if it didn't have a theme." I am not implying that Lewis was avaricious, for the profits from the sales of *Gideon's Trumpet,* or a good portion of the profits, go into a trust fund for the benefit of Clarence Earl Gideon's children.[30]

The theme, as he explained it to Ann and me, was that at the first trial, Gideon was unrepresented and alone, facing state prosecutors, while in the Supreme Court, he was represented by Abe Fortas and his law firm. In contrast, the state was represented by me, a lawyer working on his own at nights and weekends, with the secretarial help of only his wife.

I let him know this was not a very accurate picture of what had taken place. Much of my work in the case had been accomplished in Tallahassee over a six-month period, from March to mid-September 1962. There I had Judge Bowen and other lawyers in the Criminal Appeals section of the Attorney General's Office to consult with.

During the final three months, from mid-September through December, I worked on the case at night and on weekends. But that was my choice. Chesterfield Smith, the head of the firm, assured me that it would be all right for me to work on the case and use the law firm's secretaries and resources for that purpose during regular working hours. As it was, I had discussions with members of the firm during working hours about the case. I went to lunch with partners and other associates, and a frequent topic of discussion was my progress on the brief in the *Gideon* case. One of those partners was Smith, who later, in 1973–74 became the president of the American Bar Association. The Watergate scandal was taking place at the time, and Smith was an outspoken critic of Richard Nixon, advocating the appointment of a

Justice Stephen H. Grimes of the Florida
Supreme Court. Courtesy of the State
Archives of Florida.

special prosecutor to investigate Nixon's involvement in the burglary of the
Democratic Party headquarters at the Watergate complex.

Other partners who talked with me about the case included Stephen H.
Grimes, a future justice and chief justice of the Florida Supreme Court, and
Warren E. Hall Jr. Hall had been a partner in an Atlanta law firm and the
lawyer for the Teamsters Union and Jimmy Hoffa. I had not been disadvan-
taged through lack of expert advice and assistance. Furthermore, having my
wife, Ann, as my secretary was not a handicap. She had served as a personal
secretary to the Secretary of State of Florida, Thomas "Tom" Burton Adams
Jr., and had to have been one of the best secretaries in Florida.

We would have to wait for the publication of *Gideon's Trumpet* to find out
how Lewis would put this theme into words. The book was to be published
the following year, in 1964.

Lewis told me that he was in the Supreme Court's courtroom every day
and that when the decision in *Gideon* was announced, he would phone me
immediately and inform me about the Court's decision. I thanked him and
let him know that I would appreciate such a call.

Back in Bartow, we copied each of the papers in our files that he wanted
for his book. Then we mailed all the copies to Anthony Lewis.

# 14

## The Supreme Court's Decision

In mid-February 1963, I was notified by the Office of the Attorney General that H. G. Cochran Jr. was no longer the director of the Florida Division of Corrections. He had been replaced by a new permanent director, Louie Wainwright. I sent a letter to the Clerk of the Supreme Court advising the Court of this change. I did not receive a response from the Office of the Clerk.

On Monday, March 18, 1963, around noon, I received a phone call from Anthony Lewis. He told me that the Supreme Court had decided our case. Gideon had won by a unanimous vote. I had been expecting that the Court would rule on behalf of Gideon. I was disappointed that there wasn't at least one dissent, but the news was not unexpected. There were separate concurring opinions by some Justices in the case.

He also told me that the name of the case had been changed to *Gideon v. Wainwright*. The name had been *Gideon v. Cochran* from January 1962, when Clarence Gideon filed his petition for certiorari in the Supreme Court, until March 18, 1963, but now it was to have this new name.

Lewis read the opinions to me over the phone and promised to mail printed versions. My reaction to his reading of the main opinion by Justice Black was that it seemed very short and did not discuss some of the important issues in the case, such as how the decision applied to misdemeanor cases, or whether the decision was to apply retroactively or only prospectively. Also, it was difficult to understand how the decision could have been reached so soon. Decisions in the most important cases usually are announced near the end of the term of the Court, in very late June or during the first couple of days of July. This decision had been made very quickly. I was even more astounded when I learned that the decisions in the three companion cases—*Douglas v. California*, *Draper v. Washington*, and *Lane v. Brown*—also were announced by the Court on March 18, 1963. Two months after the oral arguments was a very short period of time for the Court's members to decide each of these cases and write their opinions, including concurrences and dissents.

Louie Wainwright. Photo by Donn Dughi (Donald Gregory), courtesy of the State Archives of Florida.

In the opinion for the Court in *Gideon*, written by Justice Black, he said that *Betts v. Brady* was being overruled and that the Sixth Amendment's right to counsel provision was now applicable in state courts. In other words, it had been "incorporated" into the Fourteenth Amendment, presumably the Due Process Clause. The holding applied in noncapital felony cases and a fortiori (with even stronger reason) to capital cases. In other words, *Gideon* imposed an automatic right to counsel constitutional requirement for indigent defendants in all felony cases.[1]

In the opinion, Black said that "the Court in *Betts v. Brady* made an abrupt break with its own well-considered precedents,"[2] and then he added that the

Court was now "returning to these old precedents."[3] Since he was referring to "precedents," using the plural, he must have been referring not only to *Powell v. Alabama*, which had been the case preceding *Betts* that had applied in state courts under the Due Process Clause of the Fourteenth Amendment, but he also must have been referring to *Johnson v. Zerbst*, even though that case could not be considered "precedent," since it had only applied in federal courts, pursuant to the Sixth Amendment. Also, *Betts* had not constituted an "abrupt break" from *Powell*. Instead, it had been an extension of the reasoning of *Powell*, which applied in capital cases to *Betts*, which applied in noncapital cases.

Justice John Harlan made this very clear in his concurring opinion. He said, in part:

> I agree that *Betts v. Brady* should be overruled, but consider it to be entitled to a more respectful burial. . . .
>
> I cannot subscribe to the view that *Betts v. Brady* represented "an abrupt break with its own well-considered precedents." . . . In 1932, in *Powell v. Alabama*, . . . a capital case, this Court declared that under the particular facts there presented—"the ignorance and illiteracy of the defendants, their youth, the circumstances of public hostility . . . and above all that they stood in deadly peril of their lives" . . .—the state court had a duty to assign counsel for the trial as a necessary requisite of due process of law. It is evident that these limiting facts were not added to the opinion as an after-thought; they were repeatedly emphasized . . . and were clearly regarded as important to the results.
>
> Thus when this Court, a decade later, decided *Betts v. Brady*, it did no more than to admit of the possible existence of special circumstances in noncapital as well as capital trials, while at the same time insisting that such circumstances be shown in order to establish a denial of due process. The right to appointed counsel had been recognized as being considerably broader in federal prosecutions, see *Johnson v. Zerbst*, . . . but to have imposed these requirements on the States would indeed have been "an abrupt break" with the almost immediate past. The declaration that the right to appointed counsel in state prosecutions, as established in *Powell v. Alabama*, was not limited to capital cases was in truth not a departure from, but an extension of, existing precedent.[4]

Why did Justice Black state that *Betts* had not followed earlier precedent when this was not true? One possible reason might have been that he wanted to prevent any attempt to make *Gideon* prospective only in its application. By saying that *Betts* had constituted an "abrupt break" from precedent—*Powell* and presumably the *Johnson v. Zerbst* decision—he was declaring that *Betts* was not only voidable through the overruling process but also void, a nullity as if it had never existed. And, this being the case, state courts had been wrong to ever rely on it. *Gideon*, therefore, did not change past precedent, according to Black. The real, valid precedents that the states should have followed in the years between *Betts* in 1942 and *Gideon* in 1963 were *Powell*, as Black misinterpreted it, and *Johnson v. Zerbst*, not *Betts v. Brady*. Because the states should not have relied on *Betts*, in Black's view, the states could not argue that *Gideon* should not apply retroactively to inmates convicted between 1942 and 1963 and were still in prison.

Four years later, in *Burget v. Texas*,[5] the Court said that *Gideon* was to be applied retroactively. This meant that many Florida inmates were sent back to their trial courts for new trials based on *Gideon* or to be released from custody.[6] Other states that had not automatically provided counsel to indigents also had to retry or release inmates who had been indigent and had not been represented by appointed counsel when convicted.

In his opinion, Justice Black did not specify whether the Due Process Clause or the Equal Protection Clause of the Fourteenth Amendment was the basis for the decision in *Gideon*. Instead, he merely said that the "Fourteenth Amendment," which contains both clauses, required the *Gideon* result.[7] Why wasn't he more specific about which part of the Fourteenth Amendment he was relying on? The reason, I believe, was that he would have had difficulty explaining how the decision in *Gideon* was justified under either the concept of due process or the concept of equal protection. It was easier for him to ignore those difficulties by using the "Fourteenth Amendment," thereby blurring the reason for the decision.

There would have been thorny problems involved in expressly basing the *Gideon* decision on the Due Process Clause of the Fourteenth Amendment. As explained in chapter 12, regarding the Brief for Respondent, due process, before *Gideon*, was a broad concept of fairness, and fairness was a relative concept based upon the facts and circumstances of a particular case. Due process was not susceptible to being reduced to a fixed formula, such as a black-and-white rule requiring appointment of counsel for every indigent in a felony case. Black would have had to try to explain away the merits of the "ordered liberty" concept of due process, which so many great Justices had embraced over a long period of time, and that would have been difficult for Black to do. It was easier to say that the decision was based on the Fourteenth Amendment, even though in actual fact the Court was incorporating the Sixth Amendment into the Due Process Clause of the Fourteenth Amendment.

That clause provides that "No State shall . . . deprive any person of life, liberty or property without due process of law." The Sixth Amendment's right to counsel provision was now incorporated into the Due Process Clause. Since that clause is concerned with deprivations of property as well as life and liberty, logically, the right to counsel had to extend to misdemeanors, in which a person can lose liberty or property in the form of fines. Furthermore, the right to counsel for indigents would now have to extend to civil cases involving property. However, the Court, in the *Gideon* opinion, did not discuss these issues.

Justice Black did not explain the changes to the concept of due process that were taking place as a result of the *Gideon* decision. But from today's vantage point, it is clear that the *Gideon* decision marked a major turning point in our understanding of what is meant by due process. The selective incorporation theory had now become the method for including the protections of the Bill of Rights into the Due Process Clause of the Fourteenth Amendment, making those provisions applicable in state criminal proceedings. Due process was no longer the fact-based test for determining whether the trial had been fair. Now, looking back at the case, the question was not only overall fairness but also whether a pre-requirement, or pre-rule, such as the requirement that counsel must be provided, has been followed.

Black likewise did not specifically discuss whether the Equal Protection Clause of the Fourteenth Amendment required the result in *Gideon*. That clause probably was not discussed because if the *Gideon* decision had been based on that clause, the Court would have opened up many problems. If the states were to be required as a matter of equal protection to provide counsel to indigent defendants, logically they would be required to provide indigents with the services that a rich defendant could afford, such as investigators, psychiatrists, and money for bail. This would have imposed enormous financial and practical difficulties for the states.

The question of whether *Gideon* applied to misdemeanors was left for the future. This issue was dealt with during the 1970s in *Argersinger v. Hamlin*[8] and *Scott v. Illinois*.[9] The Sixth Amendment states, "In all criminal prosecutions the accused shall . . . have the Assistance of Counsel for his defence."

Since a misdemeanor prosecution is a "criminal prosecution," and since the Sixth Amendment had now been made applicable to the states through the Fourteenth Amendment, the Court had to provide a right to counsel of some kind for indigents in misdemeanor cases in state courts. We discuss how the Court fashioned this right in chapter 18.

After reading the opinions in *Gideon*, I felt that the time for requiring counsel for indigents in criminal cases had been inevitable. It was as if there was a hugely popular tidal wave of support for requiring counsel in all criminal cases, in both federal and state trial courts, and whether the provisions of the Constitution required this result or not, the Court, as of 1963, was compelled to decide the way it did in *Gideon*.

Of the three companion cases, *Douglas v. California*[10] was the most significant. In the opinion for the Court by Justice William Douglas, the Court held that an indigent convicted defendant in a felony case is entitled to appointed counsel for the first appeal of right from the conviction. Justice Douglas also said that the basis for that decision was the "Fourteenth Amendment." There is no right to counsel for appeals mentioned in the Sixth Amendment or anywhere else in the Bill of Rights. Because such a right did not exist there, it could not have been incorporated into the Due Process Clause of the Fourteenth Amendment. That left the Equal Protection Clause as the basis for the *Douglas* decision, and there were three dissenting Justices in the case who did not believe that the Equal Protection Clause could support the decision in *Douglas*. Justice Clark and Justice Harlan wrote dissents, joined by Justice Stewart. One of the lines in Harlan's dissent reads as follows:

> The Equal Protection Clause is not apposite, and its application to cases like the present one can lead only to mischievous results.[11]

He was predicting that to be logically consistent with the decision in *Douglas* in the future, the Court would have to rule that indigent defendants must be provided all the benefits that the rich defendant has—such as money for bail. The Court could be creating significant problems for the future.

# 15

## Florida's Response and My Response

Two highly consequential actions were taken by Florida officials to comply with the March 18, 1963, *Gideon* decision. The most important was by the Florida Legislature, which, in May 1963, only two months later, created an Office of Public Defender in each of Florida's judicial circuits. The other was the Florida Supreme Court's adoption of "Rule 1," which changed the way prisoners obtained post-conviction relief.

After *Gideon,* correctional officials, judges, and prosecutors anticipated thousands of habeas corpus petitions from inmates now eligible for relief based on that decision.

A habeas petition is filed in the place where the jailor—the warden or other official having custody of the inmate—lives or works. This meant that thousands of inmates would be filing habeas petitions in circuit courts where state prisons were located, especially at Raiford. These inmates would be seeking to set aside their convictions, asking for new trials, this time with appointed counsel defending them. It would be difficult for circuit courts at towns such as Starke, near Raiford, to handle the deluge of habeas corpus petitions.

Reeves Bowen, who we met earlier in this book, an assistant attorney general in the Criminal Appeals section of the Attorney General's Office, was aware that Congress, in 1949, had enacted Title 28, Section 2255 of the United States Code, which required federal prisoners to no longer file post-conviction petitions for habeas corpus in the United States district court near the federal prison where they were incarcerated, but instead in the district court where they had been convicted. This spread the post-conviction caseload for federal inmates throughout the United States. This was a new statutory remedy based on the constitutional writ of habeas corpus. The relief that could be granted was essentially the same as relief available using the remedy of habeas corpus.

In the fall of 1962, Bowen approached the Florida Judicial Council with a request for it to ask the Florida Supreme Court to adopt a court rule patterned after the federal statute. This would require petitions for post-conviction relief by Florida inmates to be filed in the circuit court where the prisoner had been convicted. In response, the Florida Supreme Court promulgated "Rule 1." Today, Florida has a comprehensive set of criminal procedure rules, and Rule 1 has become Rule 3.850 of the Florida Rules of Criminal Procedure. It is called a "motion to vacate" rather than a "petition." The issues that can be raised and the relief that can be granted are essentially the same as in habeas corpus.

If relief is granted, the prosecutor for that circuit decides whether to re-prosecute the charges, after counsel has been appointed for the defendant, or to dismiss the case altogether and allow the inmate to go free.

It has been reported that between April 1963 and April 1966 there were 6,403 Florida inmates who filed post-conviction motions under the new procedure. Of these, 2,506 received new trials and 1,311 were released from custody with no further charges.[1] Presumably a very high percentage of these cases involved *Gideon*-based claims.

In May 1963, the Florida Legislature enacted comprehensive public defender legislation.[2] Florida has 20 judicial circuits. Some, in metropolitan areas, contain only one or perhaps two counties. Others, in rural areas, contain multiple counties. In each circuit, there is an elected state attorney, the prosecutor for that circuit. The 1963 statute created the office of public defender for each circuit. This person was to be elected by the voters for a four-year renewable term. I believe that the governor appointed the first public defender in each circuit. Public defenders could hire assistant public defenders as needed.

Of particular interest to me was a provision in the new law allowing members of The Florida Bar in good standing to volunteer to represent indigent defendants without receiving fees for their work. Such a volunteer was to be known as a "Special Assistant Public Defender."[3]

I asked the partners of the Holland firm if it would be all right for me to volunteer to become one of these defenders, and they consented to my request. I then volunteered at the circuit court, where capital cases were tried, and at the criminal court of record, where all other criminal cases were heard. I was now a volunteer special assistant public defender.

It might seem strange that the lawyer who recently argued before the Supreme Court that the states should not have to provide lawyers to indigent defendants was now a volunteer public defender. How can I explain this turn of events? My answer is that it was one thing to argue that the state should not be compelled to do something not clearly required by the Constitution, but another for me, as an individual lawyer, to volunteer to help implement a decision by the Court that now was the law of the land.

A lawyer does not always get the preferred side in a case. Lawyers take the cases entrusted to them and should do their best to help a client and a court reach the right result.

In *Gideon*, I personally believed that counsel should be provided to all indigent defendants in criminal cases. But there were legitimate issues that had to be argued and decided by the Supreme Court. No provision in the Constitution in 1962 and 1963 clearly required counsel to be automatically provided in state courts. Deciding whether parts of the Constitution should be modified through a new interpretation of those sections required substantial, serious debate.

Also, in answer to the question of what caused me to reverse course, it is an ancient tradition in the legal profession that lawyers should volunteer some of their time to help the poor. They do this as part of the privilege of being allowed to practice law. Now, the law had changed. The Court had ruled that counsel must be appointed. As a lawyer and a member of the legal profession, I considered it my responsibility to do whatever I could to help implement this new decision by the Supreme Court.

In May of 1963, the governor had yet to appoint public defenders, and volunteer lawyers were necessary to enable the courts to comply with the new *Gideon* decision. And we knew no matter how many public defenders were appointed, and no matter how many public defender offices were established, there would always be a need for volunteer lawyers to fully comply with the goals and requirements of *Gideon*.

Judge Roy Amidon, the judge of the Polk County Criminal Court of Record in Bartow, appointed me to represent several defendants in felony cases. Each was African American and housed in the jail at that court, facing charges such as robbery or burglary. I believe each one had been charged with several of these crimes. None of the clients had good defenses, and we did not go to trial in these cases. Instead, I negotiated for the lightest possible sentences, considering the nature of the offenses and the circumstances of each defendant. These cases ended in guilty pleas and sentencing hearings.

One day, I drove to Tampa to be admitted to practice before the United States District Court for the Middle District of Florida. There were four of us young lawyers being admitted that day. After each of us finished taking the oath, the judge asked us to sit in the front row while he attended briefly to another case, and then he called us to the bench and assigned each of us to represent an indigent federal criminal defendant.

I picked up the indictment in my case from the clerk. The client had been charged with failing to report for the military draft. The Vietnam War was taking place. In those days, every able-bodied male had to serve in the military in some capacity. The government had sent my client a draft notice, and he had failed to report for duty. He was in jail downstairs in the federal courthouse. I went downstairs to interview him on the day I was admitted to practice before the court.

When I asked him why he had failed to report for active duty when he received the draft notice, he told me that his main goal in his young life was to join the military. He had tried to enlist in the Air Force and Navy but had been rejected by both. He was very unhappy at being turned down. So when the draft notice arrived for him at his family home in Polk City, Florida, he thought there was no point in reporting because he was sure he was not wanted by the military and would just be turned down a third time.

This sounded like it could have been an invented story, but he seemed like a good, honest person, and I was convinced he was telling me the truth.

That same day I asked for a hearing before a magistrate to set bail. With the defendant at my side, I asked that my client be released on his own signature—on personal recognizance, on his promise to appear at all future hearings in his case. While he was free on recognizance, that same day, I took him to the Army recruitment center in downtown Tampa. He had a physical exam, which he passed, and he also passed the mental test. The recruiting sergeant said he would accept the client into the Army.

I drove the client to his home in Polk City, which was only 20 miles north of our law office in Bartow. I notified the prosecutor in our case that the Army was willing to accept the client if the charge against him could be dismissed. The prosecutor agreed to recommend to the judge that the charge be dismissed upon the defendant being sworn in as an Army recruit. A date was set for the hearing, and I asked the recruiting sergeant to meet us at the court for that hearing.

On the court day, I picked the client up at his home in Polk City, and we drove together to Tampa. At the hearing, the sergeant testified that the Army was willing to accept the client into active duty. After questioning by the judge, the client was sworn in by the sergeant, in open court, as a member of the United States Army, and simultaneously the judge dismissed the criminal charges against him. The sergeant and the client left the courtroom together. The client was very happy about now being a member of the armed services.

In another case, in Lakeland, just 12 miles to the north of our offices in Bartow, a 19-year-old man held a stiletto against a woman as she was getting into her car in the parking lot of Morrison's Cafeteria. He forced her into her car and got into the front passenger seat. He held the stiletto against her and forced her to drive 10 miles or so out of Lakeland into an orange grove. While parked in the grove, he ripped off her clothes, struck her, and forcibly raped her.

He then drove off in her car, leaving her alone, half-clothed, in the middle of the grove. Her purse was in the car, and her personal checks were in the purse. He drove to a gas station where he forged her name on one of her checks and cashed it. Later, he stopped at a store where he forged a second check, which he cashed.

Meanwhile, the victim, a married woman in her forties, had managed to find her way out of the orange grove. The sheriff's office had broadcast a description of the rapist and her car to all deputy sheriffs and police officers in the area. The car was spotted by a deputy sheriff, who stopped the car and arrested the defendant.

He was charged with seven crimes—forcible rape, a capital offense in those days; assault with the stiletto; kidnapping; assault and battery with his fists; auto theft; forgery; and passing a bad check.

The arrest occurred on a Friday, and that evening and throughout the weekend, the local TV news channels covered this horrific rape case almost nonstop. We learned the defendant's name, but the victim's name was not made public.

The Monday following these crimes, Circuit Judge William Love phoned Steve Grimes, the partner in our firm who was our best trial lawyer, and told Steve that he wanted to appoint him to represent the defendant. But he was a civil trial lawyer and had no experience in criminal cases. He told Judge Love that he would accept the appointment but asked that he also appoint me, an associate in his firm because I had had experience as an assistant attorney general in the Criminal Appeals section of the Office of the Attorney General. So Love appointed us jointly to represent the defendant.

That was at a time when a man could be put to death for the crime of forcible rape. This is no longer possible because of the Supreme Court's decision in *Coker v. Georgia*[4] in 1977. In that case, the Court held that the death penalty may only be imposed if the defendant has taken a human life.

It violates the Cruel and Unusual Punishment Clause of the Constitution[5] for a state or the federal government to put a person to death unless the victim, a human being, has been killed.

The circuit court handled capital cases, so our client was to be tried in that court. Since the charges against him were part of a single criminal enterprise, all charges were to be tried in one trial. In the meantime, he was housed in the jail one block away, in the criminal court of record building. There was no jail at the circuit court.

On the day we were appointed, Steve and I went to the jail to meet with our client. It took several months to prepare for trial, and I visited the defendant every two or three days during the preparation period. Occasionally, both Steve and I met with him, but often I was the one to visit our client. I kept him informed as to how our case was proceeding.

He claimed that before these offenses had occurred, he had been drinking and suffered an alcoholic blackout. He had experienced alcoholic blackouts in the past. Because of the blackout, he claimed, he could not remember any of the criminal acts he was charged with. He said he regained consciousness alone in the car, not knowing how he had gotten there.

Steve and I were extremely skeptical about his defense, which we were almost certain was contrived. However, it is always possible that a defendant's story is true, even if, on its face, it does not at first seem very believable.

I did research and learned that there is such a thing as an alcoholic blackout. These blackouts are similar to bouts of sleepwalking. Sleepwalking while committing an offense can constitute a defense. There must be both a criminal act and criminal intent for a person to be guilty of a serious crime. Here there were criminal acts, but there would be no intent if he had not been conscious of what he was doing.

We did not know for certain whether he was lying to us about being in an alcoholic blackout, but our research showed that this could be a legitimate defense. However, it was not a strong defense because it was likely that jurors would not believe him. Unfortunately, we had no other option.

The state attorney was seeking the death penalty. Because our client was facing the electric chair, and because we did not have a strong defense, we tried to negotiate with the state attorney to obtain a recommendation of life imprisonment in exchange for pleas of guilty. I tried to arrange a meeting with him, but he refused to meet with us. Finally, I was able to talk with him by phone, but he made it clear that he would be satisfied with nothing less than the death penalty. Florida's state attorneys are elected officials, and they have to run for re-election every four years. Ours was a high-profile case, and he might have believed he needed to pursue the death penalty in order to be re-elected.

We researched evidentiary issues that might arise at trial. Then, we prepared proposed jury instructions. We realized that our client probably would have to testify, and we prepared for direct examination of him. We had a medical doctor on call to be used as an expert witness who could testify about alcoholic blackouts. Steve and I spent a lot of time together preparing our case.

On the morning of the trial, the courtroom was packed with spectators. We sat at our counsel table with our client as juror selection began.

After several hours there was a break. The defendant was removed from the room by sheriff's deputies during the break. The state attorney walked up to where Steve and I were sitting and asked if he could speak with us. We went with him into a private room next to the courtroom. He surprised us by offering to allow our client to plead guilty to two of the lesser charges—I believe assault and battery and a bad check charge—in exchange for two concurrent sentences of one and a half to five years. He told us that if we agreed, the client probably would serve only three and a half years in prison.

We then met with our client in the same small room. We described the plea agreement that was being offered. He was ecstatic because he had been facing the death penalty and now knew that he would not die in the electric chair.

We explained to the client that the judge would not accept a guilty plea unless he was convinced of the defendant's guilt. The judge would question him to make sure that he was guilty. The client said that he understood this and was willing to undergo the questioning. We advised the state attorney that our client wished to accept the plea bargain.

During questioning by Judge Love, our client freely admitted having committed the crimes he was charged with. He was fully conscious throughout the series of crimes and even remembered the color of the victim's dress. He was sentenced in accordance with the plea bargain.

About three and a half years later, when I was no longer with the Holland firm, this client came to our office and spoke with Steve Grimes. He asked Grimes to represent him in an unrelated matter. Steve did not take the case, but he contacted me to let me know that our client did serve only three and a half years in prison.

We speculated on why the state attorney had refused to bargain with us until we were in the midst of the trial. Probably the victim, a married woman whose name had not been made known to the public, had broken down on the first day of the trial and had informed the state attorney that she could not bring herself to testify.

A Florida statute dating back to the mid- or late nineteenth century provided that an appointed attorney in a capital case was entitled to a $90 fee. So that was the fee paid to our firm for our work on the case.

Accepting court appointments and representing and helping indigent criminal defendants, appellants, and prison inmates became a major pattern of my life between 1963, after *Gideon,* and 2018 when I retired as a law faculty member at the Stetson College of Law. From 1963 to 1965 I was a part-time volunteer special assistant public defender. Beginning in 1965, I became a law professor and served on the faculties of several law schools—Emory, Ohio State, Mercer, and Stetson. For those years as a professor, I was receiving a salary that was enough for my family to live on. Therefore, I was able to spend a substantial amount of my time doing legal work for indigent defendants, appellants, and inmates, even though that work did not bring in any income.

As an assistant professor, then associate professor at the Emory Law School, beginning in January 1965, I established a legal services program for inmates of the Atlanta Penitentiary, a federal penitentiary, and called it the Legal Assistance for Inmates Program. I asked for student volunteers, and 53 signed up to help. We accepted every application. Some of our applicants already had filed their own cases in the courts, and we took over for them. Others asked us to represent them, and we first did research to determine whether there was a meritorious issue in their case. If there was merit, we would either prepare a petition for the inmate to file or would become the lawyer of record in the case. We filed motions to vacate convictions under 28 United States Code, Section 2255, and motions for reduction of sentence under Rule 35 of the Federal Rules of Criminal Procedure. We took appeals from adverse decisions by United States district courts. We brought civil actions challenging certain prison rules on constitutional grounds. Students did much of the work of the program, under my supervision.

Within three months after the program began, we had about 900 applications for legal assistance. Two different students and I would drive to the penitentiary almost every afternoon to interview clients. The students and I would work together on our cases. I had to know what was happening in each of our cases to ensure we would not miss a court filing date. I was almost always working on 30 or so active cases. I was involved in the program for three years. From 1968 to 1970, during the time I was a graduate student at Harvard Law School, I continued to handle cases before the courts for the Emory program.

During my second year as a graduate student at Harvard Law School, Charles Hollen, a friend studying for the J.D., and I established a program to provide free legal services to Massachusetts prison inmates. It was patterned after the Emory program, but there were two significant differences. First, it was to be run entirely by Harvard law students; there would not be lawyer supervision, at least not initially. Also, we made no promise that we would accept every case. Instead, we asked inmates to fill out a more comprehensive form than at Emory, and we studied the applications and voted on which cases to accept. The program was called the Prison Legal Assistance Program. The last time I checked, this program was still in existence.

I spent a total of three years in residence at Harvard. During the third full year, I was a staff attorney in a legal services program that was funded by the federal Legal Services Corporation and operated by the Harvard Law School. It was called the Community Legal Assistance Organization, but its name was changed to Cambridge and Somerville Legal Services during the year while I was there, 1970–71. There were seven lawyers in the office, and we supervised about 100 Harvard law students. We were the only program in the country providing free legal services to indigent clients in both civil and criminal cases. Wallace Sherwood and I supervised 25 senior Harvard law students in handling misdemeanor cases. The two of us also handled felony cases on our own, with research and other help from students.

It was a very busy year for me. I represented defendants in many bench trials and some jury trials. I wasn't called a "public defender," but that, in essence, is what I was. In my busiest five-day work week, I had 39 court appearances. These included arraignments, hearings to set or reduce bail, sentencing hearings, evidentiary hearings on motions to suppress evidence, legal arguments on motions to dismiss charges, and probation revocation hearings. Also included that week were two nonjury felony trials in unrelated cases, both for assault with intent to murder.

From 1971 to 1978, I was a professor and director of Clinical Programs at The Ohio State University College of Law, supervising third-year students in misdemeanors and handling felony cases, including trial level, appellate, and post-conviction cases on my own. I would estimate that I always had a caseload of about 30 to 40 cases, in addition to teaching the classroom course on Criminal Procedure.

I established civil and criminal clinical programs and taught two of them—the Criminal Defense Practicum and the Criminal Appeals and Post-Conviction Remedies Practicum. In the Criminal Defense Practicum,[6] a supervising attorney and I taught about 20 students each semester. Our goal was to teach them to become competent criminal defense lawyers. The attorney and I supervised their work in misdemeanor cases. We interviewed indigent clients with them at the local public defender office and, with the permission of the clients, brought some of those cases to the law school where we provided the defense. We sometimes used the law school's courtroom for rehearsals of our cases before going to trial. In the Criminal Appeals and Post-Conviction Remedies Practicum, I provided most of the supervision of the 12 to 15 students each semester.

I became dean and professor, beginning in 1978, at Mercer Law School, then Stetson in 1981, and stepped down from administration in 1995 and became a full-time faculty member at Stetson. At Mercer and Stetson until I retired in 2018, I continued to do legal work for indigent criminal defendants, appellants, and prison inmates. During those years I continued to teach some clinical courses. Students in those courses received academic credit for their work. In semesters when I was teaching nonclinical lecture courses or seminars I would ask for student volunteers from the courses I was teaching, to work with me on cases. I tried to get students involved as much as possible.

Thus, I spent a year and a half as an appellate-level prosecutor in the Office of the Attorney General of Florida, two years as an associate at the Holland firm and a special assistant public defender, and the rest of my career as a law professor, dean, and criminal defense lawyer, always getting students involved with me in the representation of clients. And I have answered thousands of letters from inmates, providing legal advice to them, sometimes preparing petitions for them to file and pursue in court and sometimes taking their cases and representing them in court proceedings. So from 1963 until 2018, for 55 years, my students and I provided legal help in one form or another to thousands of indigent criminal defendants, appellants, and prison inmates.

Fifty years after the *Gideon* decision, I was honored by the National Association of Criminal Defense Lawyers at their meeting in San Francisco on July 27, 2013, where I was presented with their "Champion of Indigent Defense Award." As the award was being given, the presenter spoke about the irony that I was the lawyer who, 50 years earlier, in *Gideon v. Wainwright,* had argued against providing free legal services for all indigent criminal defendants.

# 16

## Appointment of Fred Turner to Represent Gideon

W. Fred Turner is the criminal defense lawyer Judge McCrary appointed to represent Clarence Gideon after the Supreme Court remanded the case back to the circuit court in Panama City, Florida, for a retrial.

I first met Fred Turner at a dinner meeting of the St. Andrews Bay American Inn of Court, on September 14, 2000, at a restaurant in Panama City Beach, Florida. The members of the Inn had invited me to speak on the *Gideon* case, and they had invited Turner, who had been Gideon's lawyer for the second trial in 1963. Turner was 78 years old and was a retired circuit judge. I was 65 and a former dean and now a faculty member at the Stetson College of Law.

When I asked the lawyer seated next to me at the head table to point out Fred Turner, and I got my first glimpse of him, my impression was that Turner looked like the movie star and famous dancer Fred Astaire. He was about six feet tall and slender, weighing about 160 pounds. When I told the lawyer sitting next to me that Turner reminded me of Astaire, he said, "It's strange that you would say that because he's a dancer." He explained that as a criminal defense lawyer trying a case before a jury, Turner literally "danced" while moving around the courtroom. Once a local newspaper published a photo of him while trying a case, showing him whirling around with his coattails flapping behind him.

That night Turner and I talked and agreed to meet the next day. On the next day, he drove my wife, Ann, and me to the site of the Bay Harbor Pool Room. In 1957, during the summer following my first semester of law school, I worked on a Dr. Pepper truck, delivering bottles of soft drinks to grocery stores, restaurants, gas stations, and bars in the Florida Panhandle. One of the places where we delivered drinks was the Everitt Avenue area, where the Bay Harbor Pool Room had been located. On September 15, 2000, that block

W. Fred Turner. Reprinted with permission from CBS News.

looked entirely different than it had in 1957. Every one of the buildings had been demolished. The only landmarks left were the streets, the alley, and the foundations of the buildings. He showed us where the poolroom, the phone booth, the Bay Harbor Hotel (Gideon roomed there), and the porch where Irene Rhodes had sat had been located.

During the next three years, until his death at age 81 on November 23, 2003, Fred Turner and I became very close friends. He would tell me, "We are joined at the hip, Bruce, by this *Gideon* case." We corresponded extensively. We frequently talked by phone. He spent several days at an apartment in the Stetson Law School, where I was a faculty member. During that time, we ate our meals together and often talked about the *Gideon* case. We participated in panel discussions for students about the case at Stetson Law School and at the University of Tampa on or about April 19, 2001. We also participated in a panel discussion in Miami, sponsored by the Federal Defender Office for the Southern District of Florida, on March 18, 2003.

I told Fred I wanted to write about the case, and he helped by telling me everything he could remember. I would interview him, taking notes as he spoke. At other times, after we had spent a day together, I would write down everything I could remember from that day's conversations.

Fred never explicitly told me that his client had committed the crime. But he did tell me, "Gideon was a thief; he'd steal a hot stove with his bare hands." Furthermore, Gideon was offered a plea bargain by the state before the second trial in which he could plead guilty in exchange for a sentence of time already served. Fred Turner advised him to accept that plea agreement, but Gideon refused and insisted on going to trial. Turner was a very good criminal defense lawyer and would not have advised Gideon to plead guilty unless he was convinced that Gideon was, in fact, guilty.

But most telling is the presentence investigation report. After the conviction in the first trial, sentencing was postponed to allow the probation office to conduct a presentence investigation, to provide information to assist the judge in deciding what sentence to impose. A probation and parole supervisor in Bay County, Perry Wells, after the conviction, prepared a presentence investigation report in the case. Included in the report was his summary of his interview with Clarence Gideon, and one of the paragraphs in the report reads as follows:

> The Defendant admits taking items from the poolroom after finding the back door open, which he claims the operator, Mr. Strickland, does quite frequently after becoming intoxicated himself. The Defendant claims that he has been framed with the breaking and entering charge with a penalty of five years when actually he is only guilty of a misdemeanor, that being petit larceny.[1]

The report also states, "The Defendant also admits being under the influence of intoxicants at the time of the offense.... [T]he man had been drinking practically all day and was in all probability in an intoxicated condition."[2]

In the interview, the defendant claimed that he had walked through an open door. Therefore, there was no breaking, and he should have been convicted only of the misdemeanor of petit larceny. These claims were not true. The evidence showed that entry was made by breaking out the glass in a side window near the rear of the building, putting a large garbage can or a drum next to the window, and climbing through the window. But even under Gideon's version, he would have been guilty of a felony. If the door had been closed but unlocked, he would have committed a breaking, a felony, by turning the doorknob and pushing the door open in order to gain entry. If the door had been partially open and he had pushed the door a little wider to make enough space for him to enter, that also would have constituted a breaking, a felony. If he had walked through a wide-open doorway without having to push the door to make a wider opening, in order to commit a crime inside, he would have been guilty of the lesser-included offense of entering without breaking, also a felony.[3]

As a retired circuit judge, Fred Turner had the clerk of that court put together a complete copy of the Bay County circuit court file in the *Gideon* case for me. When he handled the file to me, he said, "Be sure to read the presentence investigation report."

It is clear that Clarence Gideon was the person who was in the pool hall that night, June 3, 1961, and who stole coins from the cigarette machine and the jukebox, and drank the beer and wine.

As I got to know Turner, I learned that the part of his life he was most proud of was the time he spent in the United States Army Air Corps during World War II. As a young staff officer with the legendary "Flying Tigers," he flew on planes over the Himalayan Mountains from a base in India to China to provide supplies, ammunition, and equipment to the Chinese who had retreated to the western part of China and were fighting the Japanese. These were extremely dangerous missions. Crossing over the high Himalayas was perilous, and if the plane had been shot down by the Japanese while in China, he could have been captured. And, if captured, there was a good chance the Japanese would have executed him.

After the war, Turner entered the University of Florida and graduated with a law degree in 1948. Similarly, I graduated from Stetson and became licensed as a lawyer in Florida 11 years later, in 1959.

I really liked Fred. Not only was he a good lawyer, but he also was a good person. On May 11, 2022, I received this information in an email from Gary Yates, whom I mentioned in chapter 2 of this book. Here is what he said:

> My Mom and Dad had a lot of respect for Fred Turner. I remember meeting him while I was in high school. Even then I was impressed by his caring personality and graciousness of spending time with a crazy teenager like me. I also remember playing little league baseball in the Fred Turner League at the old Daffin Park. . . .

It was not always certain that Fred Turner would become Gideon's lawyer for the second trial. Abe Fortas wrote to Clarence Gideon not long after March 18, 1963, letting him know that Gideon would need a Florida lawyer to represent him in the further proceedings that were about to take place there. In his letter, Fortas mentioned that he had written to Tobias Simon, a Florida lawyer who had been one of those who had signed the amicus brief for the American Civil Liberties Union in the Supreme Court in the *Gideon* case.[4]

On April 9, 1963, Gideon wrote to Simon, expressing hope that the Florida Civil Liberties Union would provide him with a lawyer.[5] Simon replied on April 15, letting Gideon know that a Florida Civil Liberties Union lawyer would represent him at the new trial.[6]

Shortly thereafter, Simon drove to the Raiford State Penitentiary near Starke, Florida, and interviewed Gideon for an hour and a half.[7] Tobias Simon died of cancer in 1982. During his life, he was one of the finest lawyers in the history of Florida. He was a Harvard law graduate who had become a very prominent civil rights lawyer in Miami. Even today, the Florida Supreme Court honors him by annually presenting the Tobias Simon Pro Bono Services Award to a private lawyer for exemplary volunteer legal work for the poor. Unfortunately, Simon's meeting with Gideon at the prison at Raiford did not go well. One possible reason is that Gideon kept insisting, following his victory in the Supreme Court, that he should be immediately released from confinement. He could not understand why he was to be sent back to the trial court for a new trial. He thought it would be double jeopardy to retry him.[8]

Simon must have explained to Gideon that the constitutional protection against double jeopardy, as well as other constitutional rights, can be waived and that by filing his habeas petition in the Florida Supreme Court and the petition for certiorari in the Supreme Court of the United States, he was waiving any claim of double jeopardy. In effect, in those petitions, he asked that his conviction be set aside because he had not had counsel at trial and that he should get a new trial, this time with counsel. Gideon apparently did not like hearing this from Tobias Simon. Even so, Simon was under the impression that Gideon wanted the Civil Liberties Union to represent him.[9]

The United States Supreme Court sent its "mandate" to the Supreme Court of Florida, directing that court to take steps necessary to comply with Justice Black's opinion. On May 15, the Florida Supreme Court ordered that a new trial take place.[10] Gideon was removed to the jail in Panama City for the trial. Judge McCrary set a tentative trial date of July 5, 1963.[11]

In early July, Simon and another outstanding trial lawyer from Miami, Irwin J. Block, drove to Panama City. They interviewed some witnesses and went to see Gideon at the jail. Simon described the meeting with Gideon:

> Gideon refused to be represented by either of us; he refused to be tried; he stated that the court had no power to try him. . . .[12]

The next morning, at the time set for trial, Simon and Block, the prosecutors, and Clarence Gideon met with Judge McCrary in the judge's chambers. At that meeting, Gideon made it clear that he did not want Simon or Block to represent him.[13]

McCrary excused Simon and Block. The judge then asked Gideon if there was a local lawyer whom Gideon would want to represent him, and the answer was "Fred Turner."[14] The judge agreed to appoint Turner. He set bail at $1,000, which was more than Gideon could afford, and set the trial date for August 5.[15]

After the meeting, Judge McCrary walked into the hallway and "crooked a finger" at Fred Turner, who was there to handle a divorce. Here is Turner's description of what took place next:

> I said, "what can I do for you?" He said, "I just appointed you to represent Gideon." I said, "The hell you say. I didn't even know he was [here]."[16]

The first thing Turner had to do when McCrary assigned him to the case was to talk with Gideon and make sure that Gideon really wanted Turner to represent him because Turner had been representing Gideon's wife in her suit against Gideon for divorce and child support. By the time of the second trial, the divorce was final.[17] Turner's sympathies at that point had to have been with the wife, who had been his client, but he was willing to defend Gideon if Gideon fully understood the possible conflict of interest and still wanted Turner to represent him. After receiving a thorough explanation from Turner, Gideon said he wanted Turner, and Turner agreed to represent him in his criminal case, but only if Gideon agreed that if acquitted, he would get a job and begin providing financial support to his wife and children. Gideon had not been supporting them.[18]

Why did Gideon choose Turner to be his lawyer? Turner was one of the two experienced criminal trial lawyers in the circuit. The other was Virgil Mayo. Gideon probably had talked with others at the jail and had gotten good reports about both Turner and Mayo from other prisoners. Also, Gideon had gone up against Turner in his own divorce case and probably had been impressed by Turner's ability and tenacity in seeking money from Gideon for Gideon's wife and children.

During his early meetings with Gideon in jail, Gideon was extremely angry. He told Turner that when he won his case in the Supreme Court, he expected to be immediately released from custody. He could not understand why he was to be tried again.[19] He still believed it would be double jeopardy for the state to try him again. Also, he thought the statute of limitations had run out. However, Tobias Simon had already explained to him why double jeopardy was not an obstacle. The statute of limitations is "tolled" and stops running when criminal charges are filed. In this case, the charges were filed in 1961, shortly after the crime was committed, well within the statutory period.[20] So there was no statute of limitations problem.

Turner said that Gideon had a "valise" full of motions that he wanted to be filed in his case. Turner told him, "I'll represent you only if you stop trying to be the lawyer and let me be your lawyer."[21] Turner did file a motion on July 30 to quash the charges against Gideon, asserting some of the issues that Gideon had wanted to raise. Those issues had little merit, and Turner probably filed the motion at least partially to placate his client. The motion was denied without oral argument on August 1, 1963.

Gideon wanted a change of venue. He did not think he could get a fair trial in Panama City and wanted the case moved to Tallahassee or Pensacola.[22] Turner told him that he (Turner) had grown up near Panama City and knew almost everyone in that area. He said, "Do you really want me to try the case in Tallahassee or Pensacola before a jury none of whom know me, or a jury where three out of four know me, and I will know them?" After hearing this, Gideon withdrew his request.[23]

Turner several times told me that Clarence Gideon was a friendly, very talkative person. He enjoyed being around people. He was not the sullen loner portrayed by Henry Fonda.

Turner also told me that Gideon was not motivated by being a historic figure. He was tired of being in prison and "could not do more time."[24] He just wanted out of prison, pure and simple. He was tired of prison and wanted to get out.[25]

The key witness against Gideon again was going to be Henry Cook. Turner had represented Cook in the past in a criminal case that eventually had been dismissed by the state. Cross-examining his former client during his representation of Gideon could have posed ethical problems. In a large city with numerous criminal defense lawyers available, Turner might have been required to refuse to take Gideon's case because of his prior representation of Cook. A Florida rule on ethics provides in part that

> It is unprofessional to represent conflicting interests, except by express consent of all concerned given after a full disclosure of the facts. . . . [A] lawyer represents conflicting interests when, in behalf of one client, it is his duty to contend for that which duty to another client required him to oppose.[26]

Turner explained to Gideon the extent of his involvement in the case in which he had defended Cook, and Gideon said that Turner's previous representation of this key witness in a past case did not bother him.[27] So Turner had the express consent of Gideon, but he did not have the consent of Cook.

But was getting Cook's consent necessary? Turner would not be contending "for that which duty to another client required him to oppose." Cook was no longer Turner's client. Cook was not a party in Gideon's case—he was a witness. I believe that the ethics rule contemplates conflicting financial, property, or other such interests, which were not involved in Gideon's case, with Cook as a key witness. It is doubtful that protecting a former client from embarrassment during cross-examination is the kind of interest the rule was designed to protect. I do not think Turner violated the ethics rule; I do not think he needed Cook's consent to represent Gideon.

If Turner had asked to withdraw because of conflict after learning that Cook would be the most important witness for the prosecution, it is unlikely that Judge McCrary would have granted that request. Gideon wanted Turner as his lawyer, and the number of experienced criminal trial lawyers in the circuit to choose from was very limited. McCrary would have denied the motion, ruling that any conceivable conflict of interest problems were not significant enough to require him to appoint a different lawyer for Gideon.

Turner conducted a thorough investigation of the case. One of the witnesses from the first trial he spoke with was Irene Rhodes. Rhodes told him that she did not know that Gideon had the wine bottle with him and had set it down on the ground next to the telephone booth.[28] Turner told me that he thought she was lying.[29] He also realized she was lying when she had testified at the first trial that she had picked up the bottle at the phone booth and had given it to her sick landlord. She was an alcoholic and thought her husband would divorce her if he knew she drank that wine.[30] She asked Turner not to call her as a witness because she did not want her husband to know that she had been "off the wagon" at the time of the break-in.[31] Turner decided not to call her as a witness. He did, however, expect the state to use her because she was one of the two eyewitnesses in the case, the other being Henry Cook. She could testify that Gideon emerged from the alley behind the Bay Harbor Pool Room carrying a wine bottle, and others would testify that wine had just been stolen in the break-in at the poolroom. If she tried to lie at the second trial by saying she did not see Gideon emerge from the alley with the half-empty wine bottle, the prosecutors would have used her testimony from the first trial to establish that she did see Gideon emerge from the alley that ran behind the poolroom, with the bottle of wine.

Assistant State Attorney William Harris offered a plea bargain agreement in which Gideon would be released from custody for time already served in exchange for his plea of guilty. Turner advised Gideon to accept the bargain, but Gideon insisted on going to trial.[32]

Turner had given Gideon good advice. Even before the Bay Harbor Pool Room case, Gideon had a criminal record, so even if he went to trial and was acquitted in this trial, it would not erase his prior felony conviction record. So there would have been no point in going to trial to clear his record.

It is impossible to know beforehand how a jury will decide a case. Gideon would be taking chances by going to trial. He could have ended up serving another two and a half years in prison.

On the other hand, even if he lost at trial, the chances were that he might receive a sentence of only time served or a sentence of less than the maximum of five years that he had received after the first trial. Recent publicity had been favorable to Gideon, and Judge McCrary probably admired what Gideon had accomplished through his success in the Supreme Court and might have imposed light punishment. Plus, the chance of winning an acquittal in a trial now that he had a good lawyer must have appealed to Gideon.

# 17

## The Second Gideon Trial

The second Gideon trial took place in the Circuit Court for the Fourteenth Judicial Circuit of Florida in Bay County in Panama City on August 5, 1963, exactly two years and a day after the first trial. At the second trial, Gideon was found not guilty by a jury of six men.

Why was he acquitted? The simple answer to this question, I believe, is that he was acquitted through the skill of his lawyer, Fred Turner. Of course, there was more to it, but that was the overwhelming reason why Clarence Gideon was acquitted at the second trial.

One thing that had to be explained by the defense was that coins in the cigarette machine and jukebox had been stolen from the poolroom, and shortly after the break-in, when Gideon was arrested at the downtown Panama City bar, he had a lot of coins in his possession. Where had he gotten them, if not from the poolroom? Gideon told Turner and testified at the second trial that he gambled and "ran gambling games." He said he had gotten those coins from gambling.[1] Turner was able to select a jury that included three persons he knew were gamblers and whom he believed would be sympathetic to a fellow gambler.[2] That probably was a significant factor in gaining the acquittal.

There had been two eyewitnesses to the crime—Henry Cook and Irene Rhodes. Rhodes was not used as a witness for the prosecution at the second trial. When I spent time with him, I asked Turner why she had not been called and utilized as a witness for the state. He said she had been available and did not know why the state had not called her. He was as mystified as I was about why the state had not used this eyewitness.[3]

So one of the two eyewitnesses to the crime did not testify at the second trial. And Judge McCrary allowed Turner to impeach the other eyewitness, Henry Cook, even though Cook should not have been impeached, as is shown later in this chapter.[4] After the impeachment, the jurors could assume that Cook's testimony was untrue. They could disregard his testimony. This meant that the most critical eyewitness had been neutralized. One eyewitness had not been called to testify by the state, and because of the impeachment, the testimony of the other, the most important eyewitness, could be disregarded by the jury members.

Furthermore, Turner was able to raise the possibility that Cook and his friends had been the actual burglars, not Clarence Gideon. Cook and his friends had partied the night before in Apalachicola. When they arrived home in Bay Harbor at about 5:30 or 6:00 a.m., Turner suggested they wanted to continue partying, but they were out of Cokes. According to Turner, they broke into the poolroom to get the Cokes and beer and posted Henry Cook outside on the sidewalk as a lookout.[5]

At the second trial, Frank Adams, the state attorney for the Fourteenth Judicial Circuit, was present at the counsel table with Assistant State Attorney William Harris, but Harris conducted most of the trial. The second trial took a full day, compared with the first trial, which lasted only part of one day. The transcript of the first trial is 59 pages long, while the transcript of the second trial is 141 pages in length.

The trial began with the selection of the jury. Six men were placed in the jury box and questioned by each side. Then each side could "challenge" or remove certain prospective jurors for cause. For example, if a prospective juror was related to the victim, the prosecuting witness in the case, the defense would challenge that person, and the judge would remove that prospective juror for cause. Each side may make an unlimited number of challenges for cause but must have a good reason for each. The trial judge decides whether each of these challenges should be granted.

Each side also has a limited number of peremptory challenges, which can be made for any reason. Fred Turner used peremptory challenges to exclude two prospective jurors. He told me that one of these was a "teetotaler" who would have been unsympathetic to a drinker like Clarence Gideon. And the other, Turner said, "would convict his own grandmother." His attitude, according to Turner, was that Gideon would not have been arrested if he wasn't guilty.[6] Turner accepted the two replacement jurors, both of whom he knew.

After the jury selection, the prosecution gave an opening statement to the jury. Turner was given the opportunity to make an opening statement, but he deferred making his statement. He was keeping his options open. He could give an opening statement at the close of the state's case and the beginning of testimony by his witnesses. Or he could wait until the closing argument to make his argument to the jurors on why Gideon should not be convicted.

One reason why Turner deferred his opening statement could have been that he was not yet completely sure how the testimony of the witnesses was going to develop. He was not yet certain what his theory for acquittal would be, but when all of the testimony was in, he then could tie together all the elements of his case in the closing argument. By not making an opening statement and thereby keeping his theory of the defense a secret, Turner could, and did, outsmart the prosecution. He disclosed his case theory in the closing argument when it was too late for the state to offer effective rebuttal testimony and argument.

The first and main witness for the prosecution was Henry Cook. He reiterated the testimony he had given at the first trial. He and friends had driven home from Apalachicola[7] in an old Chevrolet.[8] Cook had been dropped off by his friends at the Bay Harbor Pool Room.[9] As he stood on the sidewalk, he could see Clarence Gideon through the window of the poolroom.[10] He had known Gideon for about six months.[11] Gideon was standing by the cigarette machine, which had been broken into.[12] The face of the machine was off.[13] Money bags were on a pool table by the cigarette machine.[14]

Gideon left the poolroom by the back door. Through the window, Cook could see that the back door of the poolroom was open. He could see daylight through the darkened pool hall when Gideon opened the door.[15] Gideon walked up the dirt alley behind the poolroom to a telephone booth at the corner.[16] Cook walked up the sidewalk in front of the buildings toward the phone booth, observing Gideon through openings between buildings.[17] Gideon was carrying a pint of wine.[18] Gideon made a phone call, and a taxi came to pick him up.[19] Cook saw Irene Rhodes sitting on her porch, across the street from the phone booth.[20] Cook spoke with her, and the two of them agreed that it was Clarence Gideon they had seen.[21] It was early in the morning. The lights in the poolroom were not on, but "it was pretty light outside."[22] Cook walked back to the poolroom. It was there that he met police officers.[23] A window on the side of the poolroom near the back had been broken. There was a large can or drum placed under the window.[24]

Fred Turner began his cross-examination of Henry Cook. After questions about the answers Cook had given during direct examination by William Harris, the following exchange took place between Turner and Cook:

Q. Have you ever been convicted of a felony?

A. I "stoled" a car one time and got put on probation for it.

Q. That's what I'm talking about. The last time you testified in this case you denied that didn't you?[25]

Turner knew that Cook at one time had pleaded to and had been convicted of joyriding. Turner thought that this conviction was for a felony. However, it was for a juvenile offense. Joyriding is a felony if committed by an adult, but if the charge and conviction are for juvenile delinquency, the offense is not a felony. In fact, it is not a crime at all. It is a civil offense.[26] Technically speaking, the charge against the juvenile is for "juvenile delinquency," not joyriding, although the juvenile courts look to criminal statutes such as the joyriding statute for guidelines on whether the minor is guilty of juvenile delinquency. Juvenile courts were established at least partly to ensure that a juvenile would not have a "criminal" record and would have a fresh start when he reached 18; therefore, juvenile offenses are not considered "crimes."

It is true that at the first trial, Gideon, acting as his own lawyer, had asked the same question of Cook and had gotten a different answer:

**Q.** Have you ever been convicted of a felony?
**A.** No sir, never have.[27]

This answer during the first trial was accurate. He had been convicted of juvenile delinquency, not a felony. However, his answer during the second trial was incorrect because the juvenile joyriding conviction was not for a felony.

McCrary ordered the jurors out of the room. A debate took place about whether Turner could impeach this witness.

At one point, Turner said:

[I] am simply attacking his credibility because he testified under oath at a prior trial contrary to what he is testifying to here today, and I think the Jury has a right to know that. . . .[28]

Judge McCrary allowed Turner to proceed "to show a prior inconsistent statement."[29] The jury was brought back into the courtroom.

Turner asked further questions of Cook:

**Q.** Mr. Cook, have you ever denied, under oath, that you had been convicted of a felony? Prior to today, I'm speaking of.
**A.** Yes, I did.[30]

Harris later asked:

**Q.** What did you mean when you said you had not been convicted of a felony, and yet, you say you plead guilty to stealing an automobile?

Cook's answer was:

**A.** Well, I didn't quite understand what a felony was then.[31]

Turner moved to strike this testimony. The jurors were removed from the courtroom. Turner argued that ignorance of the law is not an excuse—that Cook should have known what is meant by the word "felony." However, Judge McCrary denied Turner's motion.[32]

The jurors were brought back into the courtroom. Harris asked further questions; then Turner asked Cook how old he was when he had pled guilty to the "felony." Cook answered, "seventeen."[33] Turner asked whether the judge in the joyriding case had explained Cook's rights to him when he pled guilty.[34] The following exchange then took place:

> A. I don't remember whether he did all that or not.
> Q. Was that Judge E. Clay Lewis, Jr., Circuit Judge?
> A. No, sir.
> Q. Which judge was it?
> A. The Juvenile Judge.
> Q. Pardon?
> A. The Juvenile Judge.[35]

It was William Harris's turn to ask questions. He elicited testimony that Bert Davenport, the local juvenile judge, had been the judge who had convicted Cook when Cook was seventeen. Harris then said, "Don't you know, Mr. Cook, that you can't be convicted, or plead guilty, to a felony in Juvenile Court?"[36] It was now obvious that Cook had not lied, but Turner objected to this comment by Harris. Judge McCrary could have cleared up the confusion caused by the incorrect assumption that the joyriding had been an adult felony. He could have ensured everyone understood that Cook had not lied. However, he sustained Turner's objection, ending the discussion of whether Cook had lied. Cook, the only eyewitness to testify, had been discredited and impeached even though he should not have been impeached. In his closing argument, Turner could now argue to the jury that Cook had lied and his testimony should not be relied upon by the jurors.

Clarence Gideon decided not to take the witness stand and testify at the first trial, but during the second trial, he did testify. He explained why he had so many coins with him at the time of his arrest. He said he had won the coins through gambling just five days before the break-in.[37] He testified that he always carried large amounts of change.[38]

He explained that on the morning of the break-in, he left his rooming house on the east side of Everitt Avenue and, although the shortest path to the phone booth would have been to cross the street and walk directly to the phone booth, he instead crossed the street and walked west until he reached the alley behind the buildings on the west side of the street. Then he walked north along the alley to reach the telephone booth.[39]

It was strange that Gideon had not taken the shorter route. The explanation he gave for walking to the alley, then north along the alley, was that there was a "drop off" on the sidewalk along the direct route, and therefore, it was easier walking when taking the longer route.[40] The real reason he testified that he took the longer way probably was that Irene Rhodes had testified at the first trial that Gideon had emerged from the alley as he walked to the phone booth, carrying a wine bottle. Gideon knew that she could be called as a rebuttal witness by the state during the second trial. To be sure that his testimony would be consistent with her previous testimony, he had to say now that he approached the telephone booth from the alley, not directly from his rooming house.

At the first trial, Rhodes and Henry Cook had identified Clarence Gideon as the man who had emerged from the alley, and both Rhodes and Cook had testified at that trial that Gideon had been carrying a half-empty wine bottle as he approached the phone booth. Gideon himself must have realized how significant the testimony about the bottle of wine was because he testified under questioning by Fred Turner that he did not drink wine.[41] That testimony was false, but it shows how critical he thought it was to convince the jurors that he had not been carrying the bottle of wine. For if he had been carrying the half-empty wine bottle, it was very likely that he had just obtained that bottle during the break-in of the poolroom just a short distance down the alley.

My wife, Ann, Fred Turner, and I had lunch together at a restaurant in Miami on March 18, 2003. We were in Miami to participate in a panel discussion regarding the *Gideon* case. During our lunch, Fred said he had been surprised when Gideon lied, saying he did not drink wine. Turner had asked him during the trial whether he had had any beer, wine, or whiskey with him when he was arrested. Gideon's answer was, "No, sir. I don't drink wine. If I had a bottle of wine I throwed it away."[42] Turner told Ann and me that he knew Gideon was a wine drinker and that Gideon's answer was a lie. Turner had not called this to the judge's attention and had not attempted to get Gideon to retract or modify this testimony. The fact that his client had lied and that Turner had not done anything to correct the erroneous testimony had bothered Turner ever since the second trial. He asked whether I thought he should have done something to rectify this false testimony.

**Route According to Gideon's Testimony**

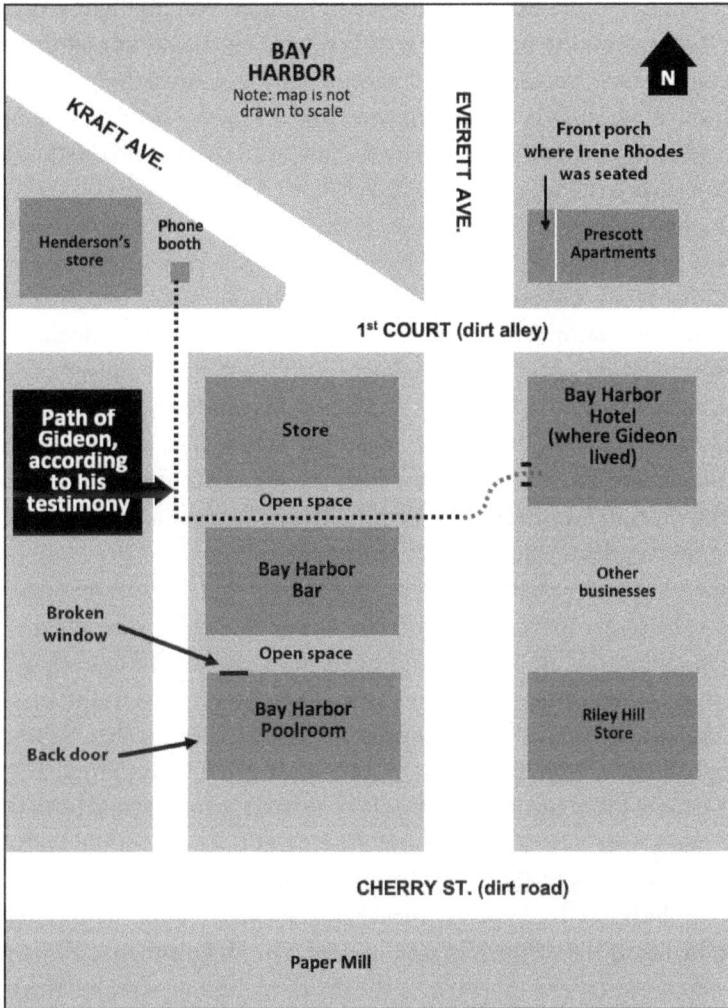

Gideon's route according to his testimony. Drawn by Lee Ann Gun.

Whether or not he drank wine was important because he had been seen with a wine bottle in the alley that ran behind the poolroom shortly after the break-in. Turner could have asked for a recess during Gideon's testimony and told Gideon that he would ask more questions which would have allowed Gideon to modify his answer. Turner could have insisted that Gideon let the jurors know he drank wine.

On the other hand, the jurors probably recognized that Gideon was an alcoholic, and alcoholics sometimes cannot admit, even to themselves, that they have a drinking problem. I told Fred that he should not let this incident bother him. I doubted that it affected the outcome in the case. Also, in the heat of a trial, it is difficult to make instantaneous decisions on issues that suddenly come up and surprise the lawyer in the way this testimony of Gideon surprised Fred.

The first witness for the defense, called by Fred Turner, was J. D. Henderson. He was the operator of Henderson's Grocery, located next to the telephone booth Gideon used to call for a taxicab on the morning of the break-in. On that morning, at approximately eight or nine o'clock, Henry Cook entered the store, and Henderson and Cook had a conversation regarding the poolroom break-in. According to Henderson, Cook had told Henderson that Cook "thought" he knew who had broken into the poolroom but added that "I'm not sure who it was." He said, "It looked like" Gideon.[43] The implication was that Cook, shortly after the crime, was not positive that it had been Gideon who he saw in the poolroom.

One of the investigating officers in the case, Duell Pitts, testified that among the stolen items were twelve bottles of "Cokes."[44] This was the only time in either trial any witness indicated that Coca-Cola bottles had been stolen in the break-in of the poolroom. Pitts also testified in the first trial but had not been asked for a list of items that had been stolen.[45] Pitts was the only witness who testified that Cokes were missing. Ira Strickland, the proprietor of the poolroom, testified in both trials as to what had been taken, and Cokes were not among the items he mentioned.[46] Undoubtedly, this testimony by Pitts in the second trial was incorrect. Cokes had not been taken in the break-in. But Fred Turner saw and seized upon an opportunity when he heard what Pitts had said. Turner now had his theory about what had happened on the morning of the break-in, and he sold his theory to the jurors.

He asked Pitts whether Gideon had Cokes with him when he was arrested.[47] He asked Preston Bray whether Gideon had Cokes with him when he got into the taxi.[48] He asked Gideon if he had had Cokes with him that morning.[49] All of them said no. Gideon had not had the Cokes that Duell Pitts had testified were stolen in the break-in.

It made sense that Clarence Gideon did not have the Cokes. He was in his early fifties, and he was an unemployed alcoholic. The jurors probably recognized that his beverages of choice were beer or wine, not Cokes. Cokes are a favorite of younger individuals, such as Henry Cook and his friends, who were in their early twenties and had been together the previous evening partying in Apalachicola. Turner would sell the jurors on the theory that the boys needed Cokes to continue partying when they arrived in Bay Harbor early in the morning of the break-in.

The court reporter did not record the closing arguments in the case, so we do not know all of what Turner said to the six jurors during his closing. Undoubtedly, he tried to convince them that Henry Cook was not truthful and that his testimony was not reliable. Fortunately, Anthony Lewis, the later author of *Gideon's Trumpet,* was a spectator at the second trial, and he took notes on what Turner said in his closing. We are much indebted to Lewis for this portion of Turner's closing argument:

> "This probationer," he said scornfully, "has been out at a dance drinking beer.... He does a peculiar thing [when he supposedly sees Gideon inside the poolroom]. He doesn't call the police. He doesn't notify the owner, he just walks to the corner and walks back [as Cook had testified].... What happened to the beer and the wine and the Cokes? I'll tell you—it left there in that old model Chevrolet. The beer ran out at midnight in Apalachicola.... Why was Cook walking back and forth? I'll give you the explanation: He was the lookout."[50]

After the acquittal, Turner must have been asked many times about the case. In answer to questions about Cook, Turner must have said more than once that Cook had not been truthful. Cook must have heard about these comments that were made by his former lawyer, and several years after the trial, Cook phoned Fred Turner to get Fred not to tell people that he had lied in the case. Fred was not at home, and his wife took the call. Cook asked her to tell Fred to "stop telling people I'm a crook."[51]

The police never charged Cook or his friends with the crime. They had not committed the offense, but Turner had raised that possibility sufficiently to enable the jurors to not find Gideon guilty beyond a reasonable doubt.

In 2003, I was in the process of writing a law review article about the *Gideon* case. The *Stetson Law Review* subsequently published that article.[52] I sent Fred a draft of the article before it was published, asking for his comments. On September 29, 2003, he wrote to me about the draft. His letter was typed on the Flying Tigers 14th Air Force Association, Inc. stationery. He was a member of the Board of Governors of that association and was entitled to use the stationery.

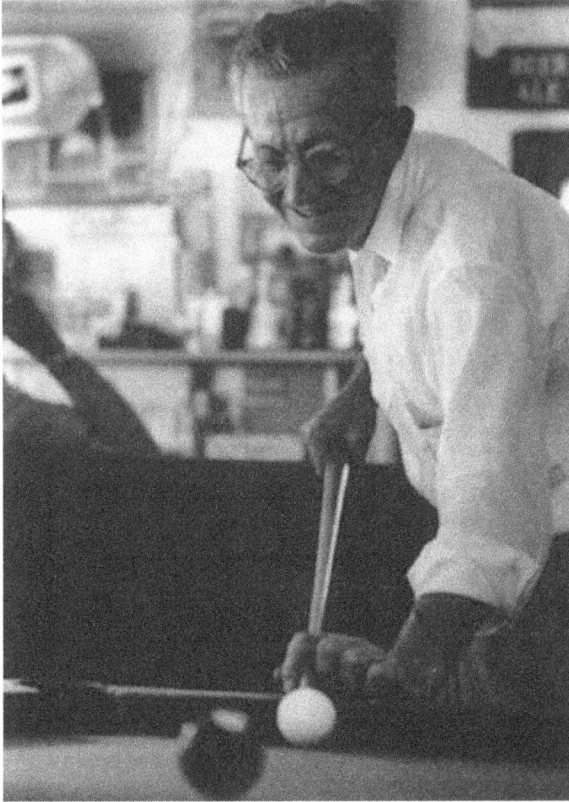

Photo of Gideon taken inside the poolroom following his acquittal at the second trial. Courtesy of Bay County Public Library, Panama City, Florida.

He began by saying:

Upon receipt of your latest revision of the Law Review Article on Gideon, I reviewed our correspondence to ascertain if there were any comments I could make and I concluded that there were none.

He then went on to say this:

Guilt or innocence (as it turned out) was not a factor in the trial of Gideon. Proof of guilt, beyond a reasonable doubt was the burden of the State, and, in the minds of the jury, was lacking in the second trial,—ergo, the acquittal.

He was telling us that, in his mind, the failure of the state to meet its burden of proving Gideon guilty beyond a reasonable doubt explained the not-guilty verdict. That certainly is part of the reason for the acquittal. But I believe that Turner was being far too modest. As I say earlier in this chapter, I believe that the main reason for the acquittal of Clarence Gideon was the skill of Gideon's lawyer, Fred Turner.

This brings to mind the ancient English common law rule that in serious criminal cases, the defendant was not entitled to the assistance of counsel for his defense. Counsel was not appointed for the defendant, and he was not entitled to be represented by a lawyer retained by him or for him by family or friends. The defendant could have a retained lawyer to explain questions of law, but that was the extent of the right to counsel in felony cases. The reason for this rule prohibiting counsel was probably the belief that a defendant in a serious criminal case should not be acquitted because of a lawyer's skill.

In this country today, we do not believe in the reason for the common law rule. We believe it is better for 10 guilty men to go free than for one innocent man to be convicted.

# 18

## The *Gideon* Legacy

### Post-1963 Developments in the Law

In 1961, when I first read the opinion of the majority by Justice Tom Clark in *Mapp v. Ohio*,[1] I was puzzled. It wasn't clear to me exactly what the Court had done in that case. Today, of course, we recognize that in *Mapp*, the Court had begun a process of selective incorporation of the criminal procedure rights for federal criminal prosecutions contained in the Fourth, Fifth, Sixth, and Eighth Amendments, one at a time, into the Due Process Clause of the Fourteenth Amendment, making those rights, or guarantees, applicable in state criminal proceedings. I believe that the *Gideon* decision, decided two years later, was the case that first made it obvious to us that the Court had embarked on this process.

In *Mapp*, the Court incorporated the Fourth Amendment's protection against unreasonable searches and seizures, including the exclusionary rule of *Weeks v. United States*,[2] into the Due Process Clause of the Fourteenth. This meant the evidence obtained through an unreasonable search or seizure can be excluded—not introduced and used by the prosecution as evidence against the defendant. It is excluded through a pretrial motion to suppress filed by the defense.

The process of selective incorporation continued with the *Gideon* decision in 1963. Then, a year later, in 1964, the Court, in *Malloy v. Hogan*,[3] incorporated the privilege against self-incrimination of the Fifth Amendment into the Fourteenth. This meant that in both state and federal criminal proceedings, individuals could not be compelled to give statements or testimony that could incriminate them.

In 1965, the Sixth Amendment's right to confront witnesses against the defendant was incorporated into the Fourteenth, in the case of *Pointer v. Texas*.[4] The right to a speedy trial, in the Sixth Amendment, was incorporated in 1967 in the case of *Klopfer v. North Carolina*.[5] During that same year, the Court incorporated the Sixth Amendment's provision guaranteeing the right of a defendant to have compulsory process for obtaining witnesses in their favor. That case was *Washington v. Texas*.[6]

The right to a jury trial by an impartial jury, contained in the Sixth Amendment, was made a part of the Due Process Clause of the Fourteenth Amendment in *Duncan v. Louisiana*[7] in 1968. The protection against double jeopardy, being tried twice for the same offense, guaranteed under the Fifth Amendment, was incorporated in 1969 in *Benton v. Maryland*.[8]

The Court also expanded upon the meaning and the extent of the right to counsel, as established on March 18, 1963, in the *Gideon* case. That same day the Court issued its decision in *Douglas v. California*.[9] The Court, in *Gideon,* had decided that at the trial level in a felony case where the defendant is indigent, he must be provided with an attorney by the state unless he knowingly waives that right. In *Douglas,* the Court held that if the defendant is convicted and wishes to take an appeal from the felony conviction and is indigent, he is entitled to the appointment of an attorney for the first appeal of right from the conviction. If he loses in that first appeal, further review could be available to the highest court in the state, called the state "supreme court" in all states except New York,[10] where the highest appellate court is the "Court of Appeals." The new right to counsel for an appeal did not extend to such a second, discretionary review, by a state supreme court.

Justice William Douglas, the Justice who wrote the majority opinion in the *Douglas* case, said the Fourteenth Amendment required that decision. The decision could not have been based on the incorporation of a provision of the Bill of Rights into the Due Process Clause of the Fourteenth Amendment, because there is no right to appeal in any of the provisions of the Bill of Rights. In fact, the Court, in *McKane v. Durston,*[11] held that there is no right to appeal at all unless the state provides such a right. So there is no right to counsel for a criminal appeal in the Bill of Rights that could be "incorporated" into the Due Process Clause of the Fourteenth Amendment. That leaves the Equal Protection Clause of the Fourteenth Amendment as the only source of the Court's authority to reach the result it did in *Douglas*.

One of the requests I had made in the Brief for Respondent and the oral arguments in *Gideon* was for the Court to consider making its decision operate prospectively if it were to overrule *Betts*. Such a decision, we hoped, would apply only to the defendants tried and convicted after the date of the *Gideon* opinion, not to prison inmates who had been convicted and sentenced between 1942 and 1963 and were still serving their sentences. The states had followed the 1942 *Betts* decision in good faith, and therefore, we tried to convince the Court that a decision overruling *Betts* should not result in the release of thousands of inmates who had been convicted before the date of the Supreme Court's *Gideon* decision. In *Burget v. Texas*,[12] however, in 1967, the Supreme Court, through Justice Douglas, stated that *Gideon* was "not limited to prospective applications."[13]

The *Gideon* case taught us that an indigent defendant is entitled to counsel for the trial or the entry of his guilty plea, but was he entitled to counsel earlier in the proceedings? In *Coleman v. Alabama*,[14] the issue was whether the right to counsel existed as early in the proceedings as a preliminary hearing. The preliminary hearing in Alabama is an evidentiary hearing that takes place before a magistrate, in some cases, before indictment, to determine whether there is probable cause to believe that the crime has been committed. If probable cause is found, the prosecution will take the case before the grand jury for an indictment.

The Court concluded that the preliminary hearing, under Alabama law, is a critical stage in a criminal proceeding. The Sixth Amendment applies not only to the trial. Instead, it applies, "In all criminal prosecutions . . . ," and according to the Court, the preliminary hearing in *Coleman* was part of the criminal prosecution. Therefore, counsel must be appointed for an indigent at least as early in the case as the preliminary hearing.

The Court applied the right to counsel in *Gideon* to an even earlier stage in the criminal process—the interrogation of a suspect in an investigation of a crime. One such case was *Escobedo v. Illinois*,[15] decided in 1964. If an investigation has become focused on a particular person because police believe that individual has committed the crime, the interrogation of that suspect is part of the "criminal prosecution." Any statements obtained should not be used by police or prosecutors if the right to counsel has not been provided to the focal suspect during the interrogation. Justice Arthur Goldberg, speaking for the majority, said:

> It would exalt form over substance to make the right to counsel, under these circumstances, depend on whether at the time of the interrogation the authorities had secured a formal indictment. Petitioner had, for all practical purposes, already been charged with murder.[16]

So the police interrogation could be considered part of "the criminal prosecution," at least in fact situations such as those in *Escobedo*.

Two years later, in *Miranda v. Arizona*,[17] the Court further elaborated upon the need for counsel during a police interrogation. The Court combined the right to counsel, under *Gideon v. Wainwright*, with the Fifth Amendment's privilege against self-incrimination in *Malloy v. Hogan*, which had been decided a year after *Gideon,* to determine that an "in custody" interrogation should not take place unless the person being questioned has had or waived the right to counsel during that interrogation. Before the interrogation begins, that person, the subject of the interrogation, must be given these four warnings:

1. He (or she) has the right to remain silent.
2. Anything he says will be used against him.
3. He has the right to counsel.
4. If indigent, a lawyer will be appointed for him.

So the Court expanded the right to counsel to interrogations, even if the interrogation takes place before formal criminal charges have been filed. These events are considered part of the "criminal prosecution," protected by the language of the Sixth Amendment and, through incorporation, by the Fourteenth Amendment. If these rules are violated, any incriminating statements made by the defendant may be excluded through a motion to suppress and not be used as evidence against him.

How far into the case does the "criminal prosecution" continue? What about sentencing? Is the sentencing stage a part of the "criminal prosecution" described in the Sixth Amendment? Should defendants have the right to appointed counsel for the sentencing if they are indigent?

Indeed, the sentencing is part of the criminal prosecution if it takes place immediately or soon after the finding of guilt in the case and it is the trial judge doing the sentencing. But what if the sentencing is delayed until weeks or months after the defendant has been found guilty?

What if the actual sentencing is done not by the trial judge in the judicial branch but by the parole board, an administrative agency in the executive branch of government?

The case of *Mempa v. Rhay*[18] provides us with answers to these questions. A Washington state sentencing scheme provided that, at the time in the case when sentencing usually takes place, the trial judge could place a defendant on probation for a period of time determined by the judge, with the sentence, in terms of time to be served, being deferred. Then, if the defendant committed another crime while on probation, a combined probation revocation/deferred sentencing hearing was held before the judge. If the judge found that the defendant had violated probation, that judge could revoke probation and was required to impose the maximum prison term sentence. The judge could recommend to the parole board that the defendant should serve less than the maximum. The judge's recommendation carried some weight, but the parole board was not bound by those recommendations. Defendants were entitled to counsel at the initial hearing when the trial judge imposed the sentence of probation but not for the combined probation revocation/ deferred sentencing proceeding.

In *Mempa*, two defendants committed additional crimes while on probation. Hearings were held in each of the cases before the trial court, and in each case, probation was revoked by the judge, and the probationer was given the maximum prison term. The probationers were not provided the right to counsel at these combined probation revocation/deferred sentencing hearings. Later, the parole board set the term for a number of years, within the statutory maximum. The judge's recommendations could be considered by the parole board in making that decision, but were not binding on the parole board.

Lawyers for the state argued that the actual sentencing had already taken place when the defendants had been placed on probation by the trial judge and that the defendants had been represented by counsel when those earlier decisions had been made. But the Supreme Court found that the combined probation revocation/deferred sentencing proceeding was the time when the more important sentencing decisions took place. And, the Court held, the defendants should have an absolute right to counsel at that hearing. The case stands for the proposition that the *Gideon* right to counsel exists in sentencing and deferred sentencing proceedings.

A case of interest when talking about probation revocation proceedings is *Gagnon v. Scarpelli*, a 1973 case.[19] A convicted defendant had been placed on probation by a Wisconsin trial court. Under Wisconsin law, he was placed in the custody of the Wisconsin Department of Public Welfare. Unfortunately, he committed another crime, and his probation was revoked not by the trial court but by that administrative agency, without a hearing and without counsel. The question was whether he should have had a hearing and been provided with counsel for the hearing. In this case, the trial judge had set the sentence, but the revocation was by the Department of Public Welfare.

The probationer filed a habeas corpus petition arguing that he should have had a hearing and counsel. The revocation was by an agency in the executive branch, not by the trial court, in the judicial branch. But even so, the revocation resulted in the loss of liberty.

When the case reached the Supreme Court, Justice Lewis Powell, speaking for the Court on the issue of whether the probationer was entitled to counsel, rejected the probationer's argument that there should have been an absolute right to counsel in the revocation proceeding. He said:

While such a rule has the appeal of simplicity, it would impose direct costs and serious collateral disadvantages without regard to the need or the likelihood in a particular case for a constructive contribution by counsel. In most cases, the probationer or parolee has been convicted of another crime or has admitted the charges against him.[20]

He went on to say:

We just find no justification for a new inflexible constitutional rule with respect to the requirement of counsel. We think, rather, that the decision as to the need for counsel must be made on a case-by-case basis in the exercise of a sound discretion by [the State Department of Public Welfare]. . . . Although the presence and participation of counsel will probably be . . . constitutionally unnecessary in most revocation hearings, there will remain certain cases in which fundamental fairness—the touchstone of due process—will require that the state provide at its expense counsel for indigent probationers or parolees.[21]

When I first read these words, I could hardly believe my eyes. Justice Powell, in 1973, had just resurrected the facts and circumstances test of *Betts v. Brady* and the "concept of ordered liberty" test for revocation decisions made by administrative agencies. Powell acknowledged what he was doing when he made this remark:

In so concluding, we are of course aware that the case-by-case approach to the right to counsel in felony prosecutions adopted in *Betts v. Brady* . . . was later rejected in favor of a per se [automatic] rule in *Gideon v. Wainwright*. We do not, however, draw from *Gideon* . . . the conclusion that a case-by-case approach to furnishing counsel is necessarily inadequate to protect constitutional rights asserted in varying types of proceedings.[22]

A probable reason for Justice Powell's reluctance to require the appointment of attorneys in these kinds of cases is that an administrative agency such as a parole board or department of public welfare is in the executive branch of government, not the judicial branch. This means that it does not have the same authority over members of the legal profession as the courts. The courts, in the judicial branch, have authority over lawyers, and can appoint them to defend indigents in criminal cases, and those appointed are expected to accept those appointments without expectation of fee.

The reasoning used by Justice Powell in *Gagnon* could be used in the future in decisions on whether there should be a right to counsel in such proceedings as

- the second appeal or discretionary review by the state supreme court;
- certiorari to the Supreme Court of the United States, including preparation of the petition for certiorari;
- habeas corpus and habeas-type proceedings;
- appeals from denials of habeas corpus petitions;
- extradition hearings;
- parole release hearings;
- prison disciplinary proceedings;
- prison classification proceedings;
- civil proceedings;
- and all types of administrative proceedings.

After *Gideon* was decided in 1963, it became necessary for the Court to determine the right to counsel in misdemeanor cases. The Sixth Amendment had been incorporated into and made a part of the Due Process Clause of the Fourteenth Amendment. The Sixth applies, "In all criminal prosecutions...," which includes misdemeanors, and for that reason the Court had to extend the right to counsel to indigent defendants in misdemeanor cases. Another reason was that the Fourteenth Amendment provides no state shall "deprive any person of life, liberty, or property, without due process of law." With the right to counsel now a part of the Due Process Clause following *Gideon*, logically, the right had to apply in any case that involved the deprivation of life, liberty, or property. In misdemeanor cases, defendants can lose liberty by being required to serve jail time and can have property taken from them in the form of fines.

The first case in which the Supreme Court ruled that the right to counsel extends to misdemeanor cases was *Argersinger v. Hamlin*,[23] decided in 1972. The petitioner had received a 90-day jail sentence for a misdemeanor while unrepresented by counsel. He filed a habeas corpus petition in the Florida Supreme Court, alleging that he had been denied the right to counsel. The Florida court denied his petition, but he won his case on petition for writ of certiorari to the United States Supreme Court. That Court, through Justice Douglas, took the position that when loss of liberty is involved, there is a constitutional right to counsel. He said:

We hold . . . that absent a knowing and intelligent waiver, no person may be imprisoned for any offense, whether classified as petty, misdemeanor or felony, unless he was represented by counsel at his trial.[24]

Another important right to counsel misdemeanor case is *Scott v. Illinois*,[25] decided in 1979. There, the defendant was convicted of theft and sentenced to a fine only, a $50 fine. He had been indigent and argued that he should have had counsel. At the Supreme Court, Justice William Rehnquist wrote the opinion for the Court, ruling against the petitioner. He said:

We . . . hold that the Sixth and the Fourteenth Amendments to the United States Constitution require only that no indigent criminal defendant be sentenced to a term of imprisonment unless the State has afforded him the right to assistance of appointed counsel in his defense.[26]

So even though the Fourteenth Amendment protects us against the deprivation of liberty or property without due process, the Court has limited the right to counsel in misdemeanors to only cases involving deprivations of liberty. Logically, based on the language of the Sixth and the Fourteenth, the right to counsel should be extended to all misdemeanors. But the Court must have realized the practical and financial problems involved in providing counsel in all misdemeanor cases and drew the line at deprivations of liberty.

But how does the trial judge know whether a misdemeanor case will result in a sentence of jail time rather than only a fine? Probably prosecutors must tell the judge, at the beginning of the case, whether they are seeking imprisonment as a possible punishment. And, if so, counsel should be appointed.

In 1967, the Court decided that the right to counsel should extend to juvenile delinquency proceedings. The case was *In re Gault*,[27] and the author of the opinion for the Court was Justice Abe Fortas. Fortas had been appointed to the Supreme Court on July 28, 1965, by President Lyndon Baines Johnson.

An adjudication in a juvenile delinquency proceeding is not a "criminal prosecution." Therefore, a juvenile in such proceeding is not expressly protected by those provisions of the Fifth and Sixth Amendments that apply in criminal proceedings and have been incorporated into the Fourteenth Amendment. However, in *In re Gault*, Justice Abe Fortas wrote that the Due Process Clause of the Fourteenth Amendment protects persons in state juvenile court adjudications.

In determining whether due process had been violated, Justice Fortas, in that case where the juvenile in the state of Arizona faced the loss of liberty, considered whether specific provisions of the Fifth and Sixth Amendments had been violated. The boy had not received written notice of the charges against him; had not been allowed to confront and cross-examine witnesses against him; had been denied the privilege against self-incrimination; and had not been provided the right to counsel. These violations amounted to a denial of his right to due process under the Fourteenth Amendment.

The decision was based on the Due Process Clause and constituted a return to the "ordered liberty" concept of due process for juvenile delinquency proceedings. Under that concept, expressed by Justices Cardozo, Frankfurter, Harlan, and others, the Due Process Clause of the Fourteenth Amendment, independently of the provisions of the Bill of Rights, can be used by the Court to make decisions ensuring basic fairness. Providing counsel to juveniles in cases in which their liberty could be taken away from them certainly was a decision required by the concept of due process. And even though the provisions of the Sixth and Fifth Amendments did not directly apply, those provisions could be looked to as guidelines in determining whether due process has been violated.

What Justice Fortas did was consistent with the position taken by Justice Frank Murphy in his dissent in *Adamson v. California,* where he agreed with the concept of total incorporation but said that even in a case where no specific guarantee of the first 10 amendments is applicable, occasions may arise "where a proceeding falls so short of conforming to fundamental standards of procedure as to warrant constitutional condemnation in terms of a lack of due process."[28]

One of the special circumstances that entitled indigent defendants to the appointment of counsel under the *Betts v. Brady* line of cases, which were based on due process, was extreme youth. Another was inexperience. Every juvenile is young and, in their brief lives, is inexperienced. Therefore, under the *Gault* decision a juvenile is entitled to appointed counsel as a matter of due process.

The right to counsel under *Gideon* does not promise that the defendant represented by appointed counsel will be acquitted, but it does require effective representation. And, unfortunately, appointment does not always result in effective representation. Convicted defendants frequently challenge their convictions through habeas corpus or other means, alleging that their lawyers were ineffective.

The Supreme Court dealt with the requirements for lawyer effectiveness in the case of *Strickland v. Washington*[29] in 1984. The Court, in that decision, developed a two-pronged test for courts to use when deciding an ineffective assistance of counsel claim. Under the first prong, called the "performance" prong, the court determines whether the attorney's representation was deficient under an objective standard of reasonableness.[30] If deficient, the court goes to the second prong, known as the "prejudice" prong. The defendant must prove that the lawyer's ineffectiveness adversely affected the case's outcome. To satisfy this prong, the defendant must show "that there is a reasonable probability that, but for counsel's unprofessional errors, the result of the proceeding would have been different."[31]

This means that the convicted defendant must satisfy the court (usually in a habeas or habeas-type proceeding) that they would have been acquitted if the lawyer had not been ineffective. As a practical matter, this is an almost impossible burden for a convicted defendant to meet. Hopefully, someday, the Court will re-examine its decision in *Strickland* and modify the prejudice prong to make it possible for the convicted defendant to obtain a new trial with different counsel in egregious cases.

In the case of *Garza v. Idaho,* decided in 2019, Justices Clarence Thomas and Neil Gorsuch, dissenting,[32] indicated that in their view *Gideon v. Wainwright* was wrongly decided. According to them, that decision involved policy choices; it had not been required by the Constitution. It was inconsistent with the original meaning of the Constitution, specifically, the historical meaning of the Sixth Amendment.

Those two Justices believe in "originalism," the concept that provisions of the Constitution should be interpreted the way they were understood at the time they were written. And, the purpose of the Sixth Amendment's right to counsel guarantee when adopted was to ensure that the English common law rule prohibiting counsel in serious criminal cases would not be followed in federal courts. Its meaning was that defendants in federal cases had the right to retained counsel, not a right to appointed counsel. It is unlikely, of course, that the views of Justices Gorsuch and Thomas will persuade the other members of the Court to overturn *Gideon.*

In *Ake v. Oklahoma,*[33] Justice Thurgood Marshall wrote the majority opinion in a case that recognizes the need for experts to assist defense counsel in preparing and presenting the case for the defendant. In *Ake,* the need was for a psychiatrist to examine the defendant and assist the lawyer in raising an insanity defense in a murder case. Justice Marshall said that due process required the state to provide a psychiatrist for the indigent defendant at state expense. That was the stated basis for the decision. My view is that also the right to counsel under *Gideon* required the state to provide a psychiatrist, for in the *Ake* case, the lawyer needed the help of the psychiatrist to provide effective representation for his client.

To effectively represent a defendant, the appointed lawyer might need other types of expert assistance. Handwriting and fingerprint experts come to mind. In a particularly complicated case, the lawyer might require the help of an expert investigator.

At the trial level, the defense lawyer who needs an expert would make a motion before that court for the appointment of the expert at state expense. If the trial judge denies that motion, there are methods of obtaining a review of that decision before going to trial. One such method, if allowed by state statute or court rules, might be an interlocutory appeal, seeking an appellate review by the intermediate court of appeal of the trial court's decision denying the defense motion. Another method is to file a complaint in the United States district court for that court to compel the state to provide funds for the expert assistance under the authority of the Federal Civil Rights Act, Title 42, Section 1983 of the United States Code.

During the 1970s, while teaching at The Ohio State University College of Law, I was the lawyer for a defendant in a case in Columbus, Ohio, in which Section 1983 was used to obtain funds from the state to hire a polygraph operator to assist in the client's defense. Our client was an intellectually disabled 19-year-old man. He and his cousin, who was about the same age, went to the cousin's girlfriend's home. It was daytime, and she was by herself. My client sat downstairs while his cousin and girlfriend went upstairs to have sex.

Unexpectedly, her father came home. The daughter appeared at the top of the stairs, wearing almost no clothes, and she screamed to her father that my client had raped her. By this time, the cousin must have left the house through an upstairs window.

The father insisted on filing charges against our client for forcible rape. When we interviewed the client, we were convinced that he was innocent. We spoke with the prosecutor to get the charges dropped, but he wouldn't dismiss the case because the father was pressing very hard for a conviction.

I decided we should use the polygraph (a lie detector) to determine whether the client was guilty. I asked the prosecutor if he would drop the rape charge if the client passed a polygraph test. The prosecutor was willing to provide a test administered by the polygraph operator employed by the prosecutor's office. If the defendant passed, the charge would be dismissed.

However, our client would have to agree that if he failed the test, he would plead guilty.

This was not satisfactory to the client or me. I did not want the client to agree to plead guilty if he failed a polygraph test. Furthermore, I first wanted a test by a private polygraph expert without having to disclose the result to the prosecution. Then, if he passed the private test, I would advise the client to submit to a test by the expert in the prosecutor's office.

We needed money for the private test. It was something like $500, but this was in the mid-1970s, and $500 in those days probably would be like $3,000 in 2025 dollars. So I filed a motion in the state trial court, asking the state to provide the money for the test. My argument was that the right to counsel, under the *Gideon* case required the state to provide funds needed by defense counsel for an indigent to be able to provide an effective defense. Also, due process required that result. In this case, having a private polygraph test to establish innocence was critical. Also, funds for a polygraph test were required under the Equal Protection Clause. A rich defendant could afford a polygraph test, and a poor defendant should have been given the money to pay for such a test when needed for an effective defense. But the state trial court judge was not persuaded by my arguments.

We then filed a lawsuit in the United States District Court in Columbus, Ohio, under Title 42, Section 1983, of the United States Code, to collect the money from the sheriff, who had funds that could be used for such purposes. United States District Judge Robert Duncan ruled for us. We received the money and hired a private polygraph operator.

The test was administered, and the client was determined to be innocent. We then agreed to allow the prosecutor's polygraph operator to administer another test. We refused to agree to plead guilty if the client failed his test, but we obtained an agreement from the prosecutor that the rape charge would be dismissed if the client passed the test. He did pass, and the charges against him were dismissed. The Federal Civil Rights Act, Title 42, Section 1983, of the United States Code, provides an extraordinary federal remedy if the state trial judge balks at providing funds to hire experts to assist in defense of an indigent individual.

In 2003, I received a phone call from Virginia ("Ginny") Sloan, the president and founder of The Constitution Project in Washington, D.C. It was around the fortieth anniversary of the *Gideon* decision. She and her organization were creating a National Right to Counsel Committee to study and report on whether the goals of *Gideon* were being realized. She invited me to join the committee, and I readily accepted her invitation.

We began our work in 2004. There were two honorary co-chairs. One was Walter F. Mondale, former vice president of the United States. He had been the Attorney General of Minnesota, who, in 1962, had urged the other state attorneys general to join him in an amicus brief in behalf of Clarence Gideon. Twenty-two states had joined. The other honorary co-chair was William S. Sessions, who had been a United States district judge for the Western District of Texas for 13 years and had served as the director of the Federal Bureau of Investigation between 1987 and 1993.

The committee had three co-chairs. One was Rhoda Billings, former justice and chief justice of the North Carolina Supreme Court. Previously, she had been a state trial judge and, at the time of our study, was a professor at Wake Forest University School of Law. One of the other co-chairs was Robert M. A. Johnson, a district attorney in Minnesota and former National District Attorneys Association President. The third was Timothy K. Lewis, a former Assistant United States Attorney, United States district judge for the Western District of Pennsylvania, and judge of the United States Court of Appeals for the Third Circuit from 1992 to 1999.

The reporters for the committee were Norman Lefstein, professor and dean emeritus of the Indiana University School of Law–Indianapolis, and Robert L. Spangenberg, research professor and founder of the Spangenberg Project, Center for Justice, Law and Society, George Mason University. I was one of 14 members, and among this group was Monroe H. Freedman, professor and former dean of Hofstra University School of Law. He was the leading scholar in the country on the subject of ethical problems facing prosecutors and criminal defense lawyers. Another member was Alan J. Crotzer, who had served almost 25 years in prison and had been exonerated based on DNA evidence. Ginny Sloan attended all our meetings. She was an outstanding leader of the committee.

Of particular interest to me was a fellow member of the committee, Abe Krash. Krash had been Abe Fortas's partner and had co-written the Petitioner's Brief in the *Gideon* case. I first met Krash in 1993, at a program at American University, on the thirtieth anniversary of the *Gideon* decision.[34] Krash and I both were speakers in the program.

In my remarks, I told the audience that Abe Fortas had been very kind to me during and immediately after the oral arguments in *Gideon*. Also, in 1966, when I was a professor at Emory Law School, and he was a Supreme Court Justice, he had been our Law Day speaker and again was very friendly and gracious. I admired him greatly.[35]

Afterward, Krash told me in a semiserious way that it had been unusual for Fortas to be so good to me because he was not known for being kind to young lawyers.

Krash and I got to know each other better as members of the National Right to Counsel Committee of the Constitution Project. He was retiring from practice at Arnold and Porter. He had served as an adjunct professor at the Georgetown Law Center and had been a visiting lecturer at the Yale Law School. He was a soft-spoken, very likable person, a gentleman in every sense. He has been completely dedicated to providing quality legal assistance to indigent defendants in criminal cases.[36] It was a privilege to get to know him while we were committee members. Sadly, he died on July 6, 2024, at the age of 97.

The committee met in Washington, D.C., approximately every six months for about five years. Then, in April 2009, our report, put into writing by Lefstein and Spangenberg, was published. It is titled *Justice Denied: America's Continuing Neglect of Our Constitutional Right to Counsel.*[37]

In the introduction, the report reminded readers that about 45 years earlier, the Court, in *Gideon,* had told us that any indigent who is hauled into court cannot be assured of a fair trial unless counsel is provided for him. The report continues:

> Yet, today, in criminal and juvenile proceedings in state courts, sometimes counsel is not provided at all, and it often is supplied in ways that make a mockery of the great promise of the *Gideon* decision and the Supreme Court's soaring rhetoric. Throughout the United States, indigent defense systems are struggling. Due to funding shortfalls, excessive caseloads, and a host of other problems, many are truly failing. . . .[38]

Our committee made 22 recommendations for improving our system for providing effective representation for indigent defendants in criminal cases. Every recommendation was significant. The most important were alluded to in the above brief excerpt from the introduction. We do not have nearly enough public defenders. Their caseloads are overwhelming, and their compensation is inadequate. Much more needs to be done today if we are to live up to the ideals of the *Gideon* decision.

# 19

## Anthony Lewis and *Gideon's Trumpet*

I met Anthony Lewis on January 15, 1963, right before the arguments in the *Gideon* case. As the reporter for the *New York Times* assigned to the Supreme Court, he was allowed to sit at a small table inside the bar in the courtroom during arguments. It was a brief exchange of simple hellos.

About a month later in February 1963, he phoned me at my office in Bartow. Workers at the *New York Times* were on strike. Since the *Times* was not being published during the strike, he had time to work on projects of his own and had decided to write a book about the *Gideon* case. He asked if he could interview me. We arranged to meet at his motel near the old Tampa Airport. Ann and I drove there and talked with Lewis for about two hours.

I had brought all my files with me. He read through them and told me which items he would like to have copies of, and afterward I made copies and mailed them to him. He explained that since he had begun working at the Court, he had wanted to write a book about the Court itself—how it functions, what happens from beginning to end when a case is filed, argued, and considered by the Justices. He had already begun writing that book. With *Gideon,* he explained, he would have a vehicle that would enable him to tie the writing he had already been doing to a specific case, making the book more interesting, not merely a dry, textbook-type description of the workings of the Court.

It was during this conversation, after hearing how I worked on the brief during the last three months, that he became excited about his intended theme for his book. The theme was a sort of David v. Goliath turned Goliath v. David theme. Gideon had not been represented by counsel at his trial but had a large Washington, D.C., law firm and a very well-known attorney representing him before the Supreme Court, while the state had only me, a young lawyer, and my wife as my secretary, in a Florida law firm, working on the case only at night and on weekends.

That theme didn't seem to me to line up with all the facts. There was more to my role in the case than those last three months at the Holland firm. And that firm was every bit the equal of Fortas's firm. It presently is known as Holland and Knight, a major national and international law firm. At the time I asked why he needed a theme as this was a nonfiction book, but he assured us that even works of nonfiction should have themes.

I was concerned the theme might not provide a completely accurate picture of the case.

The book when published did confirm his theme that there was a wide disparity between the representation Gideon received versus the legal representation for the state. I was disappointed. I felt parts just weren't factual. After getting to know Lewis and talking about the case over the years since 1963, I have an idea of the thinking behind his theme. In Lewis's view, the arguments for Gideon were overwhelming, and those for the state were practically nonexistent. I think in his mind, no lawyer should have taken and argued the case for the state. And, if a lawyer took the case, the proper thing to do would be to "confess error." (The first question he asked during our interview was why I had not confessed error in the case, a practice where one side acknowledges a mistake and by doing so, avoids lengthy litigation, basically throwing in the towel and conceding the case). The Court would never have accepted such a concession in this incredibly important case. The *Gideon* decision was not a backyard dispute between two neighbors disagreeing over the location of the property line. The consequences of the decision were momentous; the decision had to be fully vetted.

I envisioned my role in the case as something other than that of a pure advocate, merely seeking to win a case. In fact, we knew the Court wanted to overrule *Betts v. Brady.* To do that, the Court needed the strongest and most truthful and accurate arguments on each side. Only then could the Court reach the best, most honored decision possible for our nation and our legal system.

It has always been my view that although a criminal defense attorney should be a zealous advocate for a client, within the bounds of ethical constraints, a prosecutor's position is different. They represent all the people of the state and should treat all, including criminal defendants, fairly.

In 1980, 16 years after publication of *Gideon's Trumpet,* the book was made into a movie, starring actor Henry Fonda as Clarence Gideon. I had a tough time living down the image of myself on the screen. At the time of the movie's release, I was dean of Mercer University Law School in Macon, Georgia. My students joked with me about the portrayal. They noted that my character was kind of a rube, sweating profusely during the arguments, fighting off a constant barrage of Justices' questions in a thick Southern accent. I was raised in a suburb of Chicago and have a Midwestern accent, if anything. My kids informed me over the years when the actor who played me in *Gideon's Trumpet* was in a new movie or show.[1] He is better known to them as Tom Cruise's father in *Risky Business* and the chancellor of the West Beverly High School in the original *90210* TV show—not particularly likable characters either.

In the *Gideon* movie, there is a scene with two colleagues of Abe Fortas sitting in the courtroom shortly before the case was called for argument. They are talking with each other. They look at me, sitting at my counsel table, and one says, "That's Jacob; he has no chance of winning this case." The other colleague says in response, "Don't go feeling sorry for the son of a bitch until we win." That conversation could not have taken place because there had been no colleague with Fortas before or during the argument in the Supreme Court that day. He was by himself. Also, the camera shows a packed audience in the courtroom. I laugh when I think about the reality. While I was making my argument, there was only one person in the spectator section of the courtroom—my wife, Ann.

For the year after the movie came out, I felt a bit ridiculed. I understand that movies are never exact portrayals of life, but my image in the movie was hard to live down.

I was concerned when the book was published that it might adversely affect my career. In 1964, I decided to go into law school teaching, and I was apprehensive that Lewis's portrayal of me would make it difficult to get teaching jobs. That didn't happen. I first got a graduate law degree at Northwestern, then a job teaching at Emory University in 1965 as an assistant and associate professor. From there I went on to graduate study at Harvard, and a teaching position at Ohio State and then was hired as dean at Mercer School of Law and finally dean at Stetson College of Law.

I saw Anthony Lewis next on March 18, 1993, the thirtieth anniversary of the *Gideon* decision at a conference at American University, a conference celebrating the decision.[2] Justice William Brennan Jr. was the guest of honor. Chesterfield Smith, the head of the Holland firm and, at that time, former president of the American Bar Association, was there. He was a good friend and had been a mentor for me when I was an associate at the Holland firm.

Anthony Lewis gave the keynote address, and there were seven other speakers, including Abe Krash, Professor John Hart Ely,[3] and me. Ely had been a Yale law student who was a summer research intern at Fortas's firm who did some research for the Petitioner's Brief during the summer of 1962.

During the conference, Anthony Lewis and I talked. We both were older. I had grown past worrying about how I had been portrayed in the book and movie. The two of us had a great conversation. We recalled the intense questioning by the Justices during my argument.

For the next 20 years, until his death in 2013, we corresponded, had phone conversations, and saw each other at conferences and panel discussions regarding the *Gideon* case. Sometime during the late 1990s, I invited Lewis to give a keynote address at Stetson's annual Conference on Law and Higher Education. He made an excellent presentation. My colleagues and I appreciated his willingness to participate in the program.

I wrote a law review article published in 2003 by the *Stetson Law Review*.[4] In the article I briefly mentioned how in 1964 I had been disappointed by the theme used in the book. Fred Turner provided me with a lot of the information that I used in the article, and as soon as I had completed a rough draft, I sent him a copy for his comments and suggestions. When he received it, he phoned me and asked if I would mind if he sent a copy to Anthony Lewis. Apparently, the two of them had stayed in contact since the early 1960s, and Fred wanted to send Lewis a copy and then talk about it by phone with Lewis. I immediately sent Turner another copy of the draft for Lewis.

In March of 2003, I received a letter from Anthony Lewis, which I quote in pertinent part:

Dear Bruce,

I have just read your article, and I think it is wonderful. It told me many things I did not know about in the case and about you. I did not think that, after all these years, I could be caught up emotionally in an article about *Gideon,* but I was moved. I hope the *Stetson Law Review* editors understand what a gem they have.

If I knew that you had delivered Dr. Pepper to the Bay Harbor Poolroom, I had forgotten. It makes a great beginning—as the visit with Fred Turner is a perfect ending. There is so much in between that deserves comment: I wish I could go on in detail, but I won't. The main thing that comes through is your decency, your sense of a lawyer's honor. I now understand as I had not before, what you resented about my portrayal of you in the book. I did not at all appreciate how much work you did and why: because you thought a great case demanded it, even though you were sure *Betts* would be overruled.

If my criticisms of his book in the article bothered him, he accepted them without being disturbed by them.

On March 18, 2003, on the fortieth anniversary of *Gideon,* at a symposium, Anthony Lewis said this:

> In *Gideon's Trumpet,* I portray Jacob as a young assistant attorney general overmatched by the lawyer appointed by the Supreme Court to argue Gideon's case, Abe Fortas—and indeed he was, in terms of experience. But he was not overmatched, I've come belatedly to understand, in dedication or moral understanding. Even before the Supreme Court agreed to hear the case, Jacob says he and his colleagues understood that it was going to be the occasion for the overruling of *Betts v. Brady.* He did not disagree with that course. He thought it mattered how the Court took that step—how broadly, with how much understanding of the past. He worked night after night with his wife because he thought the Supreme Court was owed a proper presentation of all the considerations. So in a way, ladies and gentlemen, even though he was not the heroic figure in the case—he lost the case, he made an inexperienced argument—to me, Bruce Jacob represents the way a lawyer ought to act and think about such matters.[5]

He sent me a copy of a speech he made on March 20, 2003, describing how the ideals set forth in *Gideon* had not been realized. Here is one of the sections:

> Forty years on, how have we done? I take my answer from a recent paper by Bruce Jacob, the lawyer who represented the state of Florida in the Supreme Court, arguing against Clarence Earl Gideon's claim of a right to counsel. "I hoped that legislatures would meet the challenge," Jacob wrote. "That was at a time in my life when I still believed that legislators want to do the right thing. I no longer have that confidence in legislators. . . . [And] the record of our courts in fulfilling the hopes represented by *Gideon* is a dismal one."[6]

I realize that the Supreme Court's decision in the case was good for our country and legal system, and I did what I could as an individual lawyer to implement the decision. First, I was a volunteer Florida special assistant public defender. While at Emory Law School, I started the project providing free legal services for indigent inmates of the United States Penitentiary in Atlanta, and started a similar program for Massachusetts inmates while I was a graduate student at Harvard. I also was a legal services lawyer in a Harvard program. Then I began the clinical program to provide free legal help for indigents in criminal cases as a professor at The Ohio State University. Even as a dean and professor at two law schools I continued to do volunteer free legal work. Thus I helped thousands of indigent individuals in the criminal justice system over a period of 55 years.

Some have suggested that I did all of this because I felt guilty about the role I played in the *Gideon* case. This is not true. I love criminal law, criminal procedure, and constitutional law, and I genuinely enjoyed helping defendants and inmates with their legal problems. I enjoyed constructing legal arguments based on sections of the Fourth, Fifth, Sixth, Eighth, and Fourteenth Amendments to the Constitution. I liked to prepare and file habeas corpus petitions and to write appellate briefs and argue before the courts. Also, bringing students into each case was an effective way to teach them how to become criminal defense lawyers, appellate and post-conviction attorneys.

Ellen Podgor joined our faculty at Stetson in about 2006 after being a faculty member at the Georgia State University College of Law. For the next several years, she observed our faculty secretaries typing motions, petitions, and briefs for me on behalf of indigent defendants, appellants, and prison inmates. She learned I had been doing this throughout my career while a law teacher and dean. She decided to submit a nomination of me for the Champion of Indigent Defense Award given by the National Association of Criminal Defense Lawyers. This required getting letters of support for the nominations while keeping her efforts secret from me. One of the people she reached out to was Anthony Lewis, who provided an email of support on my behalf a week before he died on March 25, 2013.

Here is what he said:

> From the moment Bruce Jacob got the assignment as an assistant attorney general of Florida to oppose Clarence Earl Gideon's claim of a constitutional right to counsel, he knew he really hoped that the right would be established by the Supreme Court. It was. And then, Bruce Jacob devoted much of his legal life to making that right a reality in courts across the country. It was a noble endeavor, bringing luster to the legal profession and to Bruce Jacob.[7]

Even today, 12 years after his death, I often think about Anthony Lewis and how he thought enough about me to recommend me for the award while he was practically on his deathbed. As a young lawyer starting out, I did not know how to properly understand the way I had been portrayed in *Gideon's*

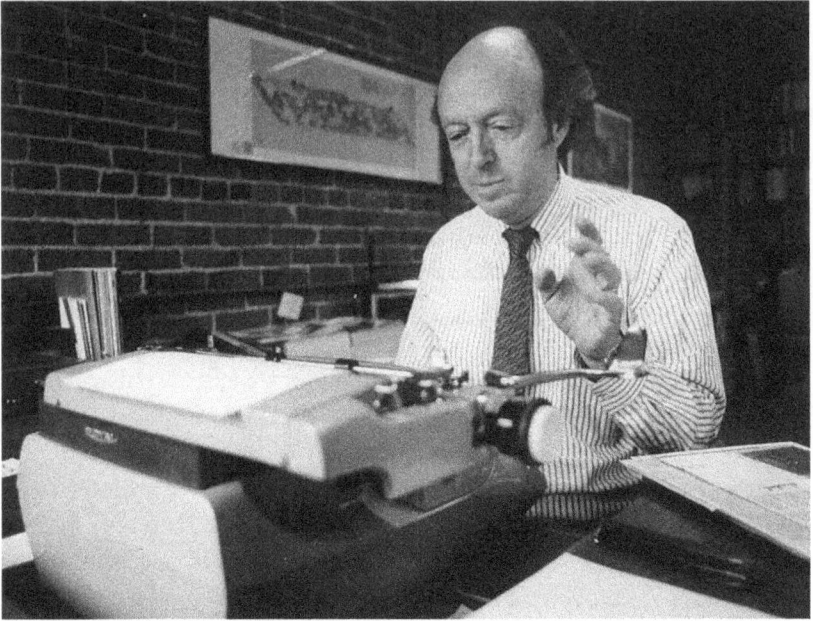

Anthony Lewis. Photo by David Ryan, *Boston Globe.*

*Trumpet,* but time does a lot for perspective, and during the 20 years between 1993 and 2013, we both had changed. I was no longer concerned about the book and the movie. Lewis had come to appreciate that there were two sides that had to be thoroughly presented in *Gideon.* And during those years we had become friends.

# 20

## Aftermath I

### Gideon

Clarence Gideon died on January 18, 1972, nine years after the arguments had taken place in the Supreme Court in his case. He was 61 years old and died of cancer. At the time of his death, he had been working at a boat marina in Fort Lauderdale, Florida. His gravesite is in the town where he was born and raised—Hannibal, Missouri. I thought I had never communicated with him, but Matthew Hofstedt, the Curator of the Supreme Court, has informed me that I did send a letter to Gideon on April 25, 1962. He had filed an answer to my typewritten response to his certiorari petition. In my letter I acknowledged receipt of his answer.[1]

### Wainwright

I did not meet either H. G. Cochran Jr. or Louie Wainwright and did not communicate with either during the early 1960s when writing the brief and arguing before the Court in the *Gideon* case, but I did meet Wainwright about 20 years later at the Stetson College of Law. It was the early 1980s, and I was the dean of the school. Wainwright was still the head of Florida's correctional system (he retired in 1987). We invited him to be the speaker at one of our "Inns of Court" dinners in our "Great Hall" for members of our student body, faculty, and guests. He accepted our invitation. I sat next to him at the head table and introduced him. He gave a very good speech. During the dinner, we had the opportunity to talk with each other. He had a very pleasant personality, and I liked him very much.

He died on December 23, 2021, in Tallahassee. He was 98 years old at the time of his death.

## Turner

Fred Turner died on November 23, 2003, at the age of 81. This was a huge loss to me personally because we had become such good friends. During that last year, we participated in the panel discussion on March 18, 2003, in Miami regarding the *Gideon* decision. The Federal Defender Office in Miami had sponsored that event. One of the other panelists was John Hart Ely, the summer intern in Fortas's office in 1962 who, in 2003, was a member of the faculty at the University of Miami Law School.

In August 2003, a ceremony commemorating the *Gideon* case was held at the Bay County Courthouse in Panama City, Florida. Fred Turner was the principal speaker and invited me to be there, but Ann and I were spending the summer in Michigan and could not attend.

He sent us a letter on August 15, and he said:

Bruce and Ann,

It was a lovely occasion and I must have signed 100 autographs. The Gideon sons (2) were there and said to me, "We hardly knew our father, he was at one time known as 'Uncle Earl' and we were raised in foster homes."

"We appreciate all you did for him." They thought my speech not too critical. Keep in touch.

Regards, Fred

Fred Turner died three months later.

## Fortas

Abe Fortas had been Lyndon Baines Johnson's lawyer in 1948 in the argument before Justice Black when Black allowed Johnson's name to remain on the ballot for the office of United States senator from Texas. Johnson won and became a senator, and Abe Fortas continued to be his personal lawyer. They became close friends as well.

In 1960, Johnson ran on the Democratic ticket for vice president of the United States with John F. Kennedy running for president. They won the election, and Johnson became the vice president of the United States in January 1961.

When President Kennedy was assassinated on November 22, 1963, Lyndon Johnson was sworn in and took over as the president of the United States. In

1964, he ran for the presidency and won a full four-year term, which began in January 1965. Fortas continued as his personal lawyer.

President Johnson wanted to appoint Abe Fortas to the Supreme Court. Fortas had not sought the position. He did not want the job, and his wife, Carolyn Agger, a tax attorney at Arnold, Fortas and Porter, did not want her husband to take the position. The salary for an Associate Justice then was $39,500 per year. The $39,500 would be the equivalent of about $395,618 in 2025.[2] It was a substantial salary, but apparently it was less than he had been earning in the practice of law. Fortas first declined Johnson's offer to be appointed to the Court. However, Johnson twisted Fortas's arm until Fortas took the job.

The appointment was made on July 28, 1965. Fortas was appointed to replace Associate Justice Arthur Goldberg, who had resigned to become our ambassador to the United Nations. The Senate easily confirmed the Fortas nomination on August 11, 1965, and he took office on October 4, 1965.

Beginning in the fall of 1965, I, too, had a new job—assistant professor of law at the Emory University School of Law in Atlanta, Georgia. Each year, our school invited a prominent judge or lawyer to be our "Law Day" speaker. Law Day was celebrated every May 1. Our dean invited Justice Abe Fortas to be our speaker for May 1, 1966, telling him that I was a faculty member, and Fortas accepted.

On the day of his speech, the dean picked him up at Atlanta's airport and told all of us in the student body and faculty that he would arrive at the school at a given time and that we could then meet the Justice. We gathered in the main lobby of our building. I was in the middle of the lobby, surrounded by dozens of students. When Justice Fortas and I shook hands, he said in his slow, deliberate voice so all could hear, "Dean, you have a good man here in Bruce Jacob." It was a very generous thing for him to say.

He gave his address outside on the Emory quadrangle. It was an excellent speech. Hundreds of Georgia lawyers, judges, and others were in the audience.

During the four years that he was on the Court, he was an outstanding judge. He wrote the opinion in *In re Gault*,[3] for example, guaranteeing due process rights for juvenile offenders facing charges in the juvenile justice system that could lead to incarceration. Another of his great opinions was the opinion for the Court in *Tinker v. Des Moines Independent Community School District*.[4] In that case, the Court held that a prohibition in a public school against the wearing of armbands by students as a form of protest against the Vietnam War violated freedom of speech protected by the First Amendment.

During his time on the Court, Fortas made some mistakes in his off-the-Court pursuits and financial affairs, eventually leading to his resignation from the Court. For one thing, he continued to work for his client of many years, President Johnson. He wrote or edited some of Johnson's speeches. He advised Johnson on the progress of the Vietnam War and served as a communications aide to Johnson. He wasn't being paid for this work. He did it out of loyalty to his good friend Lyndon Johnson and a sense of patriotism. But it arguably violated our constitutional "separation of powers" doctrine for one person to function at such a high level at the Supreme Court, in the judicial branch, and for the president, in the executive branch.

Paul Porter had been Fortas's law partner and friend. He knew that Fortas wanted to make more money, and he conceived of ways his friend could make more. He arranged for Fortas to teach a summer course at American University's Washington College of Law in Washington, D.C. There were to be nine lectures, which were to be turned into a book. Porter raised money from former clients of their law firm to fund the project, and Fortas was to receive an amount of $15,000 as remuneration for his work. That amount was equal to about $151,272 in 2025 dollars. It was a lot of money, and there was the concern that one or more of the contributors might someday have a case before the Court and expect favorable treatment from Fortas for contributing to this arrangement.

Also, a wealthy friend of Fortas's, Louis Wolfson, asked Fortas to be a member of the board of his family foundation, to attend meetings, and provide advice to the foundation. The contract provided that Fortas would receive $20,000 ($200,384 in 2025 dollars) per year for his life and the life of his wife, Carolyn Agger. Wolfson was a controversial person who owned corporations on the verge of violating federal statutes and Securities and Exchange Commission regulations. Fortas held the first $20,000 for many months, and when Wolfson was indicted for the federal crimes of selling unregistered stock and obstruction of justice in 1967, Fortas returned the $20,000 and canceled his agreement with the Wolfson Foundation.

On March 31, 1968, at the beginning of campaigns for election to the presidency, President Johnson announced that he was withdrawing from the Democratic primary, clearing the way for other candidates. He became a "lame duck" president from that point until the inauguration of the new president in January 1969.

On June 13, 1968, Chief Justice Earl Warren gave President Johnson his letter saying he wished to retire but would continue in his office until his successor could be appointed by the president and confirmed by the Senate to replace him as Chief Justice. President Johnson appointed Fortas to become Chief Justice and Homer Thornberry, a judge of the United States Court of Appeals for the Fifth Circuit, to fill Fortas's seat as Associate Justice. These nominations were made on June 26, 1968.

It was hoped that Fortas's nomination again would easily be confirmed by the Judiciary Committee and then by the whole Senate. But, unfortunately, there was opposition to the nomination.

During the hearings before the Judiciary Committee of the Senate, some opponents argued that there was no opening for the position of Chief Justice because Warren's letter was conditional, taking effect when the next Chief Justice was confirmed. It was argued that until Warren sent a letter giving a definite date for his retirement, the position was not open. Likewise, unless Fortas became Chief Justice, his position as Associate Justice was not open, and Thornberry's nomination to that position was premature.

There was opposition from senators who did not like decisions of the Warren Court, of which Fortas was a member, on the subject of pornography. Also, according to some committee members, the Warren Court was "soft" on crime.

Some committee members accused Johnson of "cronyism" for appointing two of his personal friends. In addition, Fortas was accused of spending too much time with President Johnson, doing work for the White House, arguably violating the "separation of powers" doctrine.

Fortas appeared before the Judiciary Committee, but his testimony did little to bolster his candidacy. The American University payment was a major problem. No lecturer at that law school had received anything like $15,000 for a lecture series. It was argued that donors might have expected help from him if their cases reached the Court.

Beneath the surface, some senators opposed him for antisemitic reasons. They did not want a Jew to be Chief Justice of the Supreme Court.

After a fight before the Judiciary Committee, the September 17, 1968, vote was 11 to 6 in favor of confirmation. Then, the nomination was brought to the full Senate, where a filibuster ended the nomination. Fortas withdrew his nomination on October 4, 1968.

I believe that the overarching reason for the demise of the nomination was pure politics. Lyndon Johnson had announced that he would not run again. It was an election year, and it was important to get Fortas and Thornberry confirmed as soon as possible before the presidential election in November.

Moreover, Richard Nixon was to be the candidate for the Republican Party. Nixon saw the opportunity to appoint the next Chief Justice and thereby change the direction of the Court from the liberal Warren Court to a conservative Court.

As a result of the failure to get Fortas confirmed as Chief Justice, Warren continued as Chief Justice until the end of a 1968–69 term of the Court. When he retired, President Nixon appointed Warren Burger to replace him at the beginning of the 1969–70 term. Fortas continued as an Associate Justice.

But in 1969, Wolfson's contract and payments came under scrutiny by the news media. Some suggested that Fortas might have given some advice to Wolfson in connection with Wolfson's potential federal criminal cases. Under media scrutiny, Fortas resigned from the Court on May 14, 1969. He was eventually replaced as Associate Justice by Harry Blackmun, appointed by President Nixon in 1970.

After his resignation, Fortas did not return to his former law firm, Arnold, Fortas and Porter (now Arnold and Porter). Instead, he and Howard Koven formed a new firm in Washington, D.C., under the name Fortas and Koven.

Fortas continued in the active practice of law until his death on April 5, 1982, at the age of 71. Just before his death, on March 22, 1982, he had argued a case before the Supreme Court.[5]

# 21

## Aftermath II

### End of Story

After the *Gideon* case, I continued to practice at Holland, Bevis and Smith until late August 1964. Ann and I had decided on a significant change in our lives—I would enter a different career—law school teaching. We packed our 1959 Chevrolet and headed for Chicago, where I had been admitted into the graduate program at the Northwestern University School of Law. Professors at Stetson, where I had received my first law degree, recommended that I get an LL.M., a graduate law degree, from one of the best law schools in the country, as a step toward a career in law teaching. Professor Fred Inbau, a well-known criminal law teacher, had awarded a Ford Foundation grant to me to attend Northwestern. Ann became Professor Inbau's secretary during that year. In addition to taking classes, I supervised his students in writing papers for his seminars. Inbau allowed me to teach one of his classes on the Fourth Amendment, and he gave positive feedback on my teaching. He also helped me obtain my first teaching job at the Emory University School of Law, beginning in the fall of 1965.

While an assistant professor at Emory from 1965 to 1969, I established the Legal Assistance for Inmates Program at the United States Penitentiary in Atlanta.

One of our clients was an inmate named Harold Kaufman. He had robbed a federally insured savings and loan near St. Louis, Missouri, of $11,520, including money and traveler's checks. He put the robbery proceeds in the trunk of his 1963 Nash Rambler and made his getaway driving north, across the bridge over the Mississippi River into Alton, Illinois. There the car slid on the ice and crashed into a tree. Alton police arrested him on a traffic charge and put him in jail. No inventory was taken of the car's contents, and the vehicle was hauled to a private garage.

That afternoon, FBI agents, who suspected that the Rambler was connected to the robbery, learned the car's location and searched it, finding and seizing the robbery proceeds. They did not have a warrant. A police inventory of the personal items an arrested person has with him or in his car when arrested is not considered a search and does not violate the Fourth Amendment, but this was a search for incriminating evidence, not an inventory, and because of this, a search warrant was required.

Kaufman was tried for the robbery of the savings and loan in the United States District Court in St. Louis. His appointed attorney was a civil trial lawyer, not a criminal lawyer. The lawyer apparently did not know that he could prevent the robbery proceeds found in the car's trunk from being admitted into evidence by filing a pretrial motion to suppress that evidence. He did object to the introduction of some of it during the trial, but the main defense used was insanity. Kaufman was convicted and sentenced to 20 years in prison.

In the direct appeal, the search and seizure issue was not raised. Kaufman lost that appeal.

While in prison, he learned that a motion to suppress the robbery proceeds should have been filed on his behalf at the trial level. Therefore, he filed a motion to vacate his conviction under Title 28, Section 2255 of the United States Code, asserting that Fourth Amendment issue. The district court denied the motion, and the United States Court of Appeals for the Eighth Circuit upheld that court's denial on August 4, 1967. He had 90 days from then, until November 6, 1967, to file a petition for writ of certiorari in the Supreme Court of the United States.

At this point, he was confined in the United States Penitentiary in Atlanta, and he applied to our Emory program for assistance. I asked one of our best students, William F. C. (Bill) Skinner Jr., a 25-year-old Vietnam War veteran, to work with me on the certiorari petition. We completed it and filed it with the Supreme Court on the due date of November 6, 1967.

The petition was granted on April 1, 1968. The Clerk of the Supreme Court wrote to Kaufman, asking him if he had a preference for what lawyer he would like to represent him in his case. He wrote back saying he wanted "Bruce Jacob." I was unaware of this exchange of letters, but on May 6, 1968, I received a letter from the Court appointing me as the lawyer for Kaufman.

There were two issues: (1) whether the search of the car had violated the Fourth Amendment; and (2) whether that issue could now be raised in a Section 2255 proceeding when it had not been raised before the trial court and had not been asserted in the direct appeal from the conviction. On the first issue, the facts in the case of *Preston v. United States*[1] were much like those in Kaufman's case, and the defendant in *Preston* had won.

Skinner and I worked on the brief throughout the summer of 1968. The brief was filed on August 13, 1968, and was signed by me and Bill Skinner. The oral argument was set for November 19, 1968. I phoned the clerk for permission for Skinner to sit at the counsel table with me. We were denied this request, but Skinner and his father were in the audience near me during the oral argument. At the outset of the argument, I told the Court that William Skinner, my student, had worked on the case with me and was in the audience.

Our main argument on the second issue was that any constitutional issue, including a violation of the Fourth Amendment, should be cognizable through a Section 2255 motion, even though that issue had not been previously raised. Constitutional issues are too important to be lost through the failure of a lawyer to raise such an issue in a timely fashion. Section 2255 was a statutory version of the remedy of habeas corpus, a right guaranteed by the Constitution. When those two constitutional guarantees—the Fourth Amendment and the privilege of habeas corpus are combined, as they were in *Kaufman,* my argument was that the petitioner should be allowed to raise the Fourth Amendment issue through a habeas corpus-based remedy such as 28 U.S.C., Section 2255.

Justice Fortas was one of the Justices on the bench during the oral argument.

On March 29, 1969, the decision was announced by Justice William Brennan, writing for the majority.[2] We won the case, and Justice Fortas was on our side. The case was sent back to the United States District Court in St. Louis for a new trial. An attorney was appointed there for Harold Kaufman. Kaufman pled guilty and was given a lower sentence than he had received the first time. A law review article has been written about the case by a good friend and former faculty colleague, Mark Brown.[3]

A movie was made in 1986 about Harold Kaufman. It is *A Deadly Business,* and it stars Alan Arkin as Kaufman.[4] One day about 1990, I read in the newspaper that his movie was to be shown on television that night. Ann and I watched the movie. It begins with Kaufman's release from federal prison following the victory in the Supreme Court. He goes to work for a company in New Jersey that is operated by organized crime. Some of the things they are doing seriously bother him, and he surreptitiously agrees to work as an undercover informer for the FBI. The FBI equips him with a small microphone that he wears under his clothing while engaged in conversations with his co-workers. FBI agents are nearby, in a van, recording those conversations, in which mob members talking with Kaufman admitted committing crimes. If they had discovered that they were being recorded, they might have killed Kaufman.

Based on these recordings and Kaufman's testimony, 15 to 20 organized crime figures were convicted and sent to federal prisons.

The day after I had watched the movie, as I was in my office at the Stetson Law School, the phone rang. The person on the other end said, "This is the FBI. We have Harold Kaufman, who is in the federal Witness Protection Program, on the line, and he would like to speak with you. Would you like to talk with him?" I said, "Of course." So Harold came on the line and said, "How did you like it?" I said, "You mean the movie?" He replied affirmatively. I told him I had never known anyone with this much courage—that he could have been killed while doing these recordings.

The FBI agent told me I could reach Harold anytime by phoning their offices and asking to talk with him in the Witness Protection Program. I did contact him again and had a conversation with him about 10 years later. In that phone call, he told me that because of our win in the Supreme Court, he served about 12 years less than he would have if we had not been successful. After pleading guilty, he served a couple more years, but that time had been served on a prison farm, where he was outside in the sunshine. Also, he lived in a dormitory instead of a cell and therefore was able to be among friends. I asked him why he had decided to help the FBI, after many years of a life of crime. His response was "It was you and the boys at Emory that caused me to change. Nobody before had done anything nice for me."

In 1968, while the *Kaufman* case took place, I became a graduate student at Harvard Law School. After the first year of taking courses, I was accepted into the S.J.D. (Doctor of Juridical Science) degree program, which required coursework and writing a thesis. In 1980, when the thesis was completed, and I passed the oral exam before a panel of professors, I received the degree.

Of the cases I have worked on during my career in programs at Emory, Harvard, and Ohio State, three are especially significant because they established important principles, ideas, or remedies for the use of defense lawyers in criminal cases. One was the case described in chapter 18, in which I sought money from the county sheriff to hire an expert polygraph operator to defend my client, who was charged with forcible rape but whom I strongly believed was innocent. My argument was that under *Gideon*, he was entitled to the effective assistance of counsel and that the polygraph expert was necessary to provide that effective representation. The polygraph is a useful tool for defense lawyers in negotiating with prosecutors. We established in that case that Title 42 United States Code, Section 1983, the federal civil rights statute, could be used to obtain funds from state or local governments to enable defense counsel to hire such an expert. This remedy would be available in obtaining other types of experts as well.

As just shown in this chapter, in the *Kaufman* case, I was able to demonstrate that Title 28, Section 2255 of the United States Code can be utilized after conviction to successfully assert the argument that a federal defendant was convicted on the basis of evidence obtained in violation of the Fourth Amendment's prohibition against unreasonable searches and seizures, even though that issue was not raised at the trial through a motion to suppress or on direct appeal from the conviction.

I would now like to describe the third case, in which I was able to establish that there is such a remedy as a class action habeas corpus petition.

This took place while I was teaching at The Ohio State University, in the mid-1970s. The city of Columbus had a "Workhouse" that housed persons convicted of city ordinance violations, such as drunkenness and disturbing the peace. Sentencing was in the alternative, for example, "a fine of $50 or 20 days in the Workhouse." The inmates performed many services for the city, such as cleaning the streets and hauling garbage. Many inmates were alcoholics found drunk in public who would be arrested, confined, released, rearrested, and confined again. It was a revolving door.

In 1971, the Supreme Court had decided *Tate v. Short*,[5] which held that these alternative sentencing schemes violated the Equal Protection Clause of the Fourteenth Amendment because the rich man can pay the fine and avoid imprisonment, while the poor man has to serve time in jail. This was the law of the land, but the municipal judges in Columbus completely ignored that decision.

Many inmates at the Workhouse were there in violation of *Tate v. Short*. Relatives of some of these inmates came to us at Ohio State and asked us to represent their family members who were caught up in the revolving-door cycle of being arrested over and over again and being confined for short periods after every conviction.

Habeas corpus is a civil, not a criminal, remedy. I was aware that under the Ohio Rules of Civil Procedure a civil action could proceed as a class action if the trial judge could be persuaded to allow the action to proceed in that fashion. I filed a petition for habeas corpus in the Court of Common

Pleas of Franklin County on behalf of two of our clients and asked the court to allow the case to proceed as a class action.

A common pleas court judge heard the case. I gave him a memorandum of law, which my students and I had prepared. Then the oral argument took place. Some of my students were there as observers. At first, the judge said there was no such thing as a habeas corpus class action. Such a remedy was completely unheard of. But finally, after a one-hour argument, he agreed that my argument was valid. Since habeas is a civil remedy, the civil rules of procedure had to apply. The case could and would go forward as a class action. Accordingly, he issued an order requiring the officials at the Workhouse to release any convicted inmate who had been sent there because he had been indigent and, therefore, unable to pay the fine.

Shortly after the order was issued, on Christmas Eve, when I was watching the news on television, the screen showed hundreds of Workhouse inmates being released at one time. They were shouting and screaming with joy at being freed. Eventually, about 750 Workhouse inmates were freed under that one court order issued by the judge of the court of common pleas in our case. The municipal court would sentence a convicted person to the Workhouse, but then Workhouse officials would release that person immediately under our court order.

I left Ohio State in 1978 to go to Mercer and therefore do not know what the city finally did to comply with *Tate v. Short*. The best solution, it seems to me, would have been to change its sentencing laws to distinguish between serious and not-so-serious offenses. Every convicted person, rich or poor, would serve time for serious offenses. For less serious offenses, the violator would pay a fine. If unable to pay the fine because of indigency, the fine would have to be waived. A conviction record would be maintained, but no time would be served.

Of all the cases I have worked on during my career, this is the case I am most proud of. For we were able to establish that if many persons in a jail or prison have been incarcerated illegally based on violations of the same statute, constitutional provision, or judicial decision, there is a remedy that can be used to free them all in one case—a class action based on one habeas corpus petition. Suppose several hundred persons have been convicted and sent to prison under a statute that violates the state constitution. A good lawyer could obtain the release of all of them in one class action habeas case.

I taught the ideas I had learned through those years of law practice to generations of my law students, to public defenders and private criminal defense lawyers in lectures to these groups, and in my writings.

After my seven years at Ohio State, I became the dean and professor for three and a half years at the Mercer University Law School in Macon, Georgia. Then, in 1981, I returned to the Stetson University College of Law, where I received my first law degree, as dean and professor of law. In 1995, after sixteen and a half years as dean at those two schools, I stepped down as dean and became a full-time faculty member at Stetson, but I continued to do free legal work for indigent defendants and prison inmates.

Often, I am asked how I could have been the prosecuting attorney, at the appellate level, in perhaps the most notable criminal case in our history and then spend the next 55 years of my life as a criminal defense lawyer, representing indigent persons. The answer is simple. After *Gideon* was decided, it was the law of the land, and I believed that all lawyers should do their part in fulfilling the ideals of that decision. This was a responsibility required of each of us lawyers as part of the privilege of practicing law. This was the type of law I enjoyed, and later, I combined work for defendants and inmates with the courses I was teaching law students. I used the clinical method in my teaching to help students learn to become lawyers. The clinical method is a superb way to teach law students because they can get to know the client and work on a real case in an actual courtroom, under the close supervision of a lawyer.

On April 18, 2013, I was one of four persons presented with a "Constitutional Champion" award by The Constitution Project in Washington, D.C. The other 2013 awardees were former United States Vice President Walter Mondale, Anthony Lewis (posthumously), and Abe Krash. I had the opportunity to speak with Mondale, who, as the Attorney General of Minnesota, had sponsored the amicus brief in the *Gideon* case, signed by him and other attorneys general, in favor of overruling *Betts v. Brady*. He told me that he had had very little to do with that undertaking—that Yale Kamisar, then a professor at the University of Minnesota Law School, deserved most of the credit for inviting and persuading other attorney generals to join that brief.

In 2014, the Illinois Public Defender Association created the Bruce Robert Jacob Award, which is presented to outstanding Illinois public defenders. On October 25, 2019, at its semiannual meeting, the Association presented this award to me. During the dinner meeting in which I was the guest speaker Ann and I had the privilege of sitting at a table with several Illinois public defenders who previously had received the award.

Andrew Cohen wrote an article for the March 22, 2013, edition of *Esquire Magazine* titled "The Lawyer Who Won by Losing." It was for the fiftieth anniversary of the *Gideon* decision. He began by saying:

Bruce Jacob is a remarkable man. As a young lawyer, he lost one of the most famous cases in the history of the United States Supreme Court. In fact, he got his butt kicked. But in defeat and ever since, he has reflected some of the most important and cherished values of the American justice system.

He then described my work on behalf of indigent defendants and prison inmates during the many years following *Gideon.* And he ended the article by saying this:

Here is a state lawyer, an assistant attorney general, who for decades dedicated his time helping indigent criminal defendants. Here is a lawyer who argued nobly, who lost graciously, who took nothing personally, and who put the law ahead of everything else. Bruce Jacob, you could say, is the other winner of the case of his lifetime. He may not be as famous as Clarence Earl Gideon. But he has lasted a lot longer and done a lot more good.

This is my favorite description of my involvement in the *Gideon* case and the work I have done for indigent persons since that decision in 1963.

# ACKNOWLEDGMENTS

There are many to whom I owe a great debt of gratitude for the ways they helped make this book possible. I truly could not have completed it without their assistance.

First, I wish to thank the University Press of Florida, the editorial board, and Senior Editor Sian Hunter for publishing the book. Sian was the editor who saw promise in my manuscript and accepted it for publication. Also, she has provided steady guidance for me throughout the process of editing and getting the book ready to be published. Another person at the University Press of Florida that I wish to thank for working with me during the production of the book is Managing Editor Marthe Walters, who did excellent work in preparing the manuscript. Also, thanks to Zubin Meer, who did an outstanding job of copy editing the manuscript.

Kate Bohl and I were faculty colleagues at Stetson University College of Law for a period of nine years. During that time, we became friends as well as fellow faculty members. And when she learned that I was writing this book, she immediately volunteered to help me in any way she could. She has been an inspiration to me during these many months of completing the book—getting it ready for publication. She helped me in selecting the title and suggested changing the subtitle from "A Close Look at the Supreme Court's Historic Right to Counsel Decision" to "Inside the Supreme Court's Historic Right to Counsel Decision." She worked closely with me as I made critical editorial decisions. I thank her for her sound advice and help throughout the process of preparing the manuscript and the illustrations for publication. She is a treasured friend.

Neil Skene is both a lawyer and a journalist-author. He was the Tallahassee Bureau Chief for the *St. Petersburg Times,* now the *Tampa Bay Times.* He was one of the top editors of the *Times* until 1989, when he was appointed to become the editor of the *Congressional Quarterly* in Washington, D.C., a company owned by the *Times.*

During the late 1980s, before he left for Washington, D.C., while I was dean of the Stetson Law School, Neil and I became friends. He taught the seminar on Constitutional Law for us at Stetson. Presently he practices law in Tallahassee.

He was designated to be one of the peer reviewers for this book. In that role he went far beyond what was required of him, making excellent editorial suggestions for improving the book. One was to move what was chapter 6 to the beginning, to become chapter 1. It was Neil who suggested the title of the first chapter, and he contributed the key sixth paragraph in that chapter. He advised moving much of what now is chapter 3 to later in the book. I've done as he suggested—that material now is chapter 10. Instead of disclosing that Gideon had admitted guilt, in his presentence investigation report in chapter 2, I made that disclosure later, in chapter 16, at Neil's suggestion. I could go on but won't, but the point is that the book has been vastly improved because of Neil's wonderful editorial insights.

My daughter, Lee Ann Gun, who is a journalist and editor, has assisted me over a period of several years in producing this final product. She gave me her invaluable comments for improving each draft of the manuscript. She produced three of the illustrations used in the book. And she and her husband (my son-in-law), Steve, obtained for me the exact language used in the movie *Gideon's Trumpet,* which is mentioned in chapter 19. Also, Lee Ann completely rewrote what now is chapter 19 for me, making it a much better chapter. She has given me a tremendous amount of help. I thank her very much.

My wife, Ann, was my research partner in 1962, spending long hours at four different law libraries in Florida, making notes on index cards for my use in writing the *Gideon* brief. She typed sections of the rough Brief for Respondent many times, getting it ready for the printer. She helped me prepare for the January 1963 oral arguments and was with me in the courtroom while the case was argued. And, during 2022 through 2025, over 60 years later, she typed early drafts and advised me throughout the preparation of this book. I could not have done any of this without her.

Early in the process of preparing the book we were fortunate to hire Alex Dailey, a freelance editor in Petoskey, Michigan, who typed and edited the first complete manuscript.

Our son, Bruce, helped Ann and me many times during these last several years, solving a variety of computer problems we encountered while putting the book together for publication.

I want to thank Dianne Oeste of Stetson Law School for typing and retyping chapters of the book. Shannon Edgar of Faculty Support Services and Stetson generously allowed Dianne to provide that assistance to me.

Mike Drilling, owner of Windborne Studios, in Traverse City, Michigan, provided expert help in preparing many of the illustrations for use in the book.

I want to thank our son, Brian, for the proofreading he did on early drafts of the manuscript.

Jessica Newman, of Pensacola, Florida, put together the final manuscript for submission to the University Press of Florida, and has done an outstanding job of helping me get the book ready for publication.

Again, I want to emphasize that I would not have been able to complete the book without the assistance of all these friends and family members.

# NOTES

## Preface

1 372 U.S. 335 (1963).
2 347 U.S. 483 (1954).
3 410 U.S. 113 (1973).
4 597 U.S. 215 (2022).

## Chapter 1. History at My Door

1 316 U.S. 455 (1942).
2 332 U.S. 46 (1947) and 333 U.S. 640 (1948).
3 372 U.S. 355 (1963).
4 See, respectively, Anthony Lewis, *Gideon's Trumpet* (Vintage ed., 1966) (hereinafter referred to as "Lewis"), and *Gideon's Trumpet* (Gideon Productions 1980).
5 That parking lot is where the new Capitol now stands.
6 One is Richard W. Ervin, *Freedom of Assembly and Racial Discrimination,* 10 Cleveland-Marshall Law Review 88 (1961), and the other is Richard W. Ervin and Bruce R. Jacob, *"Sit-in" Demonstrations: Are They Punishable in Florida?* 15 U. Miami L Rev. 123 (1960).
7 369 U.S. 506 (1962).

## Chapter 2. The Crime and the Arrest

1 Transcript of the second trial of Clarence Earl Gideon (August 3, 1963), 2, 10, 13, 14 (hereinafter Second Trial Transcript). Also, this is based on the Transcript of Record before the Supreme Court of the United States in the *Gideon* case, p. 19 (hereinafter Transcript of Record).
2 Second Trial Transcript, 3, 13; Transcript of Record, 17.
3 Second Trial Transcript, 13.
4 Second Trial Transcript, 16.
5 Transcript of Record, 17, 18; Second Trial Transcript, 3, 4.
6 Second Trial Transcript, 3, 45.
7 Transcript of Record, 19, 20; Second Trial Transcript, 10.
8 Second Trial Transcript, 9.
9 Second Trial Transcript, 7, 8, 22.

10 Second Trial Transcript, 5–9.

11 Second Trial Transcript, 7, 8, 22, 34.

12 Transcript of Record, 17, 18, 20, 21.

13 Second Trial Transcript, 6, 7, 20, 24, 25, 31, 56; Transcript of Record, 30, 31.

14 Second Trial Transcript, 20, 46; Transcript of Record, 29.

15 Transcript of Record, 30.

16 Transcript of Record, 30, 31.

17 Transcript of Record, 20; Second Trial Transcript, 19.

18 Transcript of Record, 18; Second Trial Transcript, 4, 5, 11, 27, 28, 29.

19 Second Trial Transcript, 35.

20 Second Trial Transcript, 31; Transcript of Record, 23.

21 Transcript of Record, 13, 14, 15, 19, 23, 24, 25, 33.

22 Transcript of Record, 13, 14, 18, 20, 24; Second Trial Transcript, 4, 5, 6, 27, 28, 29, 63, 65, 66.

23 Transcript of Record, 27.

24 Transcript of Record, 27, 28.

25 Second Trial Transcript, 89, 91.

26 Transcript of Record, 1.

27 Second Trial Transcript, 67, 68.

28 Transcript of Record, 2.

29 Transcript of Record, 3.

30 Jack King, *Clarence Earl Gideon: Unlikely World-Shaker,* Champion, June 2012, at p. 58 (hereinafter "King")

31 Lewis, 66.

32 King, 58.

33 King, 58.

34 King, 58.

35 Gideon won his case in the Supreme Court in March 1963, and the case was sent back to Panama City for a new trial, this time with a court-appointed lawyer. He was acquitted at the second trial. The lawyer, W. Fred Turner, and I became good friends between 2000 and 2003, when he died. After representing Gideon, Turner had become a Circuit Judge in Panama City. The information in the text is from interviews of Turner by the author in Panama City, Florida (September 14–15, 2000).

36 This is taken from the Presentence Investigation Report made by the Probation Office, Bay County, Florida, following Gideon's first trial, p. 2. The Presentence Investigation Report was given to me by W. Fred Turner. This report will hereinafter be referred to as "Presentence Investigation Report."

37 Presentence Investigation Report, 2.

38 Lewis, 68.

39 Presentence Investigation Report, 2.

40 Lewis, 68.

41 Lewis, 68

42 Lewis, 68, 69.

43 Criminal Registration Form, Panama City Police Department (August 4, 1961) (provided to me by W. Fred Turner.)

44 Lewis, 69.

45 Presentence Investigation Report, 3.

46 Lewis, 70

47 Presentence Investigation Report, 4; Second Trial Transcript, 118.

48 Second Trial Transcript, 117–118, and 122.

49 Second Trial Transcript, 120; Lewis, 74–75.

50 Interview with W. Fred Turner, in St. Petersburg, Florida (April 20, 2001).

51 Presentence Investigation Report, 4–5.

52 Interviews with W. Fred Turner, in Panama City, Florida (September 14–15, 2000).

53 Interview with W. Fred Turner, in St. Petersburg, Florida (April 20, 2001). Also, Presentence Investigation Report, 4–5.

## Chapter 3. The Right to Counsel Colloquy

1 Transcript of Record, 8–10.

2 Telephone interview with Jackie Wise, Secretary to Virgil Mayo, first Public Defender for the Fourteenth Circuit of Florida (March 25, 2013).

3 Telephone interview with Franklin Harrison, Attorney in Panama City, Florida (June 3, 2013).

4 Telephone interview with Jackie Wise, *supra* note 2.

5 Interview with W. Fred Turner, in St. Petersburg, Florida (April 17, 2001).

6 Telephone interview with Jackie Wise, *supra* note 2.

7 Telephone interview with Jackie Wise, *supra* note 2. Also, interview with W. Fred Turner in Panama City, Florida (September 14–15, 2000).

8 Telephone interview with Jackie Wise, *supra* note 2.

9 316 U.S. 455 (1942).

10 Mo. Ann. Stat. §545.820 (effective August 28, 1939).

11 U.S. Constitution, Article VI, the "Supremacy Clause." The Clause requires state judges to follow the Constitution and laws of the United States, including Supreme Court decisions.

12 Telephone interview with Virgil Q. Mayo, Public Defender (retired), Panama City, Florida (December 9, 2002).

13 I spoke with these lawyers on September 14 and 15, 2000, while in Panama City for a meeting of the St. Andrew Bar American Inn of Court. I was the guest speaker for the event.

14 Interview of Fred Turner on April 17, 2001, in St. Petersburg, Florida.

15 *Supra* note 13.

16 William M. Beaney, *The Right to Counsel in American Courts,* 29–30 (1955, hereinafter "Beaney").

17 The other towns were Lynn Haven and Sunnyside.

18 This law was enacted in the late nineteenth century when $90 was a large amount of money. Even in the early 1960s, the statute had not been amended to increase that amount.

19 The population figure is taken from the 1960 census. U.S. Bureau of the Census, Florida Population of Counties in Decennial Census 1900 to 1990 (Richard L. Forstall ed., 1995). In 1961, the number of violent and property crimes per 100,000 was 2,461.13, or about 1,652 for an area with a population of 67,131.

## Chapter 4. Gideon's Trial, Conviction, and Sentence

1 Transcript of Record, 10.
2 Transcript of Record, 10.
3 Transcript of Record, 10.
4 Transcript of Record, 10, 11.
5 Transcript of Record, 11.
6 Letter to me from W. Fred Turner, dated October 15, 2002.
7 His testimony can be found, Second Trial Transcript, 114–125. For a fuller description of the two trials, see Bruce R. Jacob, *The Gideon Trials,* 99 Iowa Law Review (July 2014).
8 Telephone interview with Franklin Harrison, Attorney, Panama City, Florida (June 3, 2013).
9 Telephone conversation with James White, Attorney, Panama City, Florida (June 3, 2013).
10 Telephone interview with Franklin Harrison, Attorney, Panama City, Florida (June 3, 2013).
11 Telephone conversation with James White, Attorney, Panama City, Florida (June 3, 2013).
12 Telephone conversation with James White, Attorney, Panama City, Florida (June 3, 2013).
13 Telephone conversation with James White, Attorney, Panama City, Florida (June 3, 2013).
14 Telephone interview with Franklin Harrison, Attorney, Panama City, Florida (June 3, 2013).
15 Telephone interview with Franklin Harrison, Attorney, Panama City, Florida (June 3, 2013).
16 Transcript of Record, 12.
17 Transcript of Record, 13.
18 Transcript of Record, 14.
19 Transcript of Record, 14.
20 Transcript of Record, 15.
21 Transcript of Record, 16.
22 Transcript of Record, 17.
23 Transcript of Record, 18.
24 Transcript of Record, 18.
25 Transcript of Record, 19.
26 Transcript of Record, 19.

27  Transcript of Record, 20.
28  Transcript of Record, 21.
29  Transcript of Record, 23.
30  Transcript of Record, 25.
31  Transcript of Record, 34.
32  Transcript of Record, 26.
33  Transcript of Record, 27.
34  Transcript of Record, 27.
35  Transcript of Record, 27.
36  Transcript of Record, 29.
37  Transcript of Record, 29.
38  Transcript of Record, 30.
39  Transcript of Record, 30.
40  Transcript of Record, 30.
41  Transcript of Record, 30.
42  Transcript of Record, 31.
43  Transcript of Record, 31.
44  Transcript of Record, 32.
45  Transcript of Record, 38.
46  Transcript of Record, 39.
47  Transcript of Record, 40.
48  Transcript of Record, 40
49  Transcript of Record, 41.
50  Transcript of Record, 41.
51  Transcript of Record, 41.
52  Transcript of Record, 43.

## Chapter 5. Petition for Review to the Florida Supreme Court

1  Transcript of Record, 6 and 7.
2  372 U.S. 353 (1963).
3  372 U.S. 335 (1963).
4  351 U.S. 152 (1956).
5  U.S. Constitution, Article I, Section 9, Clause 2.
6  First Amendment to the U.S. Constitution.
7  Second Amendment.
8  Fourth Amendment.
9  Fifth Amendment.
10  Sixth Amendment.
11  Eighth Amendment.
12  Florida Constitution, Article V, Section 3 (9).
13  When the United States Supreme Court decided the *Gideon* case, in 1963, the Florida Attorney General's Office realized that the circuit court at Starke, near the State Prison, and the Florida Supreme Court would be inundated with petitions

for habeas corpus from inmates seeking to set aside their convictions based on that decision. To spread the workload throughout the state's judicial system, the attorney general persuaded the Florida Judicial Council and the Florida Supreme Court to adopt Florida Criminal Procedure Rule 1, patterned after Title 28, Section 2255 of the United States Code, by requiring petitioners seeking habeas-type relief to file a motion to vacate their convictions in the circuit court where the petitioner-movant was convicted rather than at the court where incarcerated. A denial by that court can be appealed. Rule 1 now is called Florida Rule of Criminal Procedure 3.850. Habeas corpus is still a right, but only if the petitioner can show that 3.850 will not provide adequate relief. *See* Gene D. Brown, *Collateral Post-Conviction Remedies in Florida,* 20 U. Fla. L. Rev. 306 (1968).

14  Transcript of Record, 45 and 46.
15  Transcript of Record, 47; *Gideon v. Cochran,* 135 So. 2d 746 (1961).

### Chapter 6. The Petition for Writ of Certiorari to the United States Supreme Court

1  The Fifth Circuit United States Court of Appeals, in 1961, consisted of the state of Texas on the west, running to Georgia and Florida on the east, and Louisiana, Mississippi, and Alabama. Its headquarters was in New Orleans. Since then, the Fifth Circuit has been split into the Fifth Circuit on the west, with headquarters in New Orleans, and the Eleventh on the east, with headquarters in Atlanta.

2  In July 2019, the Office of the Clerk of the Supreme Court issued a "Guide for Prospective Indigent Petitioners for Writs of Certiorari," and in that "Guide" it told us that "The Court grants and hears arguments in only about 1% of the cases that are filed each Term."

3  In 1954 the law school relocated to Gulfport, adjacent to St. Petersburg, Florida, at the former Rolyat Hotel. The school still is located there.

4  My information regarding Joseph Peel and the Chillingworth murders is based on what I learned while a lawyer in the Florida Attorney General's Office from 1960 through 1962. Also, I have obtained some of the information regarding these murders from the many articles presently on the Internet regarding the Chillingworth case, as well as Peel, Holzapfel, and Lincoln.

5  The words of Gideon's petition can be found in Landmark Briefs and Arguments of the Supreme Court of the United States: Constitutional Law, vol. 57, 301–302 (Phillip B. Kurland and Gerhard Casper, eds., U. Publications of America, 1975).

### Chapter 7. The Florida Attorney General's Office

1  146 So. 2d 892 (1962).
2  307 U.S. 174 (1939).
3  554 U.S. 570 (2008).
4  561 U.S. 742 (2010).
5  597 U.S. 1 (2022).
6  143 So. 2d 193 (1962).

## Chapter 8. The Summer of 1962

1  370 U.S. 908 (1962).
2  My recollection is that around 1960, there were only about 8,000 active attorneys in Florida, in a population of 5 million. Also, I think there were only about 300,000 lawyers in the United States. Barbara A. Curran, in *American Lawyers in the 1980s: A Profession in Transition,* 20 Law and Society Review 1 (1986), stated that in 1980 there were 542,000 lawyers in the United States. If there were 542,000 in 1980, it is possible that my estimate of 300,000 in 1960 is fairly accurate. Today there are 1.3 million lawyers in our country. It is possible that the *Gideon* decision spurred some of this growth in the number of lawyers in the United States.
3  Xerox machines were not available until 1963 or 1964, so in 1962, our office made copies through a photographic process.
4  When interviewed by Anthony Lewis for his book *Gideon's Trumpet,* I gave him a copy of this letter from my files, and he included it in the book at Lewis, p. 149.
5  On April 18, 2013, I was one of four persons presented with the "Constitutional Champion" award by The Constitution Project, Washington, D.C. The other 2013 awardees were former United States Vice President Walter Mondale; Anthony Lewis, author of *Gideon's Trumpet* (posthumously); and Abe Krash, law partner and co-author (with Abe Fortas) of the Brief for Petitioner in the *Gideon* case. I had the opportunity to speak with Walter Mondale about the amicus brief, among other things. He said that almost all the credit for that brief has to be given to Yale Kamisar, who then was a professor at the University of Minnesota Law School. The amicus brief was Kamisar's idea.
6  The firm now is Holland and Knight, a national and international law firm.
7  It was very difficult to tell them I intended to leave the Attorney General's Office. They both were excellent lawyers, great teachers, and wonderful friends to me.
8  Smith later became president of the American Bar Association. He was an outstanding lawyer and another good friend and mentor.
9  Lewis, 58.
10  I gave a copy of this letter to Anthony Lewis in 1963 for his use in writing *Gideon's Trumpet.* It can be found at Lewis, p. 165.
11  367 U.S. 643 (1961).
12  He graduated from Yale Law School. And he played professional football for Pittsburgh and Detroit teams and intercollegiate football at the University of Colorado.

## Chapter 9. Marriage, the Holland Firm, and Completion of the Brief

1  The other tasks described were such things as research, interviewing clients, interviewing witnesses, and drafting documents.
2  The Court needed nine printed briefs for the Justices and some for its own library and for its records. The rest of the 40 briefs were sent by the Court to the libraries of certain selected law school libraries around the United States.
3  The Rose Printing Company had the contract to do all or most of the printing for the state. Printed briefs for the Supreme Court had to be printed by that company.

## Chapter 10. The Right to Counsel Before *Gideon*

1 Beaney, 8–12, 17–18, 27–29; *Betts v. Brady,* 316 U.S. 455 (1942); *Powell v. Alabama,* 287 U.S. 45, 62 (1932).
2 The section of the Constitution concerning ratification is Article VII.
3 Sixth Amendment to the United States Constitution.
4 Beaney, 27.
5 Beaney, 28.
6 Beaney, 28.
7 Beaney, 29.
8 Beaney, 28, 29.
9 Beaney, 29.
10 304 U.S. 458 (1938).
11 Report of the Judicial Conference of Circuit Judges, Annual Report of the Director of the Administrative Office of the United States Courts, 1940, at 113, and 1968, at 117–119.
12 Beaney, 42.
13 Beaney, 42.
14 287 U.S. 45 (1932).
15 *Id.* at 71.
16 *Id.* at 49, 53–55.
17 *Id.* at 58.
18 *Id.* at 71.
19 316 U.S. 455 (1942).
20 *Id.* at 471–472.
21 *Id.* at 472.
22 *Carnley v. Cochran,* 369 U.S. 506 (1962); *Cash v. Culver,* 358 U.S. 633 (1959).
23 *Massey v. Moore,* 348 U.S. 105 (1954); *Palmer v. Ashe,* 342 U.S. 134 (1951).
24 *Marino v. Ragen,* 332 U.S. 561 (1947).
25 *Reynolds v. Cochran,* 365 U.S. 525 (1961); *Gibbs v. Burke,* 337 U.S. 773 (1949); *Townsend v. Burke,* 334 U.S. 763 (1948); and *White v. Ragen,* 324 U.S. 760 (1945).
26 Mo. Ann. Stat. §545.820 (effective August 28, 1939).

## Chapter 11. The Brief for the Petitioner

1 Brief for Petitioner, 7–8.
2 Brief for Petitioner, 13.
3 304 U.S. 458 (1938).
4 *Id.* at 462–463.
5 Brief for Petitioner, 21.
6 Brief for Petitioner, 21 and 22, quoting from Justice Sutherland in *Powell v. Alabama,* 287 U.S. 45, 61 (1932).
7 Brief for Petitioner, 22.
8 351 U.S. 12 (1956).

9   Brief for Petitioner, 26, quoting from *Griffin v. Illinois*, 351 U.S. 12, 17–19 (1956).

10  Brief for Petitioner, 9.

11  Brief for Petitioner, 29.

12  Brief for Petitioner, 30.

13  Fortas also claimed that in eight of those thirteen states, it was the general practice to furnish legal assistance in each case where such aid was requested. *Betts v. Brady* had been decided 20 years earlier, in 1942. (Fortas was writing the brief in 1962). In *Betts,* the Court had said that "in the great majority of the states, it has been the considered judgment of the people, their representatives, and their courts that appointment of counsel is not a fundamental right, essential to a fair trial." 316 U.S. 455, 471 (1942). A lot had changed between 1942 and 1962. Now in most states, counsel was being provided to all indigent defendants.

14  *Elkins v. United States,* 364 U.S. 206, 221 (1960).

15  329 U.S. 663 (1947).

16  332 U.S. 145 (1947).

17  Brief for Petitioner, 44–46.

18  Brief for Petitioner, 9.

## Chapter 12. The Brief for the Respondent

1   287 U.S. 45 (1932).

2   304 U.S. 458 (1938).

3   316 U.S. 455 (1942).

4   351 U.S. 12 (1956).

5   There are two Due Process Clauses in the Constitution. The other is in the Fifth Amendment. It applies as a safeguard, a protection against unlawful actions by the federal government. The Fourteenth Amendment does the same for unlawful actions by state or local governments.

6   316 U.S. 455 at 462 (1942).

7   Brief for Respondent, p. 9.

8   *Snyder v. Massachusetts,* 291 U.S. 97, at 114 (1934).

9   *Palko v. Connecticut,* 302 U.S. 319, at 325 (1937). Also, Justice Black's concurrence in *Rochin v. California,* 342 U.S. 165 (1952) provided another definition of the term "due process." He said that action by police (such as pumping the stomach of a person to obtain evidence of narcotics against the will of that person) violates due process because such action is "shocking to the conscience."

10  Others included Justices Samuel Miller, David Davis, Joseph Bradley, Morrison Waite, Stanley Matthews, Horace Gray, and Melville Fuller. This information is taken from Justice Frankfurter's concurrence in *Adamson v. California,* 332 U.S. 46, 59 (1947).

11  Some would have described this as the "natural law" concept of due process. Natural law is based on the belief that there are universal standards that are inherent in humankind. As humans, we possess an innate sense of what is moral and what is not moral and a sense of what is right and wrong. What is right constitutes natural

law, and under natural law theory, the concepts of natural law and due process are virtually indistinguishable when considering the rights of defendants in criminal cases.

12  316 U.S. 455, at 474, 475 (1942).

13  *Id.* at 474.

14  399 U.S. 1, 13 (1970).

15  332 U.S. 46 (1947).

16  His dissent can be found at 332 U.S. 46, 68 (1947).

17  332 U.S. at 46, 123, and 124.

18  *Id.* at 89.

19  *Id.*

20  232 U.S. 383 (1914).

21  338 U.S. 25 (1949).

22  "Dicta" describes an expression of opinion by a judge that is not necessary to the result in the case before the court. It is not part of the law of that case and does not have the force or effect of law.

23  367 U.S. 643 (1961).

24  He does describe the effect of the Fourth Amendment upon the States "through the Due Process Clause of the Fourteenth Amendment." 367 U.S. 643–660 (1961).

25  367 U.S. 643, 682 (1961).

26  *Id.* at 678.

27  Brief for Respondent, 9, 46– 47.

28  Brief for Petitioner, 22–24.

29  Brief for Respondent, 46– 47.

30  *Betts v. Brady,* 316 U.S. 455, 473 (1942).

31  Brief for Respondent, 48.

32  Brief for Respondent, 8, 25– 26.

33  Brief for Respondent, 8, 34– 35.

34  351 U.S. 12 (1956).

35  *Id.* at 20.

36  Brief for Respondent, 53.

37  Brief for Respondent, 55– 56. It is estimated that in 2022 the prison population in Florida was about 96,000, compared with 8,000 in 1962. The state's population in 2022 was a little over four times what it was in 1962 (22 million versus 5 million). But the state's prison population was 12 times greater.

38  Brief for Respondent, 56.

39  For example, the concurring opinion of Justice Frankfurter in *Griffin v. Illinois,* 351 U.S. 12 (1956); and *Great Northern Railway Co. v. Sunburst Oil Co.,* 287 U.S. 358 (1932).

40  Brief for Petitioner, 36.

41  329 U.S. 663 (1947).

42  332 U.S. 145 (1947).

43  Brief for Respondent, 42.

44  Brief for Respondent, 42–43.

45  Brief for Respondent, 43– 44.

46  *Williams v. Kaiser,* 323 U.S. 471 (1945); *Hamilton v. Alabama,* 368 U.S. 52 (1961).

47  *Rice v. Olson,* 324 U.S. 786 (1945); *McNeal v. Culver,* 365 U.S. 109 (1961); *Chewning v. Cunningham,* 368 U.S. 443 (1962); *Pennsylvania v. ex rel Herman v. Claudy,* 350 U.S. 116 (1956).

48  *Smith v. O'Grady,* 312 U.S. 329 (1941); *Tomkins v. Missouri,* 323 U.S. 485 (1945).

49  *Carnley v. Cochran,* 369 U.S. 506 (1962); *Cash v. Culver,* 358 U.S. 633 (1959).

50  *Wade v. Mayo,* 334 U.S. 672 (1948); *Uveges v. Pennsylvania,* 335 U.S. 437 (1948); *Moore v. Michigan,* 355 U.S. 155 (1957).

51  *Wade v. Mayo,* 334 U.S. 672 (1948); *McNeal v. Culver,* 365 U.S. 109 (1961).

52  *Palmer v. Ashe,* 342 U.S. 134 (1951); *Massey v. Moore,* 348 U.S. 105 (1954).

53  *Marino v. Ragen,* 332 U.S. 561 (1947).

54  *White v. Ragen,* 324 U.S. 760 (1945); *Townsend v. Burke,* 334 U.S. 736 (1948); *Hawk v. Olson,* 326 U.S. 271 (1945); *Reynolds v. Cochran,* 365 U.S. 525 (1961); *Gibbs v. Burke,* 337 U.S. 773 (1949).

55  Brief for Petitioner, 33.

56  Brief for Respondent, 50.

57  I obtained the transcript which is used here and in the next chapter from oyez. org., *Gideon v. Wainwright*—oral argument—January 15, 1963 (Part 2) (hereinafter referred to as oyez part 2).

## Chapter 13. The Oral Arguments in Washington, D.C.

1  372 U.S. 253 (1963).

2  These remarks are taken from the Wikipedia entry on the Internet for Oliver North. (As pertains to this note and the ones that follow, Wikipedia was consulted in spring 2022, probably in March).

3  This information in these paragraphs was obtained from Wikipedia pages for the Watergate scandal, John Ehrlichman, and Charles Colson.

4  These paragraphs are from Wikipedia pages on the Watergate scandal and Archibald Cox.

5  *Nader v. Bork,* 366 F. Supp. 104 (D.D.C. 1973).

6  This is from oyez.org, *Gideon v. Wainwright*—oral argument—January 15, 1963 (Part 1).

7  *Id.*

8  372 U.S. 353 (1963).

9  372 U.S. 487 (1963).

10  372 U.S. 477 (1963).

11  These remarks regarding Lyndon Johnson's first Senate race are taken from Bruce Allen Murphy, *Fortas: The Rise and Ruin of a Supreme Court Justice* 90–96 (1988).

12  Oyez part 2, at pp. 27, 28– 29.

13  Oyez part 2, 29.

14  Oyez part 2, 29–30.

15  Oyez part 2, 34, 35– 36.

16  Oyez part 2, 39.

17 Oyez part 2, 41 and 42.

18 Oyez part 2, 60.

19 Oyez part 2, 53.

20 This is from my memory. His comment does not appear in the transcript of the argument.

21 Oyez part 2, 47–48.

22 Oyez part 2, 55.

23 Oyez part 2, 43–45.

24 There is some language in *Hamilton* that supports Justice Harlan's question: "When one pleads to a capital charge without the benefit of counsel, we do not stop to determine whether prejudice resulted." 372 U.S. 52, 55 (1961). However, the holding was based on the fact that the defendant, entitled under state law to counsel in a capital case, was denied counsel at arraignment, where "available defenses" could be irretrievably lost. I believe this holding was consistent with a special circumstances rule of *Powell* and *Betts* in which complexity of the case was considered a special circumstance.

25 Oyez part 2, 54–55.

26 277 F. Supp. 211 (N.D. Ga.1967).

27 *Johnson v. Avery,* 252 F. Supp. 783 (M.D. Tenn. 1966, reversed, 382 F. 2d 353 [6th Cir. 1967]).

28 393 U.S. 483 (1969).

29 This was an interesting experiment. Within a couple of months, after the "L.A.I." project began accepting applications for legal assistance from inmates, we had 900 applications for help out of an inmate population of 2,200 or 2,300. I was the only lawyer-supervisor during the first year, supervising 53 student volunteers. We were able to hire a staff lawyer/assistant to help me during the second year. In the following years, the staff lawyer was aided by White and Rayburn. They answered letters, did legal research and writing, and supervised law students. With their help, we were able to provide legal assistance to the 900 inmates and more. Rayburn later became a highly regarded and respected paralegal for many years in the Federal Defender Office in San Diego, California.

30 Interview with W. Fred Turner, St. Petersburg, Florida, April 20, 2001.

## Chapter 14. The Supreme Court's Decision

1 372 U.S. 335, 344–345 (1963).

2 *Id.* at 344.

3 *Id.*

4 *Id.* at 349.

5 389 U.S. 109 (1967).

6 They would be retried, this time with the benefit of appointed counsel, but if witnesses in their case were dead or unavailable, the state would have to dismiss the charges and release them from custody.

7 372 U.S. 335, at 342 (1963).

8 407 U.S. 25 (1972).

9   440 U.S. 367 (1979).

10   372 U.S. 353 (1963).

11   *Id.* at 361.

## Chapter 15. Florida's Response and My Response

1   Gene D. Brown, *Collateral Post-Conviction Remedies in Florida,* 20 U. Fla. L. Rev. 306, 308 (1968).

2   The details of this law have changed over time, but it can be found in Chapter 27 of the Florida Statutes.

3   This provision now can be found at Florida Statutes, Chapter 27, Section 27.53 (2) (2023).

4   433 U.S. 584 (1977).

5   This clause is found in the Eighth Amendment to the Constitution.

6   The supervising attorneys included LeRoy Pernell and Dennis Balske.

## Chapter 16. Appointment of Fred Turner to Represent Gideon

1   Presentence Investigation Report, 1, and Letter from Fred Turner to me (September 29, 2003).

2   Presentence Investigation Report, 1, and Letter from Fred Turner to me (September 29, 2003).

3   Florida Statutes § 810.03 (1961).

4   Lewis, 234, 235.

5   Lewis, 234, 235. Also, G. S. Prentzas, *Gideon v. Wainwright: The Right to Free Legal Counsel,* at 71 (2007) (hereinafter referred to as "Prentzas").

6   Lewis, 235.

7   Lewis, 235. Also, Prentzas, 71.

8   Prentzas, 71. Also see Bruce R. Jacob, *The Gideon Trials,* 99 Iowa Law Review 2059, 2081 (2014) (hereinafter "The *Gideon* Trials").

9   Lewis, 235.

10   Lewis, 235–236.

11   Lewis, 236.

12   Lewis, 236.

13   Lewis, 236–237; Prentzas, 71; The *Gideon* Trials, 2082; and Bruce R. Jacob, *Memories of and Reflections About Gideon v. Wainwright,* 33 Stetson Law Review 181, 257 (2003) (hereinafter "Memories of and Reflections").

14   Lewis, 237; Prentzas, 72; Abbe Smith, *Gideon Was a Prisoner: On Criminal Defense in a Time of Mass Incarceration,* 70 Washington and Lee Law Review 1363, 1372 (2013).

15   Lewis, 238; and Memories of and Reflections, 259.

16   Interviews with W. Fred Turner in Panama City, Florida (September 14–15, 2000), and in St. Petersburg, Florida (April 20, 2001). Also, I have discussed all of this in my articles, The *Gideon* Trials, 2081–2082, and Memories of and Reflections, 257–258.

17   The *Gideon* Trials, 2084.

18  Interview with W. Fred Turner, in Panama City, Florida (September 14–15, 2000).
19  Interview with W. Fred Turner, in Panama City, Florida (September 14–15, 2000).
20  Interview with W. Fred Turner, in Panama City, Florida (September 14–15, 2000).
21  Interview with W. Fred Turner, in St. Petersburg, Florida (April 17, 2001).
22  Interview with W. Fred Turner, in St. Petersburg, Florida (April 20, 2001).
23  Interviews with W. Fred Turner, in Panama City, Florida (September 14–15, 2000), and in St. Petersburg, Florida (April 17, 2001).
24  Interview with W. Fred Turner, in Panama City, Florida (September 14–15, 2000).
25  Interview with W. Fred Turner, in Panama City, Florida (September 14–15, 2000). Also, see The *Gideon* Trials, 2084.
26  Florida Code of Ethics Rules, B (6) (1992).
27  Interview with W. Fred Turner in Panama City, Florida (September 14–15, 2000).
28  Interview with W. Fred Turner in Panama City, Florida (September 14–15, 2000).
29  Interview with W. Fred Turner in Panama City, Florida (September 14–15, 2000).
30  Interview with W. Fred Turner in Panama City, Florida (September 14–15, 2000).
31  Interview with W. Fred Turner in Panama City, Florida (September 14–15, 2000).
32  *Gideon Brought New Order to Court,* Orlando Sentinel, March 21, 1988, at B3.

## Chapter 17. The Second Gideon Trial

1  Second Trial Transcript, 114–115, 123–124.
2  Interview with W. Fred Turner, in St. Petersburg, Florida (April 17, 2001).
3  Interview with W. Fred Turner, in St. Petersburg, Florida (April 20, 2001).
4  Second Trial Transcript, 35–44. Also, The *Gideon* Trials, 2089–2093.
5  The *Gideon* Trials, 2097–2098; Lewis, 248.
6  Interview with W. Fred Turner, in St. Petersburg, Florida (April 17, 2001).
7  Second Trial Transcript, 12–13.
8  Second Trial Transcript, 14.
9  Second Trial Transcript, 13.
10  Second Trial Transcript, 3–4.
11  Second Trial Transcript, 3.
12  Second Trial Transcript, 3–4.
13  Second Trial Transcript, 4.
14  Second Trial Transcript, 4.
15  Second Trial Transcript, 9, 21.
16  Second Trial Transcript, 5.
17  Second Trial Transcript, 5.
18  Second Trial Transcript, 6, 34.
19  Second Trial Transcript, 6, 34.
20  Second Trial Transcript, 6, 34.
21  Second Trial Transcript, 31.
22  Second Trial Transcript, 10.
23  Second Trial Transcript, 11.
24  Second Trial Transcript, 12.
25  Second Trial Transcript, 35, 36.

26  See cases cited in The *Gideon* Trials, 2089, footnote 24. Those cases include *In re Gault,* 387 U.S. 1, 23 (1967); *In re Poff,* 135 F. Supp. 224 (D.C. Cir. 1955); *Ex Parte Jones,* 93 P. 2d 185 (Cal. Dist. Ct. App. 1939), and *Ogden v. State,* 156 N.W. 476 (Wis. 1916).

27  Transcript of Record, 19.

28  Second Trial Transcript, 41.

29  Second Trial Transcript, 42.

30  Second Trial Transcript, 42.

31  Second Trial Transcript, 48–49.

32  Second Trial Transcript, 54–55.

33  Second Trial Transcript, 56.

34  Second Trial Transcript, 58.

35  Second Trial Transcript, 58–59.

36  Second Trial Transcript, 60.

37  Second Trial Transcript, 122–123.

38  Second Trial Transcript, 123–125.

39  Second Trial Transcript, 126–127.

40  Second Trial Transcript, 126–127.

41  Second Trial Transcript, 115.

42  Second Trial Transcript, 115.

43  Second Trial Transcript, 106.

44  Second Trial Transcript, 88.

45  Transcript of Record, 24, 25.

46  Transcript of Record, 13; Second Trial Transcript, 68.

47  Second Trial Transcript, 89.

48  Second Trial Transcript, 96–97.

49  Second Trial Transcript, 113.

50  Lewis, 248.

51  Interview with W. Fred Turner, in St. Petersburg, Florida (April 17, 2001).

52  Memories of and Reflections.

## Chapter 18. The *Gideon* Legacy

 1  367 U.S. 643 (1961).

 2  232 U.S. 383 (1914).

 3  378 U.S. 1 (1964).

 4  380 U.S. 400 (1965).

 5  386 U.S. 213 (1967).

 6  388 U.S. 14 (1967).

 7  391 U.S. 145 (1968).

 8  395 U.S. 784 (1969).

 9  372 U.S. 353 (1963).

10  In New York the trial court is called a "supreme" court, and the highest-level appellate court is the New York Court of Appeals.

11  153 U.S.684 (1894).

12  389 U.S. 109 (1967).

13  *Id.* at 114.

14  399 U.S. 1 (1970).

15  378 U.S. 478 (1964).

16  *Id.* at 486.

17  384 U.S. 436 (1966).

18  389 U.S. 128 (1967).

19  411 U.S. 778 (1973).

20  *Id.* at 787.

21  *Id.* at 790.

22  *Id.* at 788.

23  407 U.S. 25 (1972).

24  *Id.* at 37.

25  440 U.S. 367 (1979).

26  *Id.* at 373, 374.

27  387 U.S. 1 (1967).

28  332 U.S. 46, 124 (1947).

29  466 U.S. 668 (1984).

30  *Id.* at 688.

31  *Id.* at 694.

32  139 S. Ct. 738 (2019).

33  470 U.S. 68 (1986).

34  43 American University Law Review 1 (1993–94).

35  *Id.* at 39, 41

36  Bruce R. Jacob, *Remembering Gideon's Lawyers,* Champion, June 2012, at p. 16.

37  Justice Denied: America's Continuing Neglect of Our Constitutional Right to Counsel, Report of the National Right to Counsel Committee of The Constitution Project, April 2009. The report is available at the following web page of Open Society Foundations, https://www.opensocietyfoundations.org/publications/ justice-denied-americas-continuing-neglect-our-constitutional-right-counsel #publications_download.

38  *Id.* at 2.

## Chapter 19. Anthony Lewis and *Gideon's Trumpet*

1  The actor was Nicholas Pryor.

2  It was called the Conference on the Thirtieth Anniversary of the United States Supreme Court's Decision in *Gideon v. Wainwright: Gideon* and the Public Service Role of Lawyers in Advancing Equal Justice. It was hosted by the "Consortium for the National Equal Justice Library and the Washington College of Law of the American University." An article containing the remarks of each of the speakers can be found at 43 American University Law Review 1 (1993–94).

3  Ely had an illustrious career after graduating from Yale. He went into law teaching and taught at Harvard and Yale law schools and was the dean at Stanford Law

School. When he died in 2003, he was a professor at the University of Miami School of Law.

4 Memories of and Reflections.

5 Symposium, *Gideon at 40: Facing the Crisis, Fulfilling the Promise,* 41 American Criminal Law Review 135, 149 (2004).

6 Address at the Office of the Orlando Public Defender, March 20, 2003.

7 This is from an article by Curtis Krueger in The *Tampa Bay Times,* April 12, 2015, at p. 2. The title of the article is "Stetson Law Prof Took Gideon Case to Supreme Court, but Believed in the Other Side."

## Chapter 20. Aftermath I

1 Bruce Jacob to Clarence Earl Gideon, April 25, 1962, Clarence Earl Gideon Papers, Series I, Folder 11, Office of the Curator, Supreme Court of the United States.

2 Inflation between the mid-1960s and 2025 is the cause of the enormous difference between an associate justice's salary then and now. Actually, the salaries have not kept up with inflation. An associate justice's salary today is $303,600. The Chief Justice's salary then was $40,000 per year ($404,622 in 2025 dollars) and $317,500 in 2025.

3 387 U.S. 1 (1967).

4 393 U.S. 503 (1969).

5 The information regarding Abe Fortas is from my memory of the events reported in newspapers at the time. Also, I read and used information from Bruce Allen Murphy, *Fortas: The Rise and Ruin of a Supreme Court Justice* (1988).

## Chapter 21. Aftermath II

1 376 U.S. 364 (1964).

2 394 U.S. 217 (1969).

3 Mark Brown, *Bruce's Other Supreme Court Case,* 48 Stetson Law Review 313 (2019).

4 *A Deadly Business* (Thebaut Frey Productions, Taft Entertainment Television 1986).

5 401 U.S. 395 (1971).

# INDEX

Bruce R. Jacob is professor emeritus and dean emeritus of the Stetson University School of Law, where he received his law degree in 1959. After arguing *Gideon* at the U.S. Supreme Court, Jacob resigned his state assistant attorney general position, becoming a volunteer public defender while in private practice and teaching at Emory, Ohio State, and Mercer universities before returning to Stetson.

www.ingramcontent.com/pod-product-compliance
Lightning Source LLC
Chambersburg PA
CBHW030304100426
42812CB00002B/556